Hist

D0398617

DATE		

MARK TWAIN: The Man and His Work

PHOTOGRAPH BY ALBERT BIGELOW PAINE

EDWARD WAGENKNECHT

Mark Twain

THE MAN AND HIS WORK

Third Edition

With a Commentary on Mark Twain Criticism
and Scholarship Since 1960

UNIVERSITY OF OKLAHOMA PRESS

NORMAN

Some Other Books by Edward Wagenknecht

As Far As Yesterday: Memories and Reflections (1968); *Cavalcade of the American Novel* (1952); *Cavalcade of the English Novel* (1943); *Chicago* (1964); *Dickens and the Scandalmongers* (1965); *Edgar Allan Poe: The Man Behind the Legend* (1963); *Geraldine Farrar: An Authorized Record of Her Career* (1929); *A Guide to Bernard Shaw* (1929); *Harriet Beecher Stowe: The Known and the Unknown* (1965); *Jenny Lind* (1931); *Lillian Gish, An Interpretation* (1927); *Longfellow, A Full-Length Portrait* (1955); *The Man Charles Dickens: A Victorian Portrait* (1966); *Merely Players* (1966); *The Movies in the Age of Innocence* (1962); *Mrs. Longfellow: Selected Letters and Journals* (1956); *Nathaniel Hawthorne, Man and Writer* (1961); *A Preface to Literature* (1954); *Seven Daughters of the Theater* (1964); *The Personality of Chaucer* (1968); *The Personality of Milton* (1970); *The Seven Worlds of Theodore Roosevelt* (1958); *Utopia Americana* (1920); *Values in Literature* (1928); *Washington Irving: Moderation Displayed* (1962).

International Standard Book Number: 0-8061-0737-5

Library of Congress Catalog Card Number: 67-15630

Once more, inevitably, after twenty-five years

but now with greatly enriched meaning

to Dorothy

Preface

Mark Twain: The Man and His Work was first published, by the Yale University Press, in 1935, as my contribution to the centenary celebration of Mark Twain's birth. The author wished to call it "Mark Twain: A Centenary Portrait," but the publishers objected, and he reluctantly agreed to accept their title, which, since the book is a psychograph, very imperfectly indicated its character. The volume enjoyed a remarkably generous press, was at once accepted as a standard book on Mark Twain, and has continued to be cited frequently in Mark Twain books and articles clear down to the present day. It has, however, long been out of print, and I have welcomed the willingness of the University of Oklahoma Press to permit me to rewrite it for this present edition. The old title, still inappropriate, has been retained because it is against the policy of the Press to alter the title of a republished book.

Though I have made no general alterations in the plan of my book, it has, nevertheless, been so thoroughly rewritten and revised that few paragraphs have escaped alteration. There is a

good deal of material which is entirely new. Though Albert Bigelow Paine had made many of the basic materials needed for Mark
Twain study available before 1935, most of the really serious historical and critical study has been done since that date. I have
read it all, have reconsidered my view of Mark Twain in the light
of its findings, and have tried to incorporate its essence, so that,
in addition to containing my own vision of Mark Twain, this volume may claim to be as adequate a summary of the state of Mark
Twain knowledge as of 1960 as it was as of 1935.

During his lifetime, Paine allowed nobody to consult the Mark
Twain Papers; the only manuscript material I used in my first
edition were the letters to Mrs. Fairbanks, in the Huntington
Library. These have since been printed in their entirety. After
Bernard DeVoto became literary editor of the Estate, all the materials were made available to scholars, but so long as they remained at Harvard, I was in the West, and by the time I came to
the Boston area to live, they had been moved to California. I
should very much have liked to consult them for this revision, but
under existent conditions an extended stay at Berkeley was quite
out of the question.

My most important alterations have been in Chapter III,
which, it will be noted, is the only chapter I have found it necessary to retitle. (It was formerly called "The Divine Amateur.")
In common with a great many other students of Mark Twain in
the thirties, I overstressed the idea that he was a kind of folk artist
and understressed his skill and ability as a bona fide man of letters.
I do not believe that anybody ever rebuked me for this. Certainly
Paine did not, though he was, at the outset, the godfather of my
whole enterprise, and neither did DeVoto, who not only reviewed
my book magnificently, both in *The New England Quarterly* and
on the front page of *The New York Times Book Review*, but encouraged my Mark Twain studies in every possible way. Instead,
they both thought I had not gone far enough, for about the only
criticism either made of me, privately or in print, was that I had
taken too much stock in such articles as that of Olin H. Moore on
Cervantes, in which it was shown that Mark Twain had, in some
cases, importantly employed literary sources. Today, Moore is

seen as a perspicacious pioneer of a view that has grown more and more important, and the notion that Mark Twain was a kind of unconscious artist has been demolished by many scholars. There was not a great deal left of it after Professor Gladys Carmen Bellamy had published *Mark Twain as a Literary Artist* in 1950, but even without Miss Bellamy it must have been finished off by Walter Blair's brilliant account of the making of *Huckleberry Finn*.

I *have* been rebuked, however—and quite justly—for the tentative and conjectural portrait of Joseph H. Twichell as a somewhat worldly cleric, in my first edition. Though I did not mean to be unfair to Twichell, Bliss Perry and William Lyon Phelps long ago convinced me that I had been, and I cried *"peccavi"* in a letter published in *The Saturday Review of Literature*, Vol. XVII, April 2, 1938, p. 13. This communication was not indexed; consequently nobody seems to have read it, a circumstance which largely reduces to irrelevance the treatment of my views in Kenneth R. Andrews's *Nook Farm: Mark Twain's Hartford Circle* and in Leah Audrey Strong's unpublished doctoral dissertation for Syracuse University, "Joseph Hopkins Twichell: A Biography of Mark Twain's Pastor" (1953). My comments on Twichell contained a number of factual errors, and my over-all evaluation was a snap judgment. I have never, I think, in any of my books, been guilty of a similar injustice to anybody else, and not the least of the reasons why I am grateful for the opportunity of bringing out this new edition is that it gives me an opportunity to remove and to apologize for the offense.

In my first edition, I also gave a good deal of space to debating various issues which had been raised by Van Wyck Brooks in his highly controversial book, *The Ordeal of Mark Twain*. If I treated Twichell disrespectfully, it is now my feeling that I treated, not Brooks but the Brooks thesis, with much more respect than it deserved, so much so, indeed, that in some quarters I was supposed, though inconceivably as it appears to me, to have more sympathy with it than I ever had. Thus while DeVoto's *New York Times* review of my book was subtitled "A New Biography That Silences the Frustration Theory," I rubbed my eyes when I read in the London *Times Literary Supplement* that my view of Mark Twain was virtually in agreement with that of Brooks. Whatever right *The Ordeal of Mark Twain* may have had in 1935 to be discussed at length it now seems to me to have lost; consequently there are few references to it in this edition.

I have also taken out many topical references as of 1935 (Herr Schönemann will no longer have to be distressed by my disrespectful reference to Hitler), and I have also removed a good deal of juvenility, both in thought and in expression.

Miss Patricia M. Willson, Mr. Harry Earl Jones, and Mr. Harold von Arx gave me help in connection with my first edition for which I am still grateful; I also received kindnesses of various kinds from Professors Minnie M. Brashear, Henry A. Pochmann, and Ottis B. Sperlin, as well as a number of correspondents who wrote to me in reply to my "card" in the book review journals. In connection with this present edition, Professor Henry Nash Smith, the present literary editor of the Mark Twain Estate, and his assistant, Mr. Frederick Anderson, have been very kind in answering questions, and I have received favors from Professors Adolph B. Benson, Fred W. Lorch, Alexander E. Jones, Leah Audrey Strong, Cecil B. Williams, and Mrs. Caroline Thomas Harnsberger. To all, my best thanks.

I am very grateful also, as I was in 1935, to Harper and Brothers and the Mark Twain Company for their great kindness in allowing me to quote from Mark Twain's writings, letters, etc., and from books about Mark Twain controlled by them.

Further thanks are due, and gladly extended, to the following, for permission to quote from the works indicated: The Atlantic Monthly Press (*Memories of a Hostess*, by M. A. DeWolfe Howe); Coward-McCann, Inc., and Mr. Arthur Leonard Ross, attorney for the Frank Harris Estate (*Contemporary Portraits*, Fourth Series, by Frank Harris); The Crowell Publishing Company ("Painting the Portrait of Mark Twain," by S. J. Woolf, *Collier's*, Vol. XLV); Doubleday and Company (*Life in Letters of William Dean Howells*, edited by Mildred Howells; *Midstream*, by Helen Keller; *Many Celebrities and a Few Others*, by William H. Rideing); Harcourt, Brace and Company and the author (*A Lifetime with Mark Twain*, by Mary Lawton); Houghton Mifflin Company (*The Education of Henry Adams; Crowding Memories*, by Mrs. Thomas Bailey Aldrich; *American Portraits, 1875–1900*, by Gamaliel Bradford); John Howell (*Sketches of the Sixties*, by Bret Harte and Mark Twain); Little, Brown and Company and the author (*Mark Twain's America*, by Bernard DeVoto); A. C. McClurg and Company (*Mark Twain and the Happy Island*, by Elizabeth Wallace); *The Outlook* ("Mark Twain as a Newspaper Reporter," by Frank M. White); and University of North Carolina Press (*Mark Twain, Son of Missouri*, by Minnie M. Brashear).

Edward Wagenknecht

Boston University

Contents

MARK TWAIN: The Man and His Work

CHAPTER ONE: *The Matrix*

I

MARK TWAIN WAS AN ACTOR who appeared beneath the proscenium arch of the heavens in many different roles. He was Tom Sawyer (with just a touch of Huckleberry Finn); he was Colonel Sellers; he was the Connecticut Yankee; he was Joan of Arc. As Tom Sawyer he spent his youth "drowsing in the sunshine of a summer morning . . . the great Mississippi, the magnificent Mississippi rolling its mile-wide tide along; . . . the dense forest away on the other side"; and many years later, his remembrance of things past made it possible for him to preserve as literature one of the most romantic aspects in the development of America. As Colonel Sellers he dreamed mighty dreams of power and glory, dreams of fabulous riches that were to come rolling in upon him, first from the Tennessee land, then from that marvelous typesetting machine of James Paige in which he was to sink a fortune, but always mixing on his palette the colors of fact and the colors of hope until, at last, when old age was upon him, he could remember only the things that had never happened. As the Connecticut Yankee he first vaunted his Americanism against the old culture and the old corruptions of Europe, attacking with leather-lunged frontier laughter everything that the frontier could not understand; then, widening his scope, he began to think in broadly human terms, assailing selfishness and oppression everywhere, himself gone "grailing" in behalf of a loftier dream than ever King Arthur knew. Finally, as Joan of Arc he became the embodiment of the very chivalry and idealism he had sometimes been wont to deride.

✳ A mighty figure and an impressive one upon our horizon, a figure destined for a permanent place in the American mythology —and these were the roles that he played. I have called him an actor, and I do not degrade him, for in the larger sense all creative artists are actors, whatever their special medium may be. Shakespeare creates his characters by the simple expedient of permitting them to talk themselves alive. Dickens "verifies" in his own person, as he himself expresses it, the experiences and emotions of those whom he creates. The prophet Ezekiel is not satisfied to declare his message; he must make a drama of it and act it out. And Jesus of Nazareth himself has been distinguished from other great religious teachers on this very score. Not merely the herald of his Gospel, he was his Gospel, and he reached the supreme height of his self-expression not as he uttered the words of the Sermon on the Mount but when he hung on the cross at Golgotha.

In other words, when we speak of a man's art as essentially histrionic, we intend to indicate precisely what the term does not connote in the mind of the average reader. The actor uses himself as the instrument upon which he would play. He takes upon himself that which he would represent, becomes the embodiment of his own idea. The process is essentially mystical, creative, and only the mystic can altogether understand it. The great characters of fiction are built from the inside out. Popular demand has not called them into being, nor do they conform to the "types" favored by this magazine or that publisher. They are so many emanations of the man who created them; and the life that informs them, as they go about their business in the world, in his life. Only

4

by life can life be created. The law holds in biology; it holds also in art.

All these things are true in a peculiarly intimate sense of Mark Twain. Among the great writers of the world, I know none who is closer to his material or whose success is more directly depend- ent upon his ability to assimilate it. This accounts, on the one hand, for his extraordinary vividness when he is at his best; on the other, for the many absurdities he perpetrated when he wandered out of his proper field. For this reason, too, his own personality is more important to his readers than the personalities of writers like Shakespeare, or even Henry James, who, as artists, could project themselves much farther away from the things that mat- tered to them as individuals. It is all very well to say that we are not concerned with the life of a man of genius but only with his works. But when his life and his works are one—what then?

II

Mark Twain himself attempted a summary of his life-experi- ence—and consequently of his qualifications for authorship—in a letter of 1891:

> . . . I confine myself to life with which I am familiar when pre- tending to portray life. But I confined myself to the *boy*-life out on the Mississippi because that had a peculiar charm for me, and not because I was not familiar with other phases of life. I was a *soldier* two weeks once in the beginning of the war, and was hunted like a rat the whole time. My splendid Kipling himself hasn't a more burnt-in, hard-baked, and unforgetable familiarity with that death- on-the-pale-horse-with-hell-following-after, which is a raw soldier's first fortnight in the field—and which, without any doubt, is the most tremendous fortnight and the vividest he is ever going to see.
> Yes, and I have shoveled silver tailings in a quartz-mill a couple of weeks, and acquired the last possibilities of culture in *that* direc- tion. And I've done "pocket-mining" during three months in the one little patch of ground in the whole globe where Nature con- ceals gold in pockets—or *did* before we robbed all of those pockets and exhausted, obliterated, annihilated the most curious freak

5

Nature ever indulged in. There are not thirty men left alive who, being told there was a pocket hidden on the broad slope of a mountain, would know how to go and find it, or have even the faintest idea of how to set about it; but I am one of the possible 20 or 30 who possess the secret, and I could go and put my hand on that hidden treasure with a most deadly precision.

And I've been a prospector, and know pay rock from poor when I find it—just with a touch of the tongue. And I've been a *silver* miner and know how to dig and shovel and drill and put in a blast. And so I know the mines and miners interiorly as well as Bret Harte knows them exteriorly.

And I was a newspaper reporter four years in cities, and saw the inside of many things; and was reporter in a legislature two sessions and the same in Congress one session, and thus learned to know personally three sample bodies of the smallest minds and the selfishest souls and the cowardliest hearts that God makes.

And I was some years a Mississippi pilot, and familiarly knew all the different kinds of steamboatmen—a race apart, and not like other folk.

And I was for some years a traveling "jour" printer, and wandered from city to city—and so I know *that* sect familiarly.

And I was a lecturer on the public platform a number of seasons and was a responder to toasts at all the different kinds of banquets —and so I know a great many secrets about audiences—secrets not to be got out of books, but only acquirable by experience.

And I watched over one dear project of mine for years, spent a fortune on it, and failed to make it go—and the history of that would make a large book in which a million men would see themselves as in a mirror; and they would testify and say, Verily, this is not imagination; this fellow has been there—and after would cast dust upon their heads, cursing and blaspheming.

And I am a publisher, and did pay to one author's widow (General Grant's) the largest copyright checks this world has seen— aggregating more then £80,000 in the first year.

And I have been an author for 20 years and an ass for 55.

This characteristic statement calls for some comment and amplification.

Samuel Langhorne Clemens was born, the seventh-months

child of John Marshall Clemens and Jane Lampton Clemens, in Florida, Monroe County, Missouri, on November 30, 1835.

According to his own belief,[1] he was the third son and fifth child in a family of six. His ancestry was mostly English and partly Irish through Virginia and Kentucky—"Quakers and Indian fighters, independent farmers and small slaveholders," Dixon Wecter[2] calls them. The family liked to speculate about noble ancestors (and a claim on the earlship of Durham), about their kinship with one of King Charles I's judges, and even about a strain of Spanish blood supposed to have been brought into the family by an ambassadorial Clemens. However all this may have been in fact, it importantly stimulated Mark Twain's imagination and furnished him literary material—certainly in *The American Claimant*, perhaps also, much more importantly, in connection with the Duke and the Dauphin in *Huckleberry Finn*.

When Samuel was four years old, the family removed to Hannibal, in Marion County, on the west bank of the Mississippi.

"Circled with bluffs" and "the shining river in the foreground"[3]—the river that was the highway of the nation, the river whose great historian he was to become—Hannibal, on its physical side, became, in *Tom Sawyer* and in *Huckleberry Finn*, a part of the literature of the world. Mark Twain gave us the Missouri countryside also, notably in those magnificent passages in his autobiography in which he describes his summers on his Uncle John Quarles's farm, near Florida. Not even "The Eve of St. Agnes" is richer in sense-impressions than those descriptions.

There were only 450 people in Hannibal when Mark Twain came there, but it held 3,000 and was the second city in the state by the time he left. Though it was rude enough even in Mark Twain's idealized memory of it, it was not quite the cultural wilderness it has sometimes been represented. A good many of its

[1] Samuel C. Webster (*Mark Twain, Business Man,* 44), who descends from Mark Twain's sister Pamela, claims that there was yet another child, Pleasants Hannibal, who died at the age of three months, before Mark Twain was born. This fact, if it is a fact, Mark Twain never knew, and when Webster mentioned it to him, he refused to accept it.

[2] Much the best account of Mark Twain's ancestors is in Dixon Wecter, *Sam Clemens of Hannibal,* chapters I–II.

[3] Albert Bigelow Paine, *Mark Twain: A Biography,* I, 26.

families, like Mark Twain's own, had come from the South, and they brought something of tradition and background with them. Carriages, wagons, omnibuses, river boats, and flour were manufactured in Hannibal. The Marion Female Academy was housed in the Christian church, and the Reverend Daniel Emerson's English and Classical School held its sessions in the First Presbyterian church. There were five newspapers, three bookstores, and a public library in which Mark Twain's older brother Orion was a shareholder. Hannibal papers advertised the better British and American magazines, and newspaper "fillers" drew freely upon the classics and upon standard English writers, particularly of the eighteenth century.[4]

Little sympathy existed at any time between Mark Twain and his father. The boy's volatile temperament apparently lay beyond the range of the father's understanding, as also, in all likelihood, did that of the mother from whom he inherited it. John Marshall Clemens was an austere man, in religion a freethinker, in ethical conduct an undeviating puritan, a lawyer by profession, a merchant by necessity, an unselfish leader in all community enterprises. In all likelihood, Mark Twain owed more to him than he ever realized. Mark's almost fanatical financial rectitude was that of John Marshall Clemens all over again; so was the element of stability in his complex character which, with his genius, differentiated him from his lovable but impractical brother Orion. It would be interesting to know to what extent, if any, his religious apostasy was influenced by his father's example. When he was dying, John Marshall Clemens was asked by a clergyman whether he believed in Christ and in the saving blood of Christ; he answered, "I do." The son died without benefit of clergy, but he is reported to have pressed his daughter's hand and murmured, "Good-by, dear, if we meet —." Even in minor matters there are resemblances between the two. The father, also, was absent-minded, and he anticipated Mark's interest in inventions within his limited means when he tinkered with a perpetual motion machine.

With the mother the case was very different. Her tempera-

4 See Minnie M. Brashear, *Mark Twain, Son of Missouri*, especially chapter II.

8

ment was Mark Twain's temperament, and her influence upon him can be seen at every turn. It was not at all the narrowing influence which some writers have described. Jane Lampton Clemens was a Presbyterian, but she was not a fanatic, and her religion was never a burden to her. She was an intensely social being—in her youth a Kentucky belle devoted to dancing. She loved the theater and hated housekeeping. At one period she smoked a pipe.

From her Mark Twain inherited many specific tastes and tendencies—his love of red, his tenderness toward all animals, especially cats, his quick, impulsive emotion, his lifelong habit of protecting the outcast and unfortunate. No stray animal was ever turned away from Jane Clemens's door. At one time she was feeding nineteen cats. But she kept no birds, for she could not endure to think of any creature deprived of its freedom.

She had her son's curiosity also. With her it took the special form of investigating strange religions, which she considered carefully but without committing herself to them. She was capable of great indignation and of dauntless courage. Once she opened her door to a fugitive girl whom her brutal father was pursuing with a rope, then planted herself in it and gave the brute such a tongue-lashing that he slunk away. Like her son, she mingled freely, in her conversation, fact and fiction. Like him, she was unconventional, as when she heard two men on a train arguing about where Mark Twain was born and turned around and told them. "I'm his mother," she said. "I ought to know. I was there." Something of his cryptic gift of phrase was hers also, as shown in her remark, "Never learn to do anything. If you don't learn, you'll always find someone else to do it for you."

John Marshall Clemens died in 1847. It was Mark Twain's impression in later life that he was immediately taken out of school and apprenticed to the printing trade. It has now been shown that he remained in school at least until 1849, though he probably worked part time as many schoolboys have done.[5] This was at first in Hannibal, for his brother and others, but from June, 1853, on, elsewhere. He tarried in Washington, Philadelphia, and

[5] See Wecter, *Sam Clemens of Hannibal*, 131.

9

New York. He worked again for Orion in Keokuk, Iowa, stayed for a little while in Cincinnati, then, according to the established story, set out for South America to earn his fortune. But we now know that he did not wait until he got to New Orleans to decide instead to apprentice himself to Horace Bixby and learn piloting on the Mississippi.[6] Indeed a notebook entry shows that this glamorous profession had already appealed to him as early as 1855, when he was nineteen.[7]

To become a pilot, Mark Twain set himself "the stupendous task of learning the twelve hundred miles of the Mississippi River between St. Louis and New Orleans—of knowing it as exactly and unfailingly, even in the dark, as one knows the way to his own features." The river absorbed his energies from 1857 until the coming of the Civil War in 1861, and this period has a glamour all its own in his life, for this was when he established his independence and proved to himself and to others that he was able to do a man's work in the world. "When I find a well-drawn character in fiction or biography," he was to write in later years, "I generally take a warm personal interest in him, for the reason that I have known him before—met him on the river." Yet he may have exaggerated the importance of the Mississippi period, for the more we learn of his Hannibal and Keokuk days, the more deeply do his roots seem to sink into that soil. Nostalgia informs *Life on the Mississippi,* and the pathos of distance hovers about it. The coarser, harsher aspects of steamboat life, in an age of cutthroat competition and easy indulgences, are passed over altogether; a tired man is trying to recapture his lost youth.

Some students of Mark Twain have been of the opinion that it was as a pilot that he really found himself, adjusting himself to life, experiencing a satisfaction which not even his later trade of authorship could ever give him. There are times when Mark Twain himself supports this opinion. "I am a person who would quit authorizing in a minute to go to piloting," he wrote Howells in 1874, "if the madam would stand it." But he is writing under the spell of the enthusiasm awakened by going back to the river,

---

6 Walter Blair, *Mark Twain and "Huck Finn,"* 41.
7 Edwin H. Carpenter, Jr., *Mark Twain . . . ,* 11.

in his imagination, for his Mississippi articles: it is authorship that has inspired him even while he disclaims interest in authorship! He might have returned to piloting after the war if he had cared to do so; there was no "madam" to hold him then. Mining did not really suit him, but when he gave it up, he went on to journalism, not back to steamboating. The truth is that the pilot's life, though ideally suited to Mark Twain's needs at a critical period in his development, could never have absorbed him permanently. In his old age he used to have nightmares in which he was haunted by the horror of being obliged to go back to the river for bread.

It was during his pilot days, too, that Mark Twain experienced the first great sorrow of his life. In 1858 his younger brother Henry, drawn to the river by Sam's success, lost his life as the result of injuries sustained in the horrible *Pennsylvania* steamboat disaster. A contemporary newspaper reported that when Sam arrived at the bedside of his injured brother, "his feelings so much overcame him, at the scalded and emaciated form before him, that he sank to the floor overpowered."[8] It was the first of many disasters for which his "trained Presbyterian conscience" was to cause him to blame himself.

Mark Twain's connection with the Civil War was both brief and loose. He may have had some military connection in New Orleans; if so, we know none of the details.[9] Nor do we know a great deal more about his adventures with an informally organized Confederate group in Missouri, for "The Private History of a Campaign That Failed" mingles fact with fiction. Nevertheless the fact remains that Lieutenant Clemens shortly mustered himself out of Confederate service and went to Nevada with his brother Orion, a staunch Union man, whom President Lincoln had appointed secretary of the Territory.[10]

The journey is described in *Roughing It*. In Nevada, Mark Twain entered upon his various mining activities and came in

[8] Quoted by Fred W. Lorch, "Mark Twain and the *Pennsylvania* Disaster," *Twainian*, Vol. IX, Jan.-Feb., 1950, p. 2.

[9] See Ernest E. Leisy, ed., *The Letters of Quintus Curtius Snodgrass, ix.*

[10] Mark Twain's attitude toward the Civil War is discussed in the last chapter of this volume.

contact with many different aspects of Western life. He had drifted to Aurora, California, and was poor indeed in this world's gods when the opportunity came, late in the summer of 1862, to take a place on the staff of the Virginia City (Nevada) *Enterprise,* a paper edited by Joe Goodman in an atmosphere of frontier irresponsibility and bohemian camaraderie, flavored with a good deal in the way of sound literary taste and judgment. Here he first used the name Mark Twain,[11] and here he began to build up his West Coast reputation. In those days the journalistic hoax was still his favorite form of humor, and the consequences were not always pleasant. The results of one affair involved a precipitate retreat to San Francisco, where he found a somewhat uncongenial berth on the *Morning Call.*[12] From San Francisco, too, he found it prudent in time to retreat, but this time the circumstances were all to his credit. He had been too frank in his criticism of a corrupt police department. For three months he lived in Calaveras County, where, with Jim Gillis, he tried pocket mining on Jackass Hill. In 1865, Artemus Ward, whom Mark Twain had met briefly in Virginia City, wrote from the East coast to ask for a sketch to be included in a new book of humor. Mark Twain sent a story he had heard about a jumping frog. Arriving too late to be included in the book, "Jim Smiley and His Jumping Frog," as it was then called, appeared instead in the *Saturday Press,* on November 18, 1865; this marks the real beginning of Mark Twain's Eastern reputation.[13]

[11] "Mark Twain" is a piloting term and means two fathoms or "safe water." Samuel Clemens was afterwards under the impression that he had borrowed it from the nearly illiterate Captain Isaiah Sellers, and Paine accepted his statement, but it now seems as though this were one more example of his remembering the thing that did not happen. See Ernest E. Leisy, "Mark Twain and Isaiah Sellers," *American Literature,* Vol. XIII (1942), 398–404; George Hiram Brownell, "A Question as to the Origin of the Name 'Mark Twain'," *Twainian,* N.S. Vol. I, Feb., 1942, pp. 4–7, and cf. April, pp. 7–8 and May, pp. 3–5.

[12] For the hoaxes and other difficulties which contributed to Mark Twain's departure from Virginia City (and which are not always accurately related), see, especially, Henry Nash Smith and Frederick Anderson, eds., *Mark Twain of the "Enterprise"* and DeLancey Ferguson, " 'The Petrified Truth'," *Colophon,* N.S. Vol. II, No. 2 (1937), 189–96.

[13] *Jim Smiley and His Jumping Frog* may be read, with an introduction by Franklin J. Meine, in a little book published in Chicago by the Pocahontas Press in 1940. It was not Sam Clemens's first story or even his first appearance in the

In 1866 the Sacramento *Union* sent Mark Twain to the Sandwich (or, as we now call them, the Hawaiian) Islands; while there he brought his paper a "scoop" in the form of an interview with the survivors of the *Hornet* disaster, in which interest was very keen at the time. His initial contribution to *Harper's Magazine* dealt with the same subject, but unfortunately his name appeared as "Mark Swain." In December, 1866, he went east, as he supposed, for a visit. Unexpectedly, he lectured at Cooper Union. Still more unexpectedly, he sailed, in June, 1867, on the *Quaker City* Mediterranean steamboat excursion for Europe and the Holy Land, writing, for the *Alta California* and other papers, the travel letters which, revised in *The Innocents Abroad*, were soon to make him the most famous humorist of his time. It was indeed a momentous voyage, for both his personal and his professional future were decided by it. One day, in the Bay of Smyrna, a wealthy young man of Elmira, New York, named Charles J. Langdon, showed him a miniature reproduction of the face of his sister Olivia. With that face Mark Twain immediately fell hopelessly and everlastingly in love. In July, 1869, *The Innocents Abroad* was published, and on February 2, 1870, Samuel L. Clemens and Olivia Langdon were married.

Successful as *The Innocents Abroad* had been, it had not yet occurred to Mark Twain that he could rely for his livelihood upon authorship alone; he bought, therefore, an interest in the Buffalo *Express*. This venture did not turn out well. The first months of marriage were almost fantastically overshadowed by sickness. In August, Mrs. Clemens's father died, and on November 7, after Livy had been cruelly jolted in a cab, her first child, Langdon, was prematurely born. By the end of 1871, the Clemenses had moved to the Nook Farm neighborhood in Hartford, Connecticut, where, in 1874, Mark Twain was to build on Farmington Avenue the beautiful "English violet" house, which, now happily open to the public, is still one of the rococo show places of the

East. "The Dandy Frightening the Squatter" was published in the Boston *Carpet Bag*, May 1, 1852, when he was only sixteen years old. This tale was discovered by Mr. Meine. For Sam's cub-printer writings in the Hannibal *Journal*, when Orion injudiciously left him in charge, see Brashear, *Mark Twain, Son of Missouri*, chapter IV.

Western world. In Hartford, in 1872, little Langdon died, and in the same year *Roughing It* was published.

The years 1872 and 1873 were spent largely in England, lecturing, being entertained, and laying the foundations of a later world fame. During the Hartford years the summer months were spent at Quarry Farm, near Elmira, the home of Mrs. Clemens's sister, and here, in an open-air hilltop study, much of Mark Twain's best writing was done. During these years, again, Mark Twain became the happy father of three little girls—Susy, Clara, and Jean; he also extended his business interests, developing the tendency toward unwise investments that led finally to his business collapse. In 1873 he published, with Charles Dudley Warner, a Hartford neighbor, his first extended piece of fiction, *The Gilded Age*. In 1876 came *The Adventures of Tom Sawyer*. A trip to Europe yielded *A Tramp Abroad* in 1880. *The Prince and the Pauper*, a serious historical juvenile came out in 1881. In 1883 *Life on the Mississippi* appeared, to be followed a year later by *Adventures of Huckleberry Finn*. In 1889 came an earnest, extended satire, *A Connecticut Yankee in King Arthur's Court*.

In 1891, harassed by financial difficulties, Clemens closed his Hartford house and moved with his family to Europe. A long struggle ended in 1894 when the failure of both the Paige typesetter and the Charles L. Webster publishing company left Mark Twain nearly $100,000 in debt. Like Sir Walter Scott before him, he refused to take advantage of the bankruptcy laws and set out in the summer of 1895, in the company of Mrs. Clemens and their second daughter, Clara, for a lecture tour of the world. Opening in Cleveland, he gave twenty-four midsummer lectures in the United States before sailing across the Pacific from Vancouver, B. C. His success was all that could have been hoped for—even in India and Ceylon the response was enthusiastic—but just as the burden of debt had been lifted, Susy, Mark Twain's eldest daughter, whom he so passionately loved, and who had inherited so much of his own great spirit, died suddenly, across the ocean from him in Hartford, and half the reawakening glory of life died with her.

The books continued—*The American Claimant*, his least effective long story, in 1891; *Tom Sawyer Abroad* and *Pudd'nhead Wilson*, both partial successes, in 1894; then, in 1896, both *Tom Sawyer, Detective* and a long, serious historical novel, *Personal Recollections of Joan of Arc*, which was written for love and serialized without his name in *Harper's Magazine*, because he wanted it to be judged on its own merits. *Following the Equator*, his last travel book, came along in 1897, to tell the story of the world tour and pay off the last of his debts.

The Clemens family remained in Europe until 1900, when they returned to America, though not to Hartford, for Mrs. Clemens felt she could never bear to see the Hartford house again. In 1903, when her health finally broke, they removed to Florence, and it was here, in an old Italian villa, on June 5, 1904, that the much-loved Livy died. Feeling singularly helpless without her, Mark Twain and his two remaining daughters brought her body and their possessions and themselves back to America; with characteristic thoughtfulness, President Theodore Roosevelt personally ordered that they be extended the courtesy of the Port of New York.

They took a house on lower Fifth Avenue, and Mark Twain resumed his writing. He wrote enormously during the last years of his life, but much of what he wrote remained unfinished and unpublished. Mrs. Clemens had always opposed the publication of his "gospel" of determinism, *What Is Man?*. It was privately printed, unsigned, in 1906, but it was not added to his collected works until 1917. *The Mysterious Stranger*, his last important work of fiction, was published in a special format, with illustrations by N. C. Wyeth which Mark Twain would have loved, in 1916. The last books—all brief, all save the second quite unimportant—that their author himself saw through the press were *Christian Science* and *Extract from Captain Stormfield's Visit to Heaven*,[14] both in 1907, and *Is Shakespeare Dead?* in 1909. Yet he was always writing, always when he was not playing billiards, or cursing the war lords, or playing with cats and little girls. He

---

[14] *Captain Stormfield* is an early work, but for some reason Mark Twain always considered it very shocking. The full text was not printed until *Report from Paradise* appeared in 1952.

filled the magazines, and he filled the public eye. The reporters were after him continually; no public occasion was complete without him. A series of academic honors was climaxed wonderfully in 1907 when Oxford University draped his venerable whiteness with the scarlet robes of a Doctor of Letters. In 1908 he moved to his beautiful new house, "Stormfield," at Redding, Connecticut. On the day before Christmas, 1909, life struck at him for the last time, when his youngest daughter, Jean, was taken with an epileptic seizure and died in her bath. Halley's Comet had blazed in the skies just before Mark Twain was born in 1835. It was due back in 1910, and he had said he would go out with it. It reached its maximum splendor on April 19. On April 21, Mark Twain quietly died.

III

All that was fifty years and more ago, and a great deal of water has run under our bridges since, but we have had nobody to take his place. He is one of the great archetypal Americans, and one can no more think of the late nineteenth and early twentieth century without thinking of him than one can think of the Civil War years without seeing in imagination the long, gaunt figure of Abraham Lincoln. For that matter, probably the very best thing ever said about him was said by William Dean Howells when he called him "the Lincoln of our literature."

To be sure, it was often his personality, rather than his art, by which his contemporaries were enthralled. We have had great writers since Mark Twain, and we shall have others in the future, but it is not likely, these swiftly moving days, that another will capture the imagination of the public as he captured it and hold it so long.

At home he was called "the belle of New York." Abroad, he described himself as "self-appointed ambassador-at-large of the United States of America—without salary." Royalty and nobility, brains and character gravitated to him during his foreign residences, and in the early days, before the family had quite got used to the wonder of it, Jean expressed the astonishment of all in the famous remark which her father was never quite sure he could take as a compliment: "Why, papa, if this goes on, pretty soon there won't be anybody left for you to meet except God." Convinced democrat though he was, he could not help being flattered by such attentions, and it is astonishing to see with what easy grace he adapts himself, accepting homage with the ease of one born to the purple, unfailingly courteous, and completely free from the brashness of spirit which so often appears as an attempt to cover up a fundamental, deep-seated uncertainty or embarrassment. There are few more delightful anecdotes than the account of how, on a public occasion in Vienna, he was stopped by a guard as he attempted to pass a certain barrier, only to have the officer in charge rush up in great excitement. "Let him pass," he cried. "*Lieber Gott!* Don't you see it's Herr Mark Twain."

As we look back upon him now, there seems a curious dream quality in his life. As Gamaliel Bradford expresses it, "During the first decade of the twentieth century he drifted in his white dream garments—as Emily Dickinson did in solitude—through dream crowds who applauded him and looked up to him and loved him." And this impression is firmly rooted in the kind of man he was. "Mark Twain," says his biographer, "lived curiously apart from the actualities of life."

He was tremendously interested in dreams always, and he had a rich, sometimes terrible, dream life of his own. Like most artists he could dream awake as well as sleeping: when Mrs. Clemens was ill at York Harbor, he went about, for all the world like St. Francis of Assisi, pinning up notices on the trees warning the birds not to sing too loudly. "We are such stuff as dreams are made on," wrote Shakespeare at the close of his career, and Mark Twain develops the same conception much more elaborately in *The Mysterious Stranger*. Sometimes it even seemed to him that his own life had been a dream:

> I dreamed I was born and grew up and was a pilot on the Mississippi and a miner and a journalist in Nevada and a pilgrim in the *Quaker City* and had a wife and children and went to live in a villa at Florence—and this dream goes on and on and sometimes seems so real that I almost believe it is real. I wonder if it is? But there is

no way to tell, for if one applies tests they would be part of the dream too, and so would simply aid the deceit.

And again, he sums up the whole human pageant in words which are as beautiful as they are sad:

> Old Age, white-headed, the temple empty, the idols broken, the worshippers in their graves, nothing left but You, a remnant, a tradition, belated fag-end of a foolish dream, a dream that was so ingeniously dreamed that it seemed real all the time; nothing left but You, center of a snowy desolation, perched on the ice-summit, gazing out over the stages of the long *trek* and asking Yourself, "Would you do it again if you had the chance?"

However spectacularly a man with such a temperament may behave upon the stage of the world, it must be clear that his inner life will be even more intense and richer. If we would understand Mark Twain as man and artist, it is time, then, to turn to the world within as he built it up through the various agencies that became available for his use.

CHAPTER TWO: *The World Within*

I

FOR AESTHETIC EXPERIENCE in general Mark Twain was well prepared if love for the beauties of nature constitutes such prepara-
tion. Even in boyhood he had the genuine Romantic passion.
"He pitied the dead leaf and the murmuring dried weed of November," writes Albert Bigelow Paine, "because their brief lives
were ended, and they would never know the summer again or grow
glad with another spring." Here the melancholy note predominates, as it often does in Tom Sawyer's meditations, as it did with
Byron, Shelley, and Keats, and some of Mark Twain's nature passages in that first heir of his invention, *The Innocents Abroad*,
can almost be quoted in the same breath with the outpourings of
the Romantic poets.

"It was heaven and hell and sunset and rainbows and the
aurora all fused into one divine harmony," he writes of the autumn splendors, "and you couldn't look at it and keep the tears
back." He is "drunk . . . with the autumn foliage." He must shut
his eyes when he shaves: "This painted dream distracts my hand

and threatens my throat. And I have to stop and write this post-script to quiet my mind and lower my temperature, so that I can go and stand between the windows again and without peril resume." These raptures did not decline as he grew older. At Storm-field, during his last days, he so loved the glorious New England countryside that he never wished to go to the city again.

Mark Twain's most famous piece of descriptive writing is the picture of the ice storm in *Following the Equator*,[1] but it was not the spectacular aspects of nature that enthralled him most. The austere aspirations of Switzerland and the sensuous seductions of Hawaii held him, but so did the quiet, unspectacular beauties of rural England, which he viewed with "rapture and ecstasy." Running water always excited him, and there is nothing lovelier in his books than his pictures of Hannibal under the shadow of night, or of dawn breaking over the mighty river. The experiences of his youth gave him a measuring rod which he never ceased to use. So he watches the sunset in Florence and drinks in its glories, but he declares that it cannot be compared with the sunsets on the Mississippi. And neither Como nor Galilee could dim for him his memories of Lake Tahoe.

In the face of the grander aspects of nature, Mark Twain was always inclined to be impressed by the pettiness and the insignificance of man and his fevered, hectic doings. So he writes his mother from Carson City in 1861:

> I said we are situated in a flat, sandy desert. True. And surrounded on all sides by such prodigious mountains that when you stand at a distance from Carson and gaze at them awhile,—until, by mentally measuring them, and comparing them with things of smaller size, you begin to conceive of their grandeur, and next to feel their vastness expanding your soul like a balloon, and ultimately find yourself growing, and swelling, and spreading into a colossus, and I say when this point is reached, you look disdainfully down upon the insignificant village of Carson, reposing like a cheap print away yonder at the foot of the big hills, and in that instant you are seized with a burning desire to stretch forth your hand, put the city in your pocket, and walk off with it.

[1] Chapter XXIII.

At Niagara, too, it seemed to him that tourists and photographers combined to show what a miserable race human beings are:

Any day, in the hands of these photographers, you may see stately pictures of papa and mamma, Johnny and Bub and Sis, or a couple of country cousins, all smiling hideously, and all disposed in studied and uncomfortable attitudes in their carriage, and all looming up in their grand and awe-inspiring imbecility before the snubbed and diminished presentment of that majestic presence, whose ministering spirits are the rainbows, whose voice is the thunder, whose awful front is veiled in clouds, who was monarch here dead and forgotten ages before this hackful of small reptiles was deemed temporarily necessary to fill a crack in the world's unnoted myriads, and will still be monarch here ages and decades after they shall have gathered themselves to their blood relations, the other worms, and been mingled with the unremembering dust.

But the mood is not always angry:

O Switzerland! the further it recedes into the enriching haze of time, the more intolerably delicious the charm of it and the cheer of it and the glory and majesty and solemnity and pathos of it grow. Those mountains had a soul; they thought; they spoke,—one couldn't hear it with the ears of the body, but what a voice it was! —and how real. Deep down in my memory it is sounding yet. Alp calleth unto Alp!—that stately old Scriptural wording is the right one for God's Alps and God's ocean. How puny we were in that awful presence—and how painless it was to be so; how fitting and right it semed, and how stingless was the sense of our unspeakable insignificance. And Lord how pervading were the repose and peace and blessedness that poured out of the heart of the invisible Great Spirit of the Mountains.

II

But how much of this sensitiveness and enthusiasm can he carry over into his experience of the arts, where special technical training is needed for full appreciation?

Architecture he met in many different forms in the course of his wanderings. He praises, blames, judges, and generalizes. He

21

was immensely impressed by the ruins at Ephesus, and he was "carried away, infatuated, entranced with the wonders of the Alhambra and the supernatural beauty of the Alcazar." St. Mark's Cathedral, on the other hand, struck him as a miracle of ineptitude, and he found that it had the same fascination for him as hopelessly bad poetry. In 1868 he thought the Washington Monument an atrocity that ought to be either completed or torn down.

When he lived in Italy, he became considerably interested in the construction of the Italian villa. His own house in Hartford, designed for him by Edwin T. Potter, was anything but conventional; he even required the architect to give him a window over one of the fireplaces so that he could watch the snow falling and the flames leaping up to meet it. He got his own Italian villa when John Mead Howells designed Stormfield for him, but he had nothing to do with its planning, for he took up the position that he did not want to see it or hear anything about it until he moved in and saw the cat purring on the hearth. He had the excellent taste to appreciate it immediately, however, and he took pains to explain to Helen Keller that its architecture was "exactly suited to the natural surroundings; that the dark cedars and pines, which were always green, made a singularly beautiful setting for the white villa."

Concerning sculpture he says little. Late in life, when he was in Washington, he went to Rock Creek Cemetery to see Saint-Gaudens' bronze woman at the grave of Mrs. Henry Adams. He was greatly impressed and had a picture of it framed to keep on his mantel. But he seems to have been much more interested in painting than in sculpture, as, with his passion for color, he might well be expected to be.

His first contact with the arts of brush and pencil was made in the Mississippi Valley via the media of chromo reproductions of famous paintings, steel engravings of Biblical and historical subjects, and landscape daubs by the ambitious young lady of the family. His description in *The Gilded Age* of "the marvelous Historical Paintings" that one must look at in the Capitol at Washington—"and what have you done that you should suffer thus?" —may go back to impressions derived from his first visit to that city, though he could not then have seen the statue of "Mr. Lincoln as petrified by a young lady artist for ten thousand dollars." In New York in 1867 he responded warmly to Bierstadt's "The Domes of the Yosemite," and recorded in some detail his impressions of the paintings at the Academy of Design. (He already disliked the Old Masters.) One day in San Francisco he saw a new picture of Samson and Delilah. He wanted to write about that picture, but his editor—apparently considering art criticism beyond him—was discouraging. Mark was not to be daunted, however, and this is what he turned in:

> Now what is the first thing you see in looking at this picture? . . . Is it the gleaming eyes and fine face of Samson, or the muscular Philistine gazing furtively at the lovely Delilah? Or is it the rich drapery or the truth to nature of that pretty foot? No, sir. The first thing that catches the eye is the scissors on the floor at her feet. Them scissors is too modern. There wasn't no scissors like them in them days, by a damned sight!

Mark Twain's strictures on the Old Masters are so familiar that it seems unnecessary to give them here in detail. To the *Quaker City* pilgrim all saints, martyrs, and madonnas looked alike, and all were alike uninteresting. When he did like a picture, he always discovered that it was an unvalued specimen of the painter's art which he had chosen, and he always liked the copies better than the originals because their colors were brighter. Botticelli roused his special antipathy; he went through life thinking up hard things to say about Botticelli. But the Yankee hits savagely at Raphael—especially at his "Miraculous Draught of Fishes," "where he puts in a miracle of his own—puts three men into a canoe which wouldn't have held a dog without upsetting"—and others do not escape by any means scot-free. There are exceptions, to be sure. A Virgin of Murillo's catches him off guard, and he quite falls in love with her, and Raphael's "Transfiguration" he calls "wonderfully beautiful."

Some of these judgments were reached on non-aesthetic grounds. Mark Twain's hatred of kings and priests influenced him more than he perhaps realized. The painter's "nauseous adulation of princely patrons was more prominent to me and chained my attention more surely than the charms of color and expression which are claimed to be in the pictures." It was unfortunate for Mark Twain that the princely patrons were, in so many cases, such unmitigated scoundrels.

> Raphael pictured such infernal villains as Catherine and Marie de Medici seated in heaven and conversing familiarly with the Virgin Mary and the angels (to say nothing of higher personages), and yet my friends abuse me because I am a little prejudiced against the old masters—because I fail sometimes to see the beauty that is in their productions. I cannot help but see it, now and then, but I keep on protesting against the groveling spirit that could persuade those masters to prostitute their noble talents to the adulation of such monsters as the French, Venetian, and Florentine princes of two and three hundred years ago, all the same.

The limitations of all this as art criticism are clear enough, but it is only fair to Mark Twain to remember that he has much good authority behind him in his refusal to consider the merits of a piece of art apart from the health of the society which produced it.[2]

How much did Mark Twain grow through the years in his ability to appreciate paintings? When he went back to the Old Masters on the *Tramp Abroad* tour, he found "a mellow richness, a subdued color" that he had not been aware of before, or at least he could believe that these things had once been present, and he withdraws his former statement that the copies are better than the originals. He changed his mind about Turner, too. Once he had hated him, but now he could not get past the place where his pictures were exhibited in the National Gallery. He still cannot

---

[2] I cannot agree with Miss Bellamy's view (*Mark Twain as a Literary Artist*, 211) that Mark Twain's tendency to prefer pictures to their originals reflects his dissatisfaction with life; certainly I do not believe that that "was merely a minor expression of his general conception of beauty as unreal." It was, I should say, rather, a major expression of his basically aesthetic nature. Is artistic expression "unreal"? Mark Twain always imagined natural phenomena before seeing them as much greater and more beautiful than they were or could be, and remembered them the same way afterwards.

see beyond the truth or falsity of realistic detail, however—"Paul Veronese's dogs do not resemble dogs; all the horses look like bladders on legs"—and he is still strongly inclined to confuse art with morals and to create a moral issue where none exists: "The most of the picture is a manifest impossibility,—that is to say, a lie; and only rigid cultivation can enable a man to find truth in a lie." Late in life he writes, "I am more reconciled to the old masters now than I was when I was ignorant of art." Yet as late as 1899 he condemns them afresh quite on the old grounds: "The office of art seems to be to grovel in the dirt before Emperors and this and that and the other damned breed of priests."[3]

III

His musical pilgrimage was more interesting. Music, of course, was a frontier tradition. "Incurably musical," writes Bernard DeVoto, "Americans working westward carried with them fiddles and a folk art. While the frontier was still a boundary of exploration, the wayfarer expected to find a fiddle or a banjo hanging beside the rifle in the shanty where he sought hospitality." In Hannibal, Mrs. Holliday had a piano with drum attachment, and Sam Clemens and Laura Hawkins used to love to go there and thrill to the audible pyrotechnics of "The Battle of Prague." Sam himself had what Howells was later to describe as a fine tenor voice, and he seems to have done some entertaining on the river boats in his pilot days. Later, William R. Gillis tells us, he charmed his cronies in California with his singing and guitar playing.

What he sang we do not know, but we may be sure it was not Mozart. He has no taste, he assures us, rejoices to classify himself with the barbarians and glories in his barbarism. "I suppose it is very low-grade music—I know it *must* be low-grade music—because it so delighted me, it so warmed me, moved me, stirred me, uplifted me, enraptured me, that at times I could have cried, and

---

[3] On magazine and book illustrators Mark Twain's taste seems to have been safe. He praises George du Maurier in *Following the Equator*, and he appreciated the pictures which Dan Beard and E. W. Kemble did for him. He also admired Abbey, Smedley, Frost, Remington, and Pyle.

at others split my throat with shouting." And he continues: "I have never heard enough classic music to be able to enjoy it, and the simple truth is I detest it. Not mildly, but with all my heart."

But this was not quite the truth, nor was the truth simple. He comes closer to the truth when he writes, "I dislike the opera because I want to love it and can't." For years he shied away from classical music, perhaps because he did not wish to prove to himself that his capacity for musical appreciation was altogether lacking. Taken to hear Leschetitzky, he was impressed only by the pianist's wonderful memory and the nimbleness of his fingers, and he was willing to have Gabrilowitsch come to dinner only if Clara would promise not to ask him to play.

He was abnormally sensitive to sounds always, could not endure the ticking of a clock and had to have the programs for his readings printed upon a special paper that would not rattle. He was not quite without his contacts with standard music even in his early days. Both Ole Bull and Henrietta Sontag are mentioned in an 1853 letter to the Muscatine *Journal* from Philadelphia, but it is not clear that he heard them. Later he knew Ole Bull and thought very highly of him. But he had his first contacts with the opera long before he went to Europe, and there is one 1869 letter to Livy in which he is quite ecstatic about a fine church choir in Pittsburgh. "It was the very ecstasy of harmony! . . . What worship was in the music! How it preached, how it pleaded! And how earthy & merely human seemed the clergyman's poor, vapid declamation! *He* couldn't make us comprehend Christ desolate & forsaken, but the music did!"

Two of Mark Twain's daughters were musically gifted. Clara became a well-known singer, and Susy's voice was judged of potentially Wagnerian caliber by no less an authority than Blanche Marchesi. When Clara sang her first Italian air for her father, he was very impatient; he would not even listen to Schubert; instead he asked for an old Scotch air. Later, however, upon his daughter's urging, he agreed to have a piano-organ known as the Orchestrelle installed in his Fifth Avenue home. Using this agency—as, during these latter days, so many have used the phonograph—he learned to love Beethoven, Schubert, Chopin, and Brahms so

26

much that when the time came to go away for the summer, the Orchestrelle had to go with him. He even had it played as Jean's body was carried out of Stormfield the last Christmastide of his life.

At the opera Mark Twain began by loving the familiar tunes and agonizing through the recitative. It was inevitable that he should have some interesting experiences with Wagner. "I trust I know as well as anybody that singing is one of the most entrancing and bewitching and moving and eloquent of all the vehicles invented by man for the conveying of feeling; but it seems to me that the chief virtue of song is melody, air, rhythm, or what you please to call it, and that when this feature is absent what remains is a picture with the color left out." At Mannheim he attended a performance of *Lohengrin*. "The banging and slamming and booming and crashing were something beyond belief. The racking and pitiless pain of it remains stored up in my memory alongside the memory of the time I had my teeth fixed."

Time came, however, when the family made a shrine of Bayreuth, and then Mark Twain simply had to endure it. He became accustomed to the orchestration first, but he still could not endure the singing; indeed he thought it might be better if the opera could be performed in pantomime! On the other hand, the "Wedding March" in *Lohengrin* was a lovely thing, and he had never heard anything "so solemn and impressive and so divinely beautiful as *Tannhäuser*. It ought to be used as a religious service." See how his strength and weakness are blended in such an utterance as the following, the culture seeker standing beside the realist, with his stalwart honesty and his rather naïve village-atheist fear of being fooled: "I feel strongly out of place here. Sometimes I feel like the sane person in a community of the mad; sometimes I feel like the one blind man where all others see; the one groping savage in the college of the learned, and always, during service, I feel like a heretic in heaven." But before he finished, he had found good things to say not only about *Lohengrin* and *Tannhäuser* but about *Tristan und Isolde* and *Parsifal* as well.

Fortunately, however, there was one type of music—music of quality, of dignity and beauty, music utterly free from all pretensions of "arti-ness"—that Mark Twain drank in with his mother's milk and which became a part of his very being. I speak, of course, of the Negro spirituals. When the Jubilee Singers came to Lucerne in 1897, they took him back to his youth and made him see that the same truth holds in music which he had already discerned in literature, that the finest art is not exotic but grows its sturdy stock straight out of the earth, and that people do not have to learn to love it, for the simple reason that it explains them to themselves. "Arduous and painstaking cultivation" had not "diminished or artificialized" the spirituals, he found; it had only "reinforced" their "eloquence and beauty." "Away back in the beginning," this music had "made all other vocal music cheap; and that early notion is emphasized now. It is utterly beautiful to me; and it moves me infinitely more than any other music can. I think that in the Jubilees and their songs America had produced the perfectest flower of the ages; and I wish it were a foreign product so that she would worship it and lavish money on it and go properly crazy over it." This is perhaps the loveliest passage in all Mark Twain's criticism; it shows him at his best, as he was when he allowed the sensitiveness that was in him to respond unhampered to the finest things with which he came in contact. He himself sang spirituals to Mrs. Clemens the night she died. He sang them on other occasions, too, one of which has been beautifully described by his servant Katy Leary:

> I heard about one night when there was a company at the Warners' and Mr. Clemens was there, and it was a perfectly lovely night and there was a full moon outside and no lights in the house. They was just settin' there in the music room, looking out at the moonlight. And suddenly Mr. Clemens got right up without any warning and begun to sing one of them negro Spirituals. A lady that was there told me he just stood up with both his eyes shut and begun to sing kind of soft like—a faint sound, just as if there was wind in the trees, she said; and he kept right on singin' kind o' low and sweet, and it was beautiful and made your heart ache somehow. And he kept on singin' and singin' and became kind of lost in it, and he was all lit up—his face was. 'Twas somethin' from another world, she said, and when he got through, he put his two hands up

to his head, just as though all the sorrow of the negroes was upon him; and then he begun to sing, "Nobody Knows the Trouble I Got, Nobody Knows but Jesus." That was one of them negro spirituals songs, and when he come to the end, to the Glory Halle-luiah, he gave a great shout—just like the negroes do—he shouted out the Glory, Glory, Halleluiah! They said it was wonderful and none of them would forget it as long as they lived.

Surely the influence of the spirituals shows in Mark Twain's never failing love and sympathy for the Negro race. There are echoes of them, too, in his loveliest prose.

IV

We come now to the art that Mark Twain understood best, and which became his own—literature. *Huckleberry Finn* tells us about the books generally available in Midwestern frontier house-holds—the Bible, *The Pilgrim's Progress, Friendship's Offering,* the Speeches of Henry Clay, and Dr. Gunn's *Family Medicine. Life on the Mississippi* adds, among others, Ossian, *Alonzo and Melissa, Ivanhoe,* and Godey's *Lady's Book.*

Because Sam Clemens did not care much for school, it is often assumed that he grew up largely without books; this is a mistake. There is an interesting speech in *Tom Sawyer Abroad,* where Huck Finn is quite out of character: "Tom said we was right in the midst of the *Arabian Nights* now. He said it was right along here that one of the cutest things in that book happened; so we looked down and watched while he told us about it, because there ain't anything that is so interesting to look at as a place that a book has talked about." The unlettered Huck could never have felt that way about it. But Sam Clemens could and did, and so did Tom Sawyer, who was a good deal of a bookworm himself and got the ideas for many of his adventures out of what he had read.

The early biography of Mark Twain by Will Clemens quotes his mother as saying, "He was always a great boy for history, and could never get tired of that kind of reading; but he hadn't any use for schoolhouses and text-books." In her old age, Laura Haw-kins, Becky Thatcher's original, recalled his once borrowing her nickel to buy a Sam Slick book from a Yankee pedlar and going about reading it and chuckling over it. He could even read prescribed books when he wanted to read them; he had read the Bible through, for example, before he was fifteen.[4] By the time he made his visit to New York, at eighteen, the reading habit was firmly established. "You ask me where I spend my evenings," he writes home to Pamela. "Where would you suppose with a free printers' library containing more than 4,000 volumes within a quarter of a mile of me, and nobody at home to talk to?"

We hear a good deal of his reading during his Mississippi days; how, for example, he tried to read *The Fortunes of Nigel* behind a barrel, where the master caught him and "read him a lecture upon the ruinous effects of reading." He read more in Nevada, and a great deal more in San Francisco, and when he became engaged, he conjured up enchanting pictures of his wife and himself sitting through long winter evenings, studying together, and reading favorite authors, and so fixing them in their minds.

It should also be remembered, of course, that the frontier itself existed as literature. Bernard DeVoto described its characteristics clearly—fantasy and realism side by side, burlesque and extravaganza closely connected with satire—and Franklin J. Meine illustrated its quality in his *Tall Tales of the Southwest*. DeVoto speaks of four of Mark Twain's important predecessors in the field of frontier humor—Augustus Longstreet, J. J. Hooper, George W. Harris, and William Tappan Thompson. To these Miss Bellamy has now added John Phoenix. *The Jumping Frog*, *The Innocents Abroad*, and, in a measure, *A Connecticut Yankee* inherited a tradition; they did not create one. The unlettered Mark Twain, like the unlettered Robert Burns, is a creature of fancy.

V

The mature Mark Twain may have read erratically and unsystematically, as he did many other things, but he certainly read

---

[4] The suggestion of Coleman O. Parsons that the Satan of *The Mysterious Stranger* was influenced by the Jesus of the New Testament Apocrypha, though startling, is not unreasonable. See his "The Background of 'The Mysterious Stranger'," *American Literature*, Vol. XXXII (1960), 55–74.

vastly. He himself sums up: "I like history, biography, travels, curious facts and strange happenings, and science. And I detest novels, poetry, and theology." He flaunts this non-literary point of view in the face of Rudyard Kipling: "I never read novels myself, except when the popular persecution forces me to—when people plague me to know what I think of the last book that everyone is reading." And again: "What I like to read about are facts and statistics of any kind. If they are only facts about the raising of radishes, they interest me. Just now, for instance, before you came in—I was reading an article about 'Mathematics.' Perfectly pure mathematics." There is an interesting passage in the *Autobiography* where he explains how he tried three times to read a certain factual narrative in the *Atlantic*, "but was frightened off each time before I could finish. The tale was so vivid and so real that I seemed to be living those adventures myself and sharing their intolerable perils, and the torture of it was so sharp that I was never able to follow the story to the end." This is perhaps the most cogent bit of testimony we have to show Mark Twain's capacity for being absorbed in his reading.

And of course he did read "novels, poetry, and theology," and much besides. In an 1897 letter to Sir John Adams he reports having read 232 pages of his *The Herbartian Philosophy* in bed one day between ten in the morning and midnight. "It is not fast reading," he writes modestly, "but then I cannot take things in swiftly if I wish to understand them—and also make marginal notes." Professor Blair sums up fairly and comprehensively: "He read enough French, English, and American history to become a really impressive (though opinionated) specialist in certain periods. He read books and even documents written in French; he read novels in German. He read English and American histories, memoirs, biographies, philosophical treatises, travel books, dramas, humorous stories, and novels—old and new, bad, indifferent, and great." Moreover, he shows clearly that Mark Twain not only, consciously or unconsciously, used his reading as source material for his work, but also permitted his judgment of non-literary matters to be importantly affected by it.[5]

[5] The catalog of the books Mark Twain owned when he died has been printed in part in *The Twainian*, Seventeenth Year.

The usual view is that he neglected the established classics, and he encourages us to believe this by frequently expressing his inferiority complex in this regard. Howells must have winced when he read, "I have never been able to get up high enough to be at home with high literature. But I immensely like your literature, Howells." I have no reason to suppose that the Greek and Roman writers meant anything to him. I have found two references to Dante but no proof that he read him. Cervantes he knew well and shows his influence in both *Tom Sawyer* and *A Connecticut Yankee*. He speaks of *Gil Blas* and, slightingly, of Boccaccio, both for his improprieties and his "curt and meagre fashion" of telling his stories. Dumas and Voltaire he seems to have known better.

To be sure, it is unsafe to argue from silence. Mark Twain is not often considered a reader of Goethe. Yet in 1884 he asked Charles Webster to get him an unbound copy of Bayard Taylor's translation of *Faust*, so that he could divide it up into 100-page sections and bind them in flexible covers for reading in bed. Bunyan's theology made him *persona non grata* to Mark; he made Huckleberry Finn speak of Christian as "a man that left his family, it didn't say why," and he once remarked that he would rather be damned to Bunyan's heaven than read Henry James. For all that, he knew his Bunyan, and at one time, in one of his frequent flashes of anticipating the future, he dreamed up what would today be described as a motion picture version of *The Pilgrim's Progress*.

In a stray magazine article he expresses a kind of conventional affection for Chaucer, the only pre-Shakespearean poet he mentions. Spenser is "Spencer." No pre-Shakespearean dramatist appears, and of Shakespeare's contemporaries there is only Ben Jonson. In one of his speeches he declares that nobody has read *Paradise Lost*, and that nobody wants to read it or any other classic. He himself seems to have read it, however, and early in life, for an admonitory letter to Orion cites "the Arch-Fiend's terrible energy" as "the grandest thing" in the poem.

Shakespeare himself fares decidedly better. Aside from *Is Shakespeare Dead?*—that curious contribution to the Baconian controversy—Pochmann lists twenty allusions to Shakespeare in Mark Twain's writings, nearly twice as many as to any other writer. He speaks of the profound moral lessons to be learned from *Othello* and *Lear*. He was extremely fond of *Romeo and Juliet*, and once, under the spell of a glamorous Sothern and Marlowe production of that play, he told Paine that he considered it "Lord Bacon's" greatest achievement. Jervis Langdon says he frequently read Shakespeare aloud to his family, and there is an interesting passage in an unpublished manuscript, "Comments on English Fiction" (c.1870), quoted by Langdon, in which he uses some great passages from the Bible, the Gettysburg Address, and six lines from Prospero's valedictory as his touchstones of style.

Of the great English novelists, Dickens was, by all means, the most important. Mark Twain was painfully impressed by Sterne's improprieties, at least in his courting days. He admired the Charles Reade of *The Cloister and the Hearth*. But he disliked Meredith, George Eliot, Jane Austen, Sir Walter Scott, and the Goldsmith of *The Vicar of Wakefield*, and Mrs. Clemens was once greatly humiliated by being obliged to confess that her husband had not read his Thackeray. When he wanted to damn Bret Harte, he called him as "slovenly" as Thackeray and as "dull" as Lamb. Yet there are curious contradictions in his attitude toward Dickens. The first time he ever went out in company with Olivia Langdon they heard Dickens read from *David Copperfield* in Steinway Hall, New York. One might have expected Mark Twain to be in a good mood on that occasion if he ever was, but his report in the *Alta California* views both Dickens and his reading very severely.[6] As late as 1885 he assures us solemnly that there is nothing amusing in *The Pickwick Papers*. Being a contrary creature, Mark Twain may have shied away from Dickens because Orion prodded him to read him in early life, but the chances are he read more Dickens than he liked to pretend. He certainly loved *A Tale of Two Cities*, and Professor Blair has demonstrated its influence on *Huckleberry Finn*.[7]

[6] This article has been reprinted in *The Twainian*, Vol. VII, March–April, 1948, pp. 3–4.

[7] Stuart Sherman noted the flavor of Dickens in *The Gilded Age*, but Schönemann dissents, finding Mark Twain's own environment sufficient to account for all

33

Among the Americans, he read Poe in his Keokuk days, but a 1909 letter to Howells declares Poe unreadable. Since he thought "The Murders in the Rue Morgue" the only tolerable detective story, the tales of ratiocination were apparently exempted. He speaks of "The Bells" in *A Tramp Abroad.* Pochmann thinks the treasure-digging episode in *Tom Sawyer* imitated from "The Gold-Bug," and finds suggestions of both "The Raven" and "William Watson" in "The Recent Carnival of Crime in Connecticut." Schönemann makes much of the influence of Emerson, but presents little evidence.

Mark Twain's special enthusiasm for Oliver Wendell Holmes may have been determined in part by Holmes's personal kindness, but there was also some affinity of spirit between Holmes and Clemens as humorists. (DeLancey Ferguson suggests plausibly that Mr. Brown may have been suggested by the Autocrat's John.) As a matter of fact, Mark Twain always honored the whole New England school; the ill-starred burlesque he read at the Whittier Birthday Dinner was merely an error of judgment in gauging the response of a particular audience; it implied no disrespect on Mark's part.[8] In his lecture on Artemus Ward he went out of his way to explain that, good as Ward was as a comic writer, his prod-

---

features, though he admits that Dickens may have influenced the mode of treatment. I am less interested in such matters as the alleged resemblances between Sellers and Micawber than I am in style. Sellers' description of the clock in chapter VII seems very Dickensian, and Senator Dilworthy's speech in chapter LIII (or chapter XXII of volume II) might have been modeled on the remarks of the Reverend Mr. Chadband in *Bleak House*, chapter XIX. In "My Platonic Sweetheart" the delightful scene in "a great plantation house" suggests both Dickens and Lewis Carroll.

[8] Mark Twain described three tramps in a California mining camp who called themselves Longfellow, Emerson, and Holmes and conversed in terms of garbled quotations from their works. There is a full account in Paine. Henry Nash Smith, " 'That Hideous Mistake of Poor Clemens's'," *Harvard Library Bulletin*, Vol. IX (1955), 145–80, shows that both Mark Twain and Howells greatly exaggerated the resultant shock. Longfellow was essentially right when he wrote, in reply to Mark's really abject letter of apology, "The newpapers have made all the mischief." But it was the newspapers outside of Boston, and especially in the Middle West, that were really shocked. All these matters are expertly analyzed by Professor Smith, who goes astray only when led into metaphysical subtleties by Edmund Wilson's completely unfounded observation that Mark Twain's speech "must have had behind it some real unconscious antagonism" toward the New England writers.

uct was not to be mentioned along with the humorous writings of Lowell and Holmes.

Mark Twain's inferiority complex always worked especially well in connection with poetry, but he certainly was not indifferent to verse. Consider his statement to Howells concerning one of Mildred's poems. "It cost me several chapters to say in prose what Mildred has said better with a single penful of ink. Prose wanders around with a lantern & laboriously schedules & verifies the details & particulars of a valley & its frame of crags and peaks, then Poetry comes, & lays bare the whole landscape with a single splendid flash."

He speaks of Byron, of Wordsworth, and of Shelley's "sumptuous imagery." In courting days he praised Coventry Patmore's *The Angel in the House,* but found Mrs. Browning's *Aurora Leigh* obscure. He did not care much for Tennyson, and in one of his speeches he misquotes "Locksley Hall." He liked to read aloud from William Morris's "Sir Guy of the Dolorous Blast."

Much more he enjoyed C. F. Alexander's "The Burial of Moses," *The Rubáiyat of Omar Khayyám,* Kipling's ballads, and Browning. The Alexander poem he discovered early. Though it is not quite in the taste of these latter days, it served Sam Clemens well in establishing for him a standard of taste and dignity, at the same time revealing something of what the harmonies of verbal music can achieve. *Omar* he was "wild" over from the time Fitz-Gerald's translation appeared. As for Kipling, he was "just about my level," and he loved the prose too, for he once declared that it was worth journeying to India just to learn how to appreciate *Kim.* The great surprise is Browning. One would have expected Mark Twain to hate him, as he hated James and Meredith. With the perversity so characteristic of him, he decided instead to love him. Perhaps the English poet's enthusiastic robustness was the point of connection. "That man seems to have been to you," he remarked to Howells of Tolstoy, "what Browning was to me," and one could hardly say more. The Browning readings he gave at his Hartford house were famous, and all hearers agreed that they were exquisite and wonderfully clarifying.[9]

[9] William Lyon Phelps, "Mark Twain," *Yale Review,* Vol. XXV (1936),

VI

Like most persons of literary bent, Mark Twain enjoyed the theater, though he was not consistent in his attendance, nor was the stage ever an abiding passion with him, as it was with Dickens. He first encountered the theater in Hannibal, but he came to know it much better in the West, where he attended in a professional journalistic capacity, met Adah Isaacs Menken and other theater people, and produced an amusing burlesque of *Ingomar*.[10] He "did" the theaters well when he first came to New York, writes of Lotta and *The Black Crook* and very severely criticized Barnum's Museum. In Hartford he participated in amateur theatricals, patronized the theater, helped his young neighbor, William Gillette, get started as an actor, and, in general, worked to break down conservative prejudices in a Puritan community. Once he and Mrs. Clemens made a special trip to New York to see *The Mikado*.

He speaks of Edwin Forrest, Edwin Booth, Irving and Terry, Augustin Daly, John Drew, and Ada Rehan, of David Warfield, of Sothern and Marlowe. In 1906 he appeared in New York on the same program with Sarah Bernhardt for the benefit of persecuted Jews in Russia. While Mrs. Fiske was still Minnie Maddern, he had an idea that he wanted to manage her; much later he wrote "A Horse's Tale" to aid her campaign against bullfighting. In his old age he wrote a tribute to Billie Burke—"the young, the gifted, the beautiful"—in his guest book, she being his last guest in 1908.

His most elaborate piece of dramatic criticism is his study of Adolf Wilbrandt's play, *The Master of Palmyra*.[11] He loved the old-time minstrel show, but though he foresaw motion pictures

---

291–310, points out that Mark Twain read such difficult poems as those in *Parleyings*, the first three sections of *The Ring and the Book*, *Mr. Sludge the Medium*, and *Christmas Eve and Easter Day*. But he prints the program of one reading in which Mark Twain has broken the strain of continuous Browning by interlarding selections from Uncle Remus and other humorous material.

[10] See Franklin Walker, ed., *The Washoe Giant in San Francisco*, 58–60. Late in life Mark Twain once declared that his early chores as a reporter had quite ruined the theater for him. But this does not cover the case, nor does Rodman Gilder's article, "Mark Twain Hated the Theatre," *Theatre Arts Monthly*, Vol. XXVII (Feb., 1944), 109–16.

[11] See "About Play Acting," in *The Man That Corrupted Hadleyburg*.

and television as early as the eighties, I cannot find that he took any interest in the film when it arrived.[12] Melodrama, he knew, was always on the side of the angels, and he was particularly enthusiastic about projects like the Jewish children's theater on New York's East Side, whose aim was to give children something more than melodrama. He took many children to see Maude Adams in *Peter Pan* when she was playing in New York. He ardently supported the campaign for the Shakespeare Memorial Theater in 1875, and he once made a very strong plea for an endowed theater in this country. "It would make better citizens, honest citizens. One of the best gifts a millionaire could make would be a theatre here and a theatre there. It would make . . . a real Republic, and bring about an educational level."[13]

VII

Of the books and writers whom Mark Twain particularly disliked, I have already mentioned several. Meredith is berated for his artificialities, especially in characterization. He has no right to be forever telling his readers how brilliant Diana of the Crossways is unless he is able to illustrate it! George Eliot, Hawthorne, and Henry James[14] are lumped together for what Mark thinks their tiresome overanalysis. When Clemens was an old man, Paine gave him Flaubert's *Salammbô*, hoping that since he enjoyed Suetonius, he might also relish this great picture of the ancient world. He admitted its art but declared that he would not read it again except for money. He disliked romanticism when it meant evasion,

[12] In the summer of 1909 the Edison company took some motion pictures of Mark Twain with Jean and Clara at Stormfield. This reel is now said to be in the possession of the Mark Twain Museum, Hannibal. For Mark Twain's anticipations, see his *Notebook*, 192–93.

[13] Robert A. Wiggins, "Mark Twain and the Drama," *American Literature*, Vol. XXV (1953–54), 279–86, argues for a larger influence of the drama on Mark Twain's fiction than has generally been acknowledged. Mark Twain certainly uses dramatic techniques and methods at times, and these cannot have been entirely uninfluenced by his contacts with the theater, but it should be remembered that they had been domesticated in fiction long before his time.

[14] Yet Mark Twain refers to Henry James as a master as early as 1876 and as late as 1885. In 1904, James, having met him, speaks of him as "delicious poor dear old M. T."

but he disliked literature which seemed to him deficient in idealism even more.

His four favorite "hates" among writers were the Goldsmith of *The Vicar of Wakefield*, Cooper, Scott, and Jane Austen. He attempts no analysis of Goldsmith's lovely story, but he always speaks of it with extreme contempt. Any library that does not contain *The Vicar of Wakefield* is a good library. His essay on "Fenimore Cooper's Literary Offences"[15] is one of his most ambitious pieces of literary criticism. In it he accuses Cooper of every conceivable crime against grammar, rhetoric, narrative skill, and common sense. No romantic literature could stand up against all these charges. Certainly Mark Twain's own stories could not.

"Lord, it's all so juvenile! so artificial, so shoddy; and such wax figures and skeletons and spectres." Thus he wrote to Brander Matthews concerning Scott. In a famous passage in *Life on the Mississippi* he even holds Scott responsible for the Civil War. From his mediaevalism the South derived her "jejune romanticism," and so she adopted a different social and economic system from that which prevailed in the more advanced and more hardheaded North.[16]

But this time there was a curious anticlimax. After he had finished *Rob Roy* and *Guy Mannering*, bitterly hating them the while, he got hold of *Quentin Durward*. "It was like leaving the dead to mingle with the living: it was like withdrawing from the infant class in the College of Journalism to sit under the lectures in English literature in Columbia University. I wonder who wrote *Quentin Durward*?" Now, if you are going to apply the term "jejune romanticism" to anything of Scott's, there is certainly much more of it in *Quentin Durward* than in *Rob Roy* or *Guy Mannering* or the Scottish books generally.

Yet not even against Scott does Mark Twain breathe out such

[15] Not all of this paper is included in *In Defence of Harriet Shelley*. Bernard DeVoto printed the rest of it in *New England Quarterly*, Vol. XIX (1946), 291–301.

[16] See H. J. Eckenrode, "Sir Walter Scott and the South," *North American Review*, Vol. CCVI (1917), 595–603; Grace Warren Landrum, "Sir Walter Scott and His Literary Rivals in the Old South," *American Literature*, Vol. II (1930–31), 256–76; G. Harrison Orians, "Walter Scott, Mark Twain, and the Civil War," *South Atlantic Quarterly*, Vol. XL (1941), 343–59.

fire and slaughter as he does against Jane Austen. "It seems a great pity that they allowed her to die a natural death." And then, as with so many other things, the old, familiar inferiority complex raises its head again: "When I take up one of Jane Austen's books, I feel like a barkeeper entering the kingdom of heaven." He seems to have gone back to her, as he returned to *The Vicar*, again and again. Why? Was it in the spirit in which he relished "hogwash"? Or was he seeking something that he never found? Jervis Langdon tells us that *The Vicar* was one of the themes upon which his children required him to develop improvised variations.

VIII

Among the contemporary American writers mentioned by Mark Twain are Joel Chandler Harris, James Whitcomb Riley, Booth Tarkington, Rose Terry Cooke, Will Irwin, John Hay, Witter Bynner, Angela Morgan, Willa Cather, James Branch Cabell, and the Edward Bellamy of *Looking Backward*. British writers include Bernard Shaw, H. G. Wells, Olive Schreiner, Thomas Hardy—whose *Jude the Obscure* was nearly the last thing he read—Flora Annie Steele, Marjorie Bowen, and Elizabeth Robins.

Riley's poems made a powerful nostalgic appeal to Mark Twain. He greatly admired Harris and rejected the latter's own modest view that the success of the Uncle Remus stories was due to the charming folk materials contained in them; it was also due, he insisted, to the author's literary skill. Cabell's romanticism enthralled him, as it did his great archetype, Theodore Roosevelt. The girl Marjorie Bowen attracted his attention at the very beginning of her spectacular career, and one of her early novels, *The Master of Stair*, was gratefully dedicated to him. On the other hand, *An Open Question*, by Elizabeth Robins, for once won his assent to a straight, strong piece of realistic writing, and he rashly described Miss Steele's *On the Face of the Waters* as "the finest novel ever written by a woman."

Among literary curiosa Mark Twain loved Marjorie Fleming, the Mormon Bible, Pedro Carolino's *The New Guide of the Conversation in Portuguese and English* (he contributed an introduction to Osgood's 1883 edition), and Samuel Watson Royston's novel, *The Enemy Conquered; or, Love Triumphant* (1845).[17] Sometimes he enjoyed such things because they were good, more often because they were so surpassingly, triumphantly bad. He had the artist's quick, eager response to strong contrasts, or, as he puts it in the *Autobiography*, "A thoroughly beautiful woman and a thoroughly homely woman are creations which I love to gaze upon, and which I cannot tire of gazing upon, for each is perfect in her own line, and it is *perfection*, I think, in many things, and perhaps in most things, which is the quality that fascinates us." Such perfection he found in Royston, in the precious puerilities of Mrs. Julia C. Moore, "the Sweet Singer of Michigan," and in many similar gems.

IX

Special favorites among his books Mark Twain discovered early and went on reading for the rest of his life. He loved Pepys, Lecky, Malory, Plutarch, Suetonius, and Saint-Simon. His hunger for human fellowship being what it was, he could generally be depended upon to respond to a work in which he could feel the pulse of "the warm life-blood of a master-spirit." The particular human specimens which throng the pages of Saint-Simon and Suetonius showed him the human animal at his worst, but they fascinated him too. Malory's appeal was different. He seems to have reverenced the book first of all for its style, but he was by no means indifferent to the atmosphere of romance and adventure which it conjures up.

He read many other books of a biographical nature. In his youth he read Horace Walpole's letters; in his own opinion, they exercised a strong and beneficent influence upon his style. He read Parkman, Macaulay, Carlyle, Darwin, *Two Years Before the Mast*, the autobiographies of Andrew Carnegie and Moncure D. Conway, the letters of Madame de Sévigné and of James Russell Lowell.

[17] Paine calls the author "Wolston." See Guy A. Cardwell, "Mark Twain's Failures in Comedy and *The Enemy Conquered*," *Georgia Review*, Vol. XIII (1959), 424–36.

He also greatly admired the novels of William Dean Howells, and this presents something of a problem, for Howells wrote the kind of fiction that, when it was written by others, he often claimed he disliked. In his essay on Howells, he confines himself for the most part to praising the style: "For forty years his English has been to me a continual delight and astonishment." But he admired Howells in other aspects also: "You are really my only author; I am restricted to you, I wouldn't give a damn for the rest." He praises his friend's ability to make all motives and feelings clear "without analyzing the guts out of them, the way George Eliot does." He praises him, too, because he is true to life. "The creatures of God do not act out their natures more unerringly than yours do."

Part of this, no doubt, was friendship, but friendship does not account for all of it. In the usual sense of the term novelist, Howells' skill ran far ahead of his own, and Mark Twain could not help being aware of this. And, though he sometimes claimed to dislike novels, his mature judgment told him that the serious novelist was a very important person. "There is only one expert," he declared in his attack on Paul Bourget, "who is qualified to examine the souls and the life of a people and make a valuable report—the native novelist."

So it was that he stored the well, and that life stored it for him. What, now, did he draw up out of it?

CHAPTER THREE: *The Man of Letters*

I

A GENERATION AGO, it was the fashion to regard Mark Twain as a kind of folk artist, "an improvisator . . . who composed extempore," as Van Wyck Brooks put it. The classical statement of this widely influential view was that of Constance Rourke: "He was primarily a *raconteur*, with an 'unequaled dramatic authority,' as Howells called it. He was never the conscious artist, always the improviser. He had the garrulity and the inconsequence of the earlier comic story-tellers of the stage and tavern; and his comic sense was theirs almost without alteration."

Mark Twain's friends and foes agreed. Gamaliel Bradford saw him as "the bard . . . , the old, epic popular singer, who gathered up in himself, almost unconsciously, the life and spirit of a whole nation and poured it forth, more as a voice, an instrument, than a deliberate artist." Ludwig Lewisohn compared him to "the balladists of Europe," and to Homer, who "raised into the immortal realm of the imagination the life and conflict of obscure villages among the otherwise forgotten Ionians of the isles and the Asian shore." Paine himself had already found the "culmination" of Mark Twain's genius in his oral, impromptu utterances. And, as late as 1942, DeVoto wrote of Mark Twain: "He was in the antique sense a genius: he wrote in obedience to an inner drive, he exercised little voluntary control over it, and he was unable to criticize what he had written."

Mark Twain himself was largely responsible for these impressions. "I began with the first red bar," so he wrote Elsie Leslie, who had played in *The Prince and the Pauper* on Broadway, describing the slipper he had made for her, "and without ulterior design, or plan of any sort—just as I would begin a Prince and Pauper or any other tale. And mind you it is the easiest and surest way; because if you invent two or three people and turn them loose in your manuscript, something is bound to happen to them —you can't help it; and then it will take you the rest of the book to get them out of the natural consequences of that occurrence, and so, first thing you know, there's your book all finished up and never cost you an idea."

This is playfully expressed, but it does not stand alone. When he starts to work on a novel, he declares in one of his forewords, he has no story. He "merely has some people in his mind, and an incident or two, also a locality." Nor is he planning to write a long book; all he has in mind is "a little tale; a very little tale; a six-page tale." As he proceeds, not only does his material expand indefinitely, but "the original intention (or motif) is apt to get abolished and find itself superseded by a quite different one." So it was with *Pudd'nhead Wilson*, which began as a farce with one set of characters and ended, with a quite different set, as a tragedy. And he describes the difficulties he experiences in taking the twins out of the altered story so that Roxy and her associates might occupy unhindered the foreground of the stage they had usurped for themselves.

Probably no other great writer ever wasted so much of his energy as Mark Twain. "Last summer I started 16 things wrong— 3 books and 13 mag. articles—and could only make 2 little wee things, 1500 words altogether, succeed:—only that out of piles and stacks of diligently-wrought MS., the labor of 6 weeks' unremitting effort." Even the books he did carry through to completion proceeded at a distinctly haphazard rate. "It is my habit to keep four or five books in process of erection all the time, and every summer to add a few courses of bricks to two or three of them; but I cannot forecast which of the two or three it is going to be." Sometimes, especially in later years, it was none of them, and it is doubtful that anybody else ever left so many aborted manuscripts behind him.[1]

Nor is structure generally considered the greatest of Mark Twain's achievements in the works he finished. If A *Connecticut Yankee* is a great book, as I think it is, it is great because it has enough power in it to triumph over every conceivable lack of proportion and violation of tone. Walter Blair has now shown that *Tom Sawyer* is a much better proportioned book than it has often been thought to be, though I am not sure he would go so far as to claim that Mark consciously planned all the effects he has pointed out.[2] The long-drawn-out account of the "rescue" of Nigger Jim with which *Huckleberry Finn* closes has generally been considered a blemish.[3] At one point in *Life on the Mississippi* Mark Twain writes: "Here is a story which I picked up on board the boat that night. I insert it in the place merely because it is a good story, not

[1] The best account of these is in Bernard DeVoto's moving essay, "The Symbols of Despair," in *Mark Twain at Work*.

[2] Walter Blair, "On the Structure of *Tom Sawyer*," *Modern Philology*, Vol. XXXVII (1939-40), 75-88. Lewis Leary's "Tom and Huck: Innocence on Trial," *Virginia Quarterly Review*, Vol. XXX (1954), 417-30, seems to me much less convincing. See, also, Svend Peterson's chronology for *Tom Sawyer*, "Splendid Days and Fearsome Nights," *Mark Twain Quarterly*, Vol. VIII, Winter-Spring, 1949, pp. 3-8, 10.

[3] The ending of *Huckleberry Finn* has now been earnestly defended by T. S. Eliot, in his introduction to the Chantecleer Press edition of the novel (1950), and by Lionel Trilling, in *The Liberal Imagination* (New York, Viking Press, 1950). I find the defense unconvincing, essentially for the reasons stated by Leo Marx, in "Mr. Eliot, Mr. Trilling, and Huckleberry Finn," *American Scholar*, Vol. XXII (1952-53), 423-40. Thomas A. Gullason, "The 'Fatal' Ending of *Huckleberry Finn*," *American Literature*, Vol. XXIX (1957-58), 86-91, rejects the arguments of Eliot and Trilling, then develops a quite humorless defense of his own, which attributes to Mark Twain ideas about Huck and Tom that he could possibly have held. See, also, Warren Beck, "Huck Finn at Phelps Farm," *Archives des Lettres Modernes*, Vol. III, Nos. 13-15 (1958); Barry B. Spacks, "The Thematic Function of the 'Rescue' in *Huckleberry Finn*," *Mark Twain Journal*, Vol. XI, Summer, 1959, pp. 8-9; Robert Ornstein, "The Ending of *Huckleberry Finn*," *Modern Language Notes*, Vol. LIV (1959), 678-702.

because it belongs here—for it doesn't." And by the time he began to dictate his *Autobiography* he was frankly glorifying literary anarchy: "Start at no particular time of your life; wander at your free will all over your life; talk only about the thing which interests you for the moment; drop it the moment its interest threatens to pale, and turn your talk upon the new and more interesting thing that has intruded itself into your mind meantime."

Mark Twain himself seems to have felt that he was weak in characterization also. "It is a line of characters whose fine shading and artistic development requires an abler hand than mine," he writes in one connection; "so I easily perceived that I must not make the attempt." He was right if by a gift for characterization one understands the faculty of *constructing* character, as Thackeray and Flaubert and Howells constructed it, or the ability to portray a complex type against the realized background of a highly involved civilization. On the other hand, his ability to *evoke* character, as distinct from constructing it, is very great, as many an incident in the odyssey of Huckleberry Finn or Roxy's adventures with her wayward son, and many a moment even in quite inconsequential sketches, can testify. Mrs. Judith Loftus appears but for a moment in *Huckleberry Finn*, but who in *The Canterbury Tales* is more unforgettable? And, indeed, Mark Twain's way with such casually introduced characters is close akin to Chaucer's.

II

Of course, it is no part of my purpose here to deny Mark Twain's skill as an improviser. The tales which he told his children would alone show that—the variations he played on MacDonald's *At the Back of the North Wind* or the *tours-de-force* in which he was required to weave a story around the objects on the mantel.[4] As a platform artist he was incomparable. In his early days, he longed to be a minstrel or a clown. Once, when he was very young, he even wanted to be a preacher, for the eminently practical reason that he did not believe a preacher could be damned. He lectured; he gave readings; he told stories. And his

[4] For a detailed account of some of these improvisations, see Caroline T. Harnsberger, *Mark Twain, Family Man*, 71–72.

skill was not confined to the presentation of his own work. I have already spoken of his Browning readings; his reading of one of Cable's stories haunted Howells over half a century. "He was the most perfect reader I have ever known," writes Robert Underwood Johnson. "His voice was peculiarly musical and had its own attraction, while his clear renderings of meanings in the most involved versification was sometimes like the opening of a closed door." One night in San Francisco, long before he was a celebrity, he stopped in at the *Call* about seven o'clock, just as the boys were getting ready to go to the theater. He sat down and began to reel off stories and reminiscences, and the first time anybody thought of looking at his watch it was eleven o'clock and the theaters were closed.

With acting he had less experience, but in what he did he seems to have been excellent. When he played Peter Spyle in *Loan of a Lover* in Hartford, Mrs. James T. Fields compared him to Joe Jefferson, and Augustin Daly did his best to bring him to New York. But here, if anywhere, he was an *improvisateur*, for, as W. W. Ellsworth relates, "he would put in lines, which, while very funny to those on the other side of the footlights, were decidedly embarrassing to his fellow actors. At one point I remember he began to tell the audience about the roof which he had just put on an ell of his new house and rambled on for a while, ending up that particular gag by asking Gertrude, much to her embarrassment, if she had ever put a tin roof on *her* house."

Even those who did not greatly enjoy Mark Twain's platform work testify to the skill with which he performed it. Thus H. R. Haweis tells us that his appearance was unimpressive, and that he said very little that would have been worth putting in print. Yet when it was over, and the disappointed auditor looked at his watch, he was astonished to discover that an hour and twenty minutes had passed. "It seemed ten minutes at the outside."

Once William Dean Howells asked Mark Twain to look over a manuscript from the point of view of checking the dialect. "All right, my boy," he replied, "send proof sheets *here*. I amend dialect stuff by talking and talking and *talking* it till it sounds right." He loved the human voice better than any instrument—"Bob

Ingersoll's music will sing through my memory always as the divinest that ever enchanted my ears"—and it was his opinion "that one cannot get out of finely wrought literature all that is in it by reading it mutely."

But it was not only dialect that he treated thus. He claimed to have got the whitewashing chapter in *Tom Sawyer* "cheaply" by talking it before he wrote it down. It is interesting that one critic, rejecting the idea that Mark Twain was an unconscious artist, should have set out to illustrate his processes of development by reference not to one of his published stories but to a platform reading.[5] But it would not be accurate to say that this is to give the case away, for Mark often prepared most carefully when he wished to appear most spontaneous. Sometimes his revisions substituted colloquial expressions for the more formal English which had come, as it were, more "naturally" in his first draft. Edgar Branch has shown how much of his early writing is not at all spontaneous or indigenous but very definitely and self-consciously "literary."[6] He himself praised E. W. Howe for writing as a man talks, but he could not read his own books in public until he had, in a manner, "oralized" them. He was always as particular about his "spot" on the program as the most expensive vaudeville star, and in "How To Tell a Story" he virtually wrote a treatise on the pause. "He imparted to the printed page the vivacity of the spoken word," wrote Brander Matthews, "its swiftness and its apparently unpremeditated ease." Read with the proper stress on "apparently," this statement is wholly accurate.

III

Mark Twain was not always true to the chaste mistress of his art; during the Hartford years especially, he was often absorbed in other things. "Mama and I have both been very much troubled of late," wrote Susy, "because papa, since he had been publishing General Grant's books, has seemed to forget his own." But when he saw himself and the world most clearly, there was never any

[5] John W. Hollenbach, "Mark Twain, Story-Teller, at Work," *College English*, Vol. VII (1946), 303-12.
[6] *The Literary Apprenticeship of Mark Twain*, 9, 129, 169.

doubt in his mind that "the most important feature of my life is its literary feature." If he had ever doubted this, he discovered its truth after Susy died, when he wrote like a man possessed, getting up at four or five o'clock in the morning to hold his agony at bay with his pen. "I work all the days, and trouble vanishes away when I use that magic. This book will not long stand between it and me, now; but that is no matter. I have many unwritten books to fly to for preservation; the interval between the finishing of this one and the beginning of the next will not be more than an hour, at most." In "The Turning-Point of My Life" he saw himself committed irrevocably to paper and ink at fourteen. And Paine tells us that when he was dictating his autobiography, he was inaccurate about everything except his books.

We see how much Mark Twain loved his work in his repeated insistence that it is not work but pleasure, self-indulgence. There is no work except physical labor. He could not grant that Joe Goodman had had "poor pay" for his twenty years of self-denying absorption in an intellectual task. "No, oh no. You have lived in a paradise of the intellect whose lightest joys were beyond the reach of the longest purse in Christendom." And when his daughter became a singer, he congratulated her upon having found a city of the soul in the form of an art to which she could devote herself. This was the only sure refuge against the trials of life.

But, of course, he did work at his writing. He was volatile and temperamental, and though *Life on the Mississippi* would seem to have been the book he was foreordained from before the foundation of the world to write, he never thought of writing it until Joe Twichell suggested it to him. For all that, the idea that he was undisciplined, either as a writer or as a man, is nonsense. Did he not learn two exacting trades—printing and piloting? How many of his critics can show a similar achievement? And how many men of fifty-two could memorize a list of some 500 unrelated words, as he did, merely to test out Loisette's memory system? It cannot have been easy to do the large amount of writing he did under the conditions which prevailed on the *Quaker City* cruise. And though he seems to have disliked proofreading, he did do a large amount of difficult and fruitful revision.[7]

Nor was Mark Twain anything like so innocent of serious literary theory as he has often been represented as being. The views he held are clear and definite, and they were derived from many respectable literary and intellectual sources, ranging all the way from the "inspiration" of the Romantics to the "organicism" which, as Sherwood Cummings has suggested, may have been derived from his reading of Taine. Originally they were not always quite consistent with each other, but he reconciled them in his final, personal, working formulation quite as much as it would be reasonable to expect.

In some matters—style, for example—this has always been clear. He prided himself on his skill in dialect, and an explanatory note at the beginning of *Huckleberry Finn* refers, though without precise definition, to the shadings employed, because he did not want the reader to suppose "that all these characters were trying to talk alike and not succeeding." He was fanatical about punctuation, and when he has to deal with an author he dislikes, he can be more than pernickety about grammar. Dowden's biography of Shelley, which he detests for its treatment of Harriet Westbrook, is "a literary cake-walk." He comments at some length on the clichés of Southern journalism in *Life on the Mississippi*, and his book on Christian Science attacks Mrs. Eddy for the barbarities of her style quite as heartily as for her cupidity. When he approves, as with Howells or Ingersoll, style is quite as important. He even looks for it in informational writings, which make no claim to be considered literature, and praises it when it appears. As for himself, no compliment ever pleased him more than praise of his style.

But the same point of view carries over into larger matters. When he says, "I never had any leaning toward literature, nor any desire to meddle with it, nor had ever flourished a literary pen save by accident," he is talking nonsense, and he knows it. When he says that in his own writing he puts his faith in "an automatically working taste," he probably means, as Sydney J. Krause has suggested,[8] "that he had no complete understanding of the under-

[7] For an effective summary of some of the work he did on *Huckleberry Finn*, see Blair, *Mark Twain and "Huck Finn,"* 351–54.

[8] This paragraph is importantly indebted to Krause's fine article, "Twain's Method and Theory of Composition," *Modern Philology*, Vol. LVI (1958–59),

lying methods by which his art was formed and that he felt that the creative faculties were basically unamenable to full analysis." He also meant that "he discovered his subject, not before, but *as*, he wrote," a wasteful method, as his experience proved, but one which achieved, when it was successful, an organic, rather than a mechanically superimposed, structure. He "felt that organization would occur simultaneously with his immersion in his subject and that a unique form would arise from the spontaneous adaptations to his heated imagination." Such a form "would be self-begotten to the extent that [Mark] Twain was confident that it was there for him to find if he kept writing long enough. The form might come as it would, but it would come, or the story simply would not be written, or at least would never be successfully completed." He made six wrong starts on *Joan of Arc*.

Mark Twain believed that literature of real value can be produced only by a writer who is willing to give himself, absolutely and unreservedly, to his material. "There is nothing," he writes Mrs. Fairbanks in 1868, "that makes me prouder than to be regarded by intelligent people as 'authentic.' A name I have coveted so long—& secured at last! *I* don't care anything about being humorous, or poetical, or eloquent, or anything of that kind—the end & aim of my ambition is to be authentic—is to be considered authentic." Much later in life, he lays down a rule regarding the "native novelist": "This native specialist is not qualified to begin work until he has been absorbing during twenty-five years. How much of his competency is derived from conscious 'observation'? The amount is so slight that it counts for next to nothing in the equipment. Almost the whole capital of the novelist is the slow accumulation of *un*conscious observation—absorption." The material had to be assimilated, absorbed into the author's personality, impregnated with his own sense of values. Nobody ever made

---

167–77. See, also, George Feinstein, "Mark Twain's Idea of Story Structure," *American Literature*, Vol. XVIII (1946–47), 160–63; Edgar H. Goold, Jr., "Mark Twain on the Writing of Fiction," *American Literature*, Vol. XXVI (1954–55), 52–66. A letter of Mark Twain's describing "My Methods of Writing" has been published under that title in *Mark Twain Quarterly*, Vol. VIII, Winter-Spring, 1949, p. 1.

more fun than Mark Twain of the artificial morality of the Sunday School books, but nobody was ever more sure that an author must "make the reader love the good people in the tale and hate the bad ones."

It is not surprising, then, that his best books should have been those which permitted him to draw most freely upon the memories of his early life. The sense of the past was always strong in him. He brooded over it and possessed it, and the curious detachment from the world immediately around him which was natural to his temperament reinforced this tendency. As he grew older, he dwelt more and more in the past, for the old Mississippi world that had produced him was so different from that in which he spent his later years that it tended to take on in memory the iridescent colors of a dream, and when he thought about it, it always seemed as if he were reliving a previous existence. That lovely land he held fast and made his own, safe against change, safe from the vicissitudes of actual experience. He operated on it; he turned it into the stuff of art. Victor Royce West has rightly discerned Mississippi folklore in *Joan of Arc*, and the Eseldorf of *The Mysterious Stranger* is only Hannibal with a mediaeval coloring. Moreover, there is an earlier version of *The Mysterious Stranger* in which young Satan actually comes to Hannibal and associates with Huck and Tom.

Henry Seidel Canby must in some quarters have fluttered the dovecotes when, in *Turn West, Turn East* (1951), he bluntly stated that Mark Twain wrote better than Henry James. His travel books are more "literary" than James's, for James confined himself to what he observed, where Mark Twain, like Melville, reinforced his observations with reading. Mark Twain had nothing to say about "point of view" in fiction, compared with what James said about it, but where did James ever achieve it quite so triumphantly as Mark Twain did in *Huckleberry Finn?* Take the fun and the frivolity out of Mark's letter to Elsie Leslie, already quoted, and it is not very far from James's acceptance of the Turgenev principle that the writer must always begin with his characters and not with his plot; otherwise he will force them into an unnatural and artificial line of action. Even "stream-of-consciousness" is present, as George Feinstein has noted, in some of his untutored narrators.

IV

He seems to have demanded no special concessions in the way of working conditions. When Mrs. Clemens arranged his desk for him neatly, he had to upset everything before he felt enough at home to be able to work. When he was really interested, he could work under conditions which most of us would regard as prohibitive. "I am here in Twichell's house at work, with the noise of the children and an army of carpenters to help. Of course they don't help, but neither do they hinder. It's like a boiler factory for racket, and in nailing a wooden ceiling on the room under me the hammering tickles my feet amazingly, sometimes jars my table a good deal, but I am never conscious of the racket at all, and I move my feet into positions of relief without knowing when I do it."

Sometimes he works regularly, sometimes irregularly. Once he waits weeks for a "call." Sometimes the subject takes "full charge," and the words "leap out" before he knows what is coming. Katy Leary says that when the mood was upon him, he would sometimes jump out of bed in the middle of the night and sit down to write for hours at a stretch. In his old age, he remembered having written the bulk of *The Innocents Abroad* in sixty days. On *Roughing It* he turned out between thirty and sixty-five manuscript pages a day: "I find myself so thoroughly interested in my work now (a thing I have not experienced for months) that I can't bear to lose a single moment of the inspiration." In the summer of 1883 he said he never wrote less than 2,600 words a day on *Huck*; his average was 3,000; once he did 4,000. In 1894, he speaks of having added 1,500 words to *Joan of Arc* one day, "which was a proper enough day's work though not a full one." During the next two days he wrote 6,000 words, "and that was a very large mistake. My head hasn't been worth a cent since." *Joan* was, in general, easy for him—probably because he so loved the subject. "A tale which tells itself," he calls it; "I merely have to hold the pen."

His attitude toward himself as a man of letters is modest enough. When he tells Howells that he expects to appear in the encyclopaedias of the future as "Mark Twain; history and occupation unknown—but he was personally acquainted with Howells," he is paying a graceful compliment, but it is not the kind of compliment that an arrogant writer would have paid. "The papers have found at last the courage to pull me down off my pedestal & cast slurs at me," he writes Mrs. Fairbanks in 1871—"& that is simply a popular author's death rattle. Though he wrote an *inspired* book after that, it would not save him." Five years later, he views the future no less unhopefully: "Two or three years more will see the end of my ability to do acceptable work, & then I shall have a great long compulsory holiday in which to drift around & annoy people with over-liberal visits." To "make" the *Atlantic* seemed quite beyond him, and he was astonished when Howells asked him to contribute. "I do not know that I have any printable stuff just now . . . but I shall have by and by. It is very gratifying to hear that it is wanted by anybody. I stand always prepared to hear the reverse, and am constantly surprised that it is delayed so long." When Howells or Mrs. Clemens was not available to edit his stuff for him, he looked about for somebody else. Mark Twain submitted his books to Howells; Howells did not submit his books to Mark Twain. Sometimes it even seems as though Mark Twain imposed on Howells. We may grant that it would have been ridiculous for Howells to ask Mark Twain to correct *The Rise of Silas Lapham* for him. Nevertheless only a modest man could have accepted the situation—and the relationship—as Mark Twain did. When he was on his deathbed, he told his daughter he was doubtful that the sale of his books would continue for more than a brief period following his death.[9]

For all that, he had a certain faith in his work, and as time went on, and he progressed toward world fame, it did not tend to lessen. While he was still in Nevada, he had already come to realize that some of his things were good enough to deserve a wider

[9] It must be understood, however, that Mark Twain could only be edited by someone he respected and whom he had chosen for the job. For the sad story of what happened to one self-appointed "literary kangaroo," see *Mark Twain–Howells Letters*, II, 710–11, n. 2.

audience than the one he habitually addressed. "But sometimes I throw off a pearl (there is no self-conceit about that, I beg you to observe) which ought for the eternal welfare of my race to have a more extensive circulation than is afforded by a local daily paper." When *The Jumping Frog* was widely reprinted and made his name known on the East Coast, he was uneasy. "To think that, after writing many an article a man might be excused for thinking tolerably good, those New York people should single out a villainous backwoods sketch to compliment me on!" He hated the British pirate, John C. Hotten, most of all, for adding drivel of his own to his books in order that he might copyright them in England. "My books are bad enough, just as they are written, but what must they be after Mr. John Camden Hotten has composed half-a-dozen chapters and added the same to them?" He is almost equally offended by inaccuracies in a newspaper article. "They put words into my mouth. I'd rather they had put street sweepings." Nor was it an author who thought meanly of himself who was to describe Theodore Roosevelt as "the Tom Sawyer of the political world."

Perhaps it is in connection with his *Autobiography* that we get Mark Twain's frankest expressions of his faith in posterity's interest. As his dictations absorbed him, his enthusiasm grew, and he told Paine he intended to go on until he had dictated a library, some of which would not be printed for one thousand years. "The edition of A.D. 2006 will make a stir when it comes out. I shall be hovering around taking notice, along with other dead pals." Elizabeth Wallace noticed that he seldom refused anyone permission to photograph him, and that he always faced the camera with a serious expression. "I think a photograph is a most important document, and there is nothing more damning to go down to posterity than a silly foolish smile caught and fixed forever."

He loved praise at all times, and was charmingly, almost naïvely, grateful for it. When Grace King told him how her father, in the agonies of Reconstruction, had turned for solace to *The Innocents Abroad*, how it was the first book after Shakespeare that he found money to buy, Mark's eyes filled with tears. And if he was touched by the praise of an individual, how much more thankful and proud he was when recognition came, as it were, officially, from a great university like Yale or Oxford. "Although I wouldn't cross the ocean again for the price of the ship that carried me, I am glad to do it for an Oxford degree." There was something pathetic about his gratitude. It was almost as though he needed to be reassured concerning his value.

One would not expect a man who took such a common-sense attitude toward the business of writing to be especially intractable in his dealings with editors, illustrators, and publishers. As for publishers, Mark Twain, as we shall see, was always inclined to think that they were cheating him; otherwise he was generally agreeable. When Dan Beard was chosen to illustrate the *Yankee*, Mark Twain remarked sarcastically that he hoped the artist would read the book before making his pictures, adding that he did not believe this was the usual custom with illustrators. But this request was an eminently fair one, and both Beard and Lucius Hitchcock have testified that they found him pleasant to work with. When Hitchcock was working on *A Horse's Tale*, Mark Twain was very specific in his directions, for he was eager to have Susy appear in the pictures as the heroine, yet even here he acknowledged, "I find the artist knows more about what will make a good picture than I do. What I thought a good subject for a picture isn't worth a hang, and something I should not have thought of at all makes a very good one, so I will leave all that with you." The most famous set of illustrations ever prepared for one of Mark Twain's works was of course E. W. Kemble's for *Huckleberry Finn*, and though he had some criticisms at first, he soon recognized their quality.

V

Poetry and playwriting would seem about as far out of Mark Twain's orbit as anything literary could be, yet he tried both, and the play made from *The Gilded Age* and acted by John T. Raymond was a great success. He also tried dramatizing *Tom Sawyer* and *The Prince and the Pauper*, and in 1883 he and Howells got together in an abortive attempt to revive Colonel Sellers.[10] He

[10] See Walter J. Merserve, "Colonel Sellers as a Scientist," *Modern Drama*, Vol. I (1958–59), 151–56.

collaborated with Bret Harte in a play called *Ah Sin*, which had a short run at Daly's Fifth Avenue Theater in 1877 and on the road. Once he wanted to collaborate with Howells on a tragedy based on Carlyle's life of Cromwell, and once he attempted to join forces with a Viennese dramatist in preparing plays for the Burg Theater! I am not sure whether he was serious when he told Mrs. Fairbanks that he had written a five-act play with only one character in it, the interest of the audience being centered on two other persons who do not appear at all. No such manuscript is to be found among the Mark Twain Papers. But there are still two acts extant of another darling project (he tried this one twice), that in which a book agent wanders into Elsinore (and Shakespeare's *Hamlet*), making what Mark Twain evidently thought very funny comments on the action.[11]

Theatrical producers are generally considered much "tougher" to deal with than publishers; perhaps that is why Mark Twain decided to be as difficult as possible with producers. As Samuel C. Webster writes with only pardonable exaggeration: "He seems to want to begin with the actors before he has a producer, and he has an idea that the producer is going to offer a good price for a play he's never seen, and he's not going to let him read it until he gets his terms, and then if . . . [the producer] wants to make anything out of it . . . [he] will tell him where he gets off."

Miss Brashear thinks Mark Twain wrote more doggerel and humorous verse during his Hannibal period than can now be identified. "The Aged Pilot-Man," in *Roughing It*, crude as it is, has a kind of ballad quality and manifests an elementary capacity for meter and rime. "The Derelict," the song of the fairy tree at the beginning of *Joan of Arc*, and the poem written in memory of his daughter Susy are better, and these are Mark Twain's best pieces of verse.

VI

But if poetry and drama did not come natural to him, humor did. He was a "character," an "original." He saw things differently

[11] The fullest report on this matter is "Twain's Version of *Hamlet*," *Twainian*, N.S. Vol. II, June, 1943, p. 4–6.

from other people, and he expressed them differently, as his mother had before him. He could not have lived and spoken like the ordinary, conventional man if the salvation of his soul had depended upon it. There was humor in his appearance and in his speech; Hamlin Garland found that his drawl "and a curious aloofness of glance (as though he spoke through a mask) made it difficult . . . to take his serious statements at their face value." In the early days, his humor was sometimes cruel or in bad taste, as when he found fun in stench and vomit and perpetrated practical jokes and hoaxes. He afterwards got over these things almost completely. "When a person of mature age perpetrates a practical joke it is fair evidence, I think, that he is weak in the head and hasn't enough heart to signify." But as long as he lived he was capable of issuing a public statement that the report of his death had been somewhat exaggerated, or telephoning the newspapers that it is not true that he is dying, for he would not do such a thing at his time of life.

Sometimes Mark Twain found his own works terribly funny; once, at least, he was greatly distressed by his inability to find anything humorous in them. Once he ruined a speech by laughing at his own joke. But he always wanted to be something more than a fun-maker, and he was unhappy when he thought people failed to see that "more." He fears lest his platform work is degrading him, making him a mere "buffoon"; he stipulates that "no humorous pictures" must be used to illustrate one of his stories; he likes the *Atlantic* audience, "for the simple reason that it doesn't require a 'humorist' to paint himself striped and stand on his head every fifteen minutes." As early as 1870 he declared of his department in *The Galaxy* that "these *Memoranda* are not a 'humorous' department. I would not conduct an exclusively and professedly humorous department for any one. I would always prefer to have the privilege of printing a serious and sensible remark, in case one occurred to me, without the reader's feeling obliged to consider himself outraged." On his first meeting with Helen Keller, he went out of his way to tell her that "Mark Twain" was a good name for him because "he was sometimes light and on the surface, and sometimes—'Deep,' interrupted the child." Later, when she was older, and he could talk to her heart to heart, he confided that he wished he had accomplished more. She protested. "Ah, Helen, you have a honeyed tongue; but you don't understand. I have only amused people. Their laughter has submerged me."

For all that, I do not believe, as it was once fashionable to believe, that Mark Twain was a writer forced out of his normal aesthetic development. No self-respecting man would wish to be considered merely a fun-maker, or to publish what he considered his best work, as Mark Twain published his *Joan of Arc*, unsigned, because only on that basis could he hope to win a fair hearing for it. A month to the day before he died, he wrote a little girl who had praised *The Prince and the Pauper* that he liked himself best when he was serious. I think we must allow something here for sheer human perversity—a writer always tends to value most highly what is difficult or impossible for him to do—and I suspect we come pretty close to the heart of the matter in Mark Twain's case in an 1881 letter in which he declares that he likes the *Prince* better than *Tom Sawyer* because "I haven't put any fun in it. . . . You know a body always enjoys seeing himself attempting something out of his line."[12]

[12] Much recent criticism of Huck and Tom illustrates the danger of reading Mark Twain without a sense of humor. Thus Lauriat Lane, Jr.'s defense of *Huckleberry Finn* as a great novel in the 1955 *College English* symposium is based upon quite as irrelevant grounds as William Van O'Connor's attack, as Gilbert M. Rubenstein has shown. Charles A. Allen is under the impression that if Tom Sawyer were about today, he would be considered "a juvenile delinquent" and also, inevitably, a subject for tears—"a lonely, frustrated boy who is desperately trying to obtain someone's approval"! Lionel Trilling's idea that Huck regards the river as a god is no less fuzzy-minded, though it is certainly less disgusting, than Leslie Fiedler's notion (to which it would require Mark's own vocabulary to do justice) that the relationship between Huck and Jim was homosexual. Kenneth Lynn, on the other hand, thinks Huck finds a father in Jim and compares their association to that of Eva and Uncle Tom. Their separation is "tragic." In Huck's contacts with his own father, Mr. Lynn discerns a fictional presentation of Mark Twain's relations with the "hard-hearted" John Marshall Clemens, a supposition which can only recall Bernard Shaw's reported reply to the man who accosted him on the street with "Mr. Kipling, I presume?" "If you can presume that," replied Shaw, "you can presume anything," and strode on. To Mr. Lynn, Huck's escape from the cabin is not merely a clever trick; it is "symbolic suicide and murder," and his slaughter of the pig "symbolizes his desire to end his own miserable life" and "to slay his father and the sordid animality of his ways." But he reports W. H. Auden as finding in the book "the incompatibility of love and freedom." These people cannot possibly all be right, and there is no evidence in the text that any of them are. For a refreshing contrast to such wild subjectivity, one may turn to Louis J. Budd's article, "The

For, when he stopped to reason the matter out, Mark Twain knew that humor itself is a very serious business. "Everything human is pathetic," says Pudd'nhead Wilson. "The secret source of Humor itself is not joy but sorrow. There is no humor in heaven." But here, on this earth, humor is the salt of society. "The minute it crops up all our hardnesses yield, all our irritations and resentments flit away, and a sunny spirit takes their place." As the Mysterious Stranger points out, humor is even a very important means of controlling social behavior. "For your race, in its poverty, has unquestionably one really effective weapon—laughter. Power, money, persuasion, supplication, persecution—these can lift a colossal humbug—push it a little—weaken it a little, century by century; but only laughter can blow it to rags and atoms at a blast. Against the assault of laughter nothing can stand."

Even without these considerations, however, Mark Twain would always have been impatient toward his work and his reputation in some aspects, for he was a writer always conscious of the need for improvement. As soon as the *Innocents* contract is signed, he sees himself moving onward to better things. "I shall write to the Enterprise and Alta every week, as usual, I guess, and to the Herald twice a week—occasionally to the Tribune and the Magazines . . . but I am not going to write to this, that and the other paper any more." Though the instinct of the journalist was strong in him, he was not willing to permit the public to set his tone. He promises himself that after he is married, he will be done with "literature to please the general public." But emancipation did not come so soon. In 1899 he writes Howells: "For several years I have been intending to stop writing for print as soon as I could afford it. At last I can afford it, and have put the potboiler pen away. What I have been wanting is a chance to write a book without reserves—a book which should take account of no one's feelings, and no one's prejudices, opinions, beliefs, hopes, illusions, delusions; a book which should say my say, right out of my

Southward Currents under Huck Finn's Raft," *Mississippi Valley Historical Review*, Vol. XLVI (1959), 222–37, which interprets *Huckleberry Finn* in terms of the writer's experience, not the critic's. "To see the emphasis on violence as a demonstration of Twain's neuroses, as some have done, is to ignore his sensitivity to current events."

heart, in the plainest language and without a limitation of any sort. I judged that that would be an unimaginable luxury, heaven on earth."

VII

These matters are not irrelevant toward the consideration of Mark Twain as a serious, conscious artist, for it is part of the folk-artist view that he did not understand, and could not judge, his own works. And it must be admitted that often he could not, at least while he was working on them; otherwise he must surely have abandoned such projects as the blindfold novelettes, "Simon Wheeler, Detective," "The Autobiography of a Damn Fool," and the history of the microbes long before he did. But he did finally abandon them, and the study of his manuscripts which has been made of late years shows that he finished most of the manuscripts which were worth finishing or which he could possibly have finished. We must not be misled by his threat to burn *Huckleberry Finn* unfinished, for there are other passages which show that he did understand and appreciate that book, and even that Mrs. Clemens did—"dear old Huck," she writes. In 1885 Mark thanked Joel Chandler Harris "for the good word about Huck, that abused child of mine, who has had so much mud flung at him. Somehow I can't help believing in him, and it's a great freshment to my faith to have a man back me up who has been where such boys live, and knows what he is talking about." Huck was never in any danger of getting edited into the stove, for Mark was incapable of burning a manuscript, and he abandoned work when he did, not because he did not believe in the book, but because he had encountered technical problems which must be solved before he could proceed. It is true that he showed a tendency to rate both *Joan of Arc* and *The Prince and the Pauper* higher than contemporary criticism tends to place them. Though in 1904 he agreed with William Lyon Phelps that *Huckleberry Finn* was his masterpiece, he is officially on record as regarding the *Joan of Arc* as worth all his other books together. But both *Joan* and the *Prince* are better books than many readers now suppose, and though Mark was mistaken, his errors are quite explicable. He loved and revered Joan herself too much to evaluate anything he might write about her dispassionately, and the Mississippi books were all too close to his own memory and experience to hit him with quite the same impact they bring to bear upon us. *Joan of Arc* and *The Prince and the Pauper* were the kind of literature that a writer was expected to produce in those days; so far as form and materials were concerned, they might safely be judged by comfortably established criteria. But *Huckleberry Finn* was something new in the world, and it had to be lived with for a while, as any great and original work of art does, before anybody could know how great it really was.

VIII

I have already spoken of Mark Twain's use of literary materials in his travel writings. This tendency began early; even his Philadelphia letters in the Muscatine *Journal* use material from R. A. Smith's *Philadelphia as It Is in 1852*.[13] But the tendency is not confined to travel writings or to nonfiction either. It may be doubted that any modern writer has used "sources" more freely than Mark Twain.

It was, of course, quite in accord with the philosophy of life to which he was committed in later years that he should do so. Just before he started out on his world tour, he told a newspaper interviewer in Portland, Oregon: "I don't believe an author, good, bad, or indifferent, ever lived, who created a character. It was always drawn from his recollection of someone he had known. . . . We mortals can't create, we can only copy. Some copies are good and some are bad." And what applied to characterization applied as well to other aspects of literary work.[14]

The matter may be studied in terms of general literary influences and also in terms of specific sources.

Mark Twain never wrote an essay on "Books That Have In-

[13] Fred W. Lorch, "Mark Twain's Letters in the Muscatine *Journal*," *American Literature*, Vol. XVII (1946), 348–51.

[14] Fred W. Lorch, "Mark Twain's 'Morals' Lecture During the American Phase of His World Tour of 1895–96," *American Literature*, Vol. XXVI (1944–45), 52–66. See Mark Twain's views on plagiarism and Walter Blair's interesting discussion of them, in his *Mark Twain and "Huck Finn,"* 59–60.

fluenced Me"; if he had, he must surely have begun with the Bible. Professor Pochmann counted 124 Biblical allusions in his writing —eighty-nine of them, to be sure, in the *Innocents*—far more than to any other book or writer. But not only does Mark Twain quote the Bible; he burlesques it; he takes the reader's knowledge of it absolutely for granted; he derives from it in every conceivable way. Charles W. Stoddard has described the thrilling beauty of his reading, one night in London, from the Book of Ruth. It is not difficult to agree with Paine that the limpid beauty and simplicity of Mark Twain's style at its best owe much to that well of English undefiled.

Next to the Bible, the most important influence was that of Cervantes. This was pointed out in detail by Olin H. Moore as far back as 1922.[15] This was the first literary influence to be studied in detail, and authorities on Mark Twain kicked hard against the pricks in their reluctance to accept it, but their struggles were in vain, for Mark had made his acknowledgment in *Huckleberry Finn* itself. Tom Sawyer is the Don Quixote to Huck Finn's Sancho Panza. Tom, like the Don, is an omnivorous reader who seeks to act out romantic adventures in his own experience, and some of the dialogue between the two boys follows the conversations between Don Quixote and Sancho Panza very closely. The picnic scene in *Tom Sawyer* is clearly indebted to the Don's attack upon the sheep, as well as to his adventures when he tries to halt the funeral procession. But *Tom Sawyer* did not represent Mark Twain's first use of this material; neither was it the last. Sancho and the Don had already appeared in the *Alta California* letters of 1866–67, which have now been reprinted as *Mark Twain's Travels with Mr. Brown*; in *A Connecticut Yankee*, Alisande was to enact Don Quixote and the Yankee himself his squire.

Miss Brashear feels strongly that Mark Twain was importantly influenced by eighteenth-century writers. His strong social interest expresses itself in his passion for biography, diaries, and letters —all popular forms in the age of Queen Anne. This period was also greatly interested in the "character." Miss Brashear found "Sir Roger at the Play" in the early Snodgrass letter on *Julius*

[15] "Mark Twain and *Don Quixote*," PMLA, Vol. XXXVII (1922), 324–46.

Caesar, and pointed out that *The Spectator* was well known in the Middle West. The eighteenth century was also interested in fables, moralized legends, and maxims. She was able to do little with the fables, but there are plenty of maxims. Moralized legends appear in "The Man That Corrupted Hadleyburg," "The $30,000 Bequest," "Was It Heaven or Hell?," "A Dog's Tale," and "A Horse's Tale," the last two being "almost sentimental documents to illustrate the XVIII Century doctrine of nature's social union."

Miss Brashear may have overstated the case for eighteenth-century influence upon Mark Twain; certainly his thinking was more influenced by nineteenth-century scientific writing than she believed. Swift is the eighteenth-century writer with whom it is most interesting to compare him, but little or no direct influence can here be traced. There is one vague reference to Swift in *Roughing It,* and H. W. Fisher reports that Mark Twain once denounced Swift as a sadist and masochist whom it would be a waste of time to try to explain, but Mark seems to have only the vaguest information concerning Swift: he is not even certain when he lived. Schönemann compares Swift and Mark Twain interestingly, without actually asserting influence, and finds many parallels. Swift's attitude toward animals, as providing a refuge from the contemptible character of mankind, is interesting in this connection also.[16]

Goldsmith was another matter. The Goldsmith of *The Vicar of Wakefield* was anathema, as we have seen, but the essayist was another story. Mark Twain knew him well at an early stage, and Schönemann's suggestion that he may have influenced not only the "colloquial ease" of the American's style but even his philosophy of history is not altogether unreasonable. His most direct imitation of Goldsmith was in the essay, "Goldsmith's Friend Abroad Again," that noble protest against the inhumanity shown by Americans to the Chinese on the Pacific Coast,[17] but Paul Fatout has most interestingly shown reason to suppose that Mark Twain's account of some of the circumstances of his first lecture,[18] as re-

16 See Coley B. Taylor, *Mark Twain's Margins on Thackeray's "Swift."*
17 This may now be read in *The Curious Republic of Gondour and Other Whimsical Sketches.*
18 In "Mark Twain's First Lecture: A Parallel," *Pacific Historical Review,* Vol. XXV (1956), 347–54.

lated in *Roughing It*, may be fiction, suggested by Goldsmith's experiences on the first night of *She Stoops To Conquer*, as reported by Washington Irving.

Some points about Mark Twain's use of specific sources are too obvious to require discussion. The use of Malory in *A Connecticut Yankee* has always been clear, and everybody knows that "A Double-Barrelled Detective Story" took its point of departure from Sherlock Holmes, and *Captain Stormfield's Visit to Heaven* from *The Gates Ajar*, by Elizabeth Stuart Phelps, as everybody knows also that *Tom Sawyer, Detective* Americanizes a Danish novel, *The Parson of Vejlby*, by Steen Steensen Blicher, which Mark Twain heard about through Lillie de Hegermann-Lindencrone.[19] Nobody would expect Mark Twain to be able to write *The Prince and the Pauper* or *Personal Recollections of Joan of Arc* without studying historical sources, though he did a more thorough job for the *Joan of Arc* at least than he is often given credit for, and it is surprising—and also illuminating for the understanding of his methods—that he should have used a Sut Lovingood story—American as corn on the cob—along with all his French and British materials.[20] Some of the sources that have been suggested are, of course, conjectural—like Miss Bellamy's suggestion that the death of Laura Hawkins in *The Gilded Age* is indebted to Hawthorne's description of Judge Pyncheon's end in *The House of the Seven Gables*, or Kenneth Lynn's idea that Roxy in *Pudd'nhead Wilson* may have been derived from Cassy in *Uncle Tom's Cabin*. There is no reasonable room for doubt,

[19] See J. Christian Bay, "*Tom Sawyer, Detective*: The Origin of the Plot." in *Essays Offered to Herbert Putnam by His Colleagues and Friends on His Thirtieth Anniversary as Librarian of Congress, 5 April, 1929* (Yale University Press, 1929); D. M. McKeithan, "The Source of Mark Twain's *Tom Sawyer, Detective*," in his *Court Trials in Mark Twain and Other Essays*.

[20] He had previously tried to use it in *The Prince and the Pauper* but had cut it out. See E. Hudson Long, "Sut Lovingood and Mark Twain's *Joan of Arc*," *Modern Language Notes*, Vol. LXIV (1949), 37–39, and D. M. McKeithan, "Mark Twain's Story of the Bull and the Bees," in his *Court Trials in Mark Twain*. The fullest study of the sources of *Joan of Arc* and the most important paper on that work is Albert E. Stone, Jr., "Mark Twain's *Joan of Arc*: The Child as Goddess," *American Literature*, Vol. XXXI (1959–60), 1–20. See, also, besides McKeithan's long paper on Joan's trial, Mentor L. Williams, "Mark Twain's *Joan of Arc*," *Michigan Alumnus Quarterly Review*, Vol. LIV (1948), 243–50, and Mary A. Wyman, "A Note on Mark Twain," *College English*, Vol. VII (1946), 438–43.

however, that *Tom Sawyer Abroad* uses material from Jules Verne's *Five Weeks in a Balloon*,[21] and we know that Mark Twain prepared for sending Tom and Huck out among the Indians by ordering some "personal narratives" of life on the Plains.

It may seem surprising that a work like *The Mysterious Stranger* should have had so many literary connections,[22] but the great surprise is *Huckleberry Finn*, which has now been shown to have had almost as many sources (one is tempted to say) as *The Cloister and the Hearth*, including *The Arabian Nights*, *The Lady of the Lake*, Carlyle's *The French Revolution*, *A Tale of Two Cities*, Bird's *Nick of the Woods*, Mark's own *The Prince and the Pauper*, and (for that matter!) *The Cloister and the Hearth* itself. This is much too complicated to summarize here; the reader must go to Walter Blair's amazing adventure in scholarship, *Mark Twain and "Huck Finn,"* a necessity not to be lamented since this is a reading adventure second in enlightenment and pleasure only to *Huckleberry Finn* itself and one of which no sensible admirer of Mark Twain would willingly deprive himself.[23]

If this be true, why, then, do *Huckleberry Finn* and the rest of Mark Twain's best writings make such a strong impression of freshness and originality upon us that he has actually been called a folk artist? The answer is simple. Mark Twain drew a great deal from his reading, but he also drew a great deal from life. Moreover, he used what he read like an artist, not like a reporter; he assimilated it, as Chaucer did, and made it a part of himself. By the time he got through, he himself could not have told where he had got it; neither did it matter; for when a man reads as creatively as Mark Twain read, reading and experience and imagination become one. I have already noted Paul Fatout's suggestion that his description of the circumstances surrounding his first lecture may have been borrowed from Goldsmith. But Professor Blair throws out an even more startling idea when he suggests that when Mark

[21] D. M. McKeithan, "Mark Twain's *Tom Sawyer Abroad* and Jules Verne's *Five Weeks in a Balloon*," in *Court Trials in Mark Twain*.

[22] See Coleman O. Parsons, "The Background of *The Mysterious Stranger*," *American Literature*, Vol. XXXII (1960–61), 55–74.

[23] See, also, Blair's article, "The French Revolution and *Huckleberry Finn*," *Modern Philology*, Vol. LV (1957–58), 21–35.

reported that his mother drowned kittens when she had to but always warmed the water first, he may have been thinking not about his mother but about B. P. Shillaber's Mrs. Partington! Certainly Mrs. Partington resembled Aunt Polly (who was Jane Clemens), and her picture was used for Aunt Polly in the first edition of *Tom Sawyer*.[24]

If Tom's Aunt Polly was indebted to Mark Twain's mother, then Judge Thatcher was his father, Sid was drawn from his brother Henry, and his sister Pamela furnished the original of Cousin Mary. Huck Finn is Tom Blankenship, the village vagabond; Nigger Jim was derived from Uncle Dan'l, a slave on the plantation owned by Uncle John Quarles. Tom Blankenship's father was town drunkard in Hannibal, as Huck's father is in the book, and Injun Joe was another local character, though the reality was much less vicious than the fiction. The "Duke" was a journeyman printer, whom Mark Twain met, at a later date, in Virginia City. Or at least all these identifications have been made. According to the preface, Tom Sawyer, too, was drawn from life, "but not from an individual—he is a combination of the characteristics of three boys whom I knew." It is no secret that the most important of these was named Sam Clemens.

Mark Twain used actual places as well as persons in his stories. John Quarles's farm was moved down to Arkansas both in *Huckleberry Finn* and in *Tom Sawyer, Detective*. "It was all of six hundred miles," said Mark Twain, "but it was no trouble; it was not a very large farm—five hundred acres, perhaps—but I could have done it if it had been twice as large."

I must not leave the impression that Professor Blair confines himself, in *Mark Twain and "Huck Finn,"* to describing the sources of the book in Mark Twain's reading; the sources indicated in his living are quite as impressive. Nor were the Mississippi books unique in this regard. *The Gilded Age* is full of contemporary references. Contemporary readers must have been immediately aware of the use made of the scandals involving the notorious Senator Pomeroy of Kansas, as well as the Fair-Crittenden murder

[24] Walter Blair, *Native American Humor*, 1800–1900 (American Book Company, 1937), 152; *Mark Twain and "Huck Finn,"* 62–63.

case in San Francisco,[25] and James Harvey Young has reasonably suggested that Ruth Bolton may have been taken in part from Anna Dickinson, whom Mark Twain seems to have admired. More interestingly, Fred W. Lorch has shown that many of the basic feudal concepts and practices which Mark Twain portrays and attacks in *A Connecticut Yankee* were actually observed by him in operation in the Sandwich Islands, when he visited there, and that up to a point the Yankee plays the same role in sixth-century England that the missionaries were enacting in Hawaii.[26]

Whether Mark Twain got more material from literature or from life, there would seem to be no question that the material he got from life was the more vital. What he got from books was equally useful, but he could not use it until after it had been vitalized by his experience; his experience provided him with the means of making it seem real. Life vitalized literature; literature did not simply provide a means of escape from life, as is the case with lesser writers. As he grew older, his memory relinquished its hold on facts, but it retained impressions tenaciously. He may have stretched it a little when he described Tom Sawyer as belonging "to the composite order of architecture," but there are many things in his books which do belong to that order. So the last word belonged neither to reading nor to experience but to imagination. If he made himself Goldsmith and his mother Mrs. Partington, he altered what he saw and experienced no less freely than what he had read. The St. Petersburg of *Tom Sawyer* and *Huckleberry Finn* is not Hannibal; it is a created town that has grown out of Hannibal, and the alterations made by Mark Twain have been determined by his artistic purposes. In his pages Mississippi steamboating moves away from cutthroat competition and be-

25 See Albert R. Kitzhaber, "Mark Twain's Use of the Pomeroy Case in *The Gilded Age*," *Modern Language Quarterly*, Vol. XV (1954), 42–56; Franklin Walker, "An Influence from San Francisco on Mark Twain's *The Gilded Age*," *American Literature*, Vol. VIII (1936), 63–66. Mrs. Fair's first name was Laura, but it seems amazing that Mark Twain should have given the "bad" heroine of *The Gilded Age* the name of his own childhood sweetheart, Laura Hawkins. In *Tom Sawyer*, he called her Becky Thatcher, but by the time he came to *Huckleberry Finn* he forgot what he had called her.

26 "Hawaiian Feudalism and Mark Twain's *A Connecticut Yankee in King Arthur's Court*," *American Literature*, Vol. XXX (1958–59), 50–66.

comes an idyll. The original of Widow Douglas was a woman of Hannibal, but the Widow Douglas is a much lovelier person than her prototype had been. In life, Injun Joe did not die in the cave, though he was lost there on one occasion, and Huck Finn's refusal to surrender Jim was based upon a very different set of circumstances in the life of Tom Blankenship.

✳ "The ancients stole our best thoughts," and Mark Twain's originality was the only kind that is possible for a modern writer. His art was the art that conceals art. As he himself once observed, "Shakespeare took other people's quartz and extracted the gold from it—it was a nearly valueless commodity before."

CHAPTER FOUR: *Paradoxes*

I

CHAUCER WRITES OF HIS Doctour of Phisik:

> He knew the cause of everich maladye—
> Were it of hoot, or cold, or moyste, or drye—
> And where they engendred, and of what humour.

We no longer believe, with mediaeval medical science, that our particular "complexion," or temperament, is determined by the balance of "humours" that make up our being, but the ideal of a well-rounded life still prevails. As we turn now from Mark Twain the writer to Samuel L. Clemens the man, it is important at the outset to determine the fundamental bias of his temperament as best we can, and to see him as he stands or falls in the midst of the varied influences and stimuli that life brings to bear upon him. And we may well begin with the most external and most obvious thing—his appearance.

He described himself, amusingly, in his own particular brand of German, to Bayard Taylor in 1878:

Meine Beschreibung ist vollenden: Geborn 1835; 5 Fuss 8½ inches hoch; weight doch aber about 145 pfund, sometimes ein wenig unter, sometimes ein wenig oben; dunkel braun Haar und rhotes Moustache, full Gesicht, mit sehr hohe Oren und leicht grau prachtvolles strahlenden Augen und ein Verdammtes gut moral character. Handlungkeit, Author von Bücher.

But how did he appear to others? Let us first hear Bret Harte:

His head was striking. He had the curly hair, the acquiline nose, and even the acquiline *eye*—an eye so eagle-like that a second lid would not have surprised me—of an unusual and dominant nature. His eyebrows were very very thick and bushy. His dress was careless, and his general manner one of the supreme indifference to surroundings and circumstances.

Senator William M. Stewart, of Nevada, whom Clemens served briefly as a secretary, after his return from the Mediterranean seems to have disliked him as much as any man ever did:

I was seated at my window one morning when a very disreputable looking person slouched into the room. He was arrayed in a seedy suit, which hung upon his loose frame in bunches with no style worth mentioning. A sheaf of scraggy black hair[1] leaked out of a battered old slouch hat, like stuffing from an ancient Colonial sofa, and an evil-smelling cigar butt, very much frazzled, protruded from the corner of his mouth. He had a very sinister appearance.

Mrs. James T. Fields took this snapshot at a later period:

He is forty years old, with some color in his cheeks and a heavy light-colored moustache, and overhanging light eyebrows. His eyes are grey and piercing, yet soft, and his whole face expresses great sensitiveness. He is exquisitely neat also, though careless, and his hands are small, not without delicacy. He is a small man, but his mass of hair seems the one rugged-looking thing about him.

[1] Stewart's inability even to tell the color of Mark Twain's hair does not inspire faith in his other observations. See Wecter, *Sam Clemens of Hannibal*, 260, for a report concerning an item called, "Oh, She has a Red Head," in which Mark glorified red hair by attributing it to both Adam and Jesus!

Here is a picture of Mark Twain on the platform, from a contemporary review:

His face is clean cut as a cameo. He speaks in a sort of mechanical drawl and with a most bored expression of countenance. The aggrieved way in which he gazes with tilted chin over the convulsed faces of his audience, as much as to say, "Why are you laughing?" is irresistible in the extreme. He jerks out a sentence or two and follows it with a silence that is more suggestive than words. His face is immovable while his hearers laugh, and as he waits for the merriment to subside, his right hand plays with his chin and his left finds its way to the pocket of his pants. Occasionally the corners of his mouth twitch with inward fun, but never is a desire to laugh to get the better of him. These characteristics agree so well with his description of himself in his books—Innocence victimized by the world, flesh, and Devil—that one cannot fail to establish the resemblance and laugh at the grotesque image.

Susy sees him with the eyes of love:

Papa's appearance has been described many times, but very incorrectly. He has beautiful gray hair, not any too thick or any too long, but just right; a Roman nose, which greatly improves the beauty of his features; kind blue eyes and a small mustache. He has a wonderfully shaped head and profile. He has a very good figure— in short, he is an extraordinarily fine looking man.

William Dean Howells's picture, too, has been painted with care:

Clemens was then hard upon fifty, and he had kept, as he did to the end, the slender figure of his youth, but the ashes of the burnt-out years were beginning to gray the fires of that splendid shock of red hair which he held to the height of a stature apparently greater than it was, and tilted from side to side in his undulating walk. He glimmered at you from the narrow slits of fine blue-greenish eyes, under branching brows, which with age grew more and more like a sort of plumage, and he was apt to smile into your face with a subtle but amiable perception, and yet with a sort of remote absence; you were all there for him, but he was not all there for you.

Finally, we have S. J. Woolf, the artist who painted him in 1906:

> Instead of the weather-beaten face which I had expected, I saw one softer and calmer, but no less strong, while the delicacy and refinement of his features were most noticeable. His hair, too, which I had always thought wiry, was glossy and silken. Never have I seen a head where it seemed a more integral part—its ivory-like tones melting imperceptibly into the lighter hues of the skin, so that the line of juncture was almost entirely lost. Even his hands betrayed a more actively nervous man than one would be led to imagine a former river-pilot could be.

So far the balance between sweetness and strength would seem to be well maintained.

People were impressed by his mouth—"as delicate as a woman's," says Kipling—and his eyes and his voice. George Ade thought the eyes "imperious," even though Mark had to look up at him—"a calm, penetrating, unwavering gaze," and Owen Wister speaks of "blue fire under bushy brows, steady when he fixed them on you, inquiring, penetrating, fierce, and genial at the same time." The voice, writes W. H. Rideing, was "deep and earnest like that of one of the graver musical instruments, rich and solemn, and in emotion vibrant and swelling with its own passionate feeling." When he spoke the words "two thousand years," his enunciation "seemed to make visible and tangible all the mystery, all the remoteness, and all the awe of that chilling stretch of time." A part of the charm and power of his voice was in the famous drawl he inherited from his mother, and that art played as large a share in it as accident, we may safely infer from his daughter's observation that he often lost it in private life.[2]

During his early lecture days, Mark Twain was sometimes described by the newspapers as a curiosity rather than a beauty, and in his *Autobiography* he pretends to be greatly hurt by this. "I was never ugly in my life! Forty years ago I was not so good-looking. A looking glass then lasted me three months. Now I can wear one

[2] There is a Mark Twain recording at Yale. See Mort Weisinger, "Listen! Mark Twain Speaking," *Saturday Evening Post*, Vol. CCXXI (July 3, 1948), 12.

out in two days." He took great care of his hair, quite according to a system of his own, "thoroughly scouring it with soap and water every morning, then rinsing it well; then lathering it heavily, and rubbing off the lather with a coarse towel, a process which leaves a slight coating of oil upon each hair . . . ." He was also fond of having Katy Leary massage his head.

Persons who found Mark Twain a phenomenon in his personal appearance were generally influenced by their impression of his clothes. The first time Thomas Bailey Aldrich brought him home, one dark winter's night, his astonished wife saw "a most unusual guest, clothed in a coat of sealskin, the fur worn outward; a sealskin cap well down over his ears; the cap half revealing and half concealing the mass of reddish hair underneath; the heavy mustache having the same red tint. The trousers came well below the coat, and were of a yellowish-brown color; stockings of the same tawny hue, which the low black shoes emphasized. May and December intermixed, producing strange confusion in one's preconceived ideas."

Mrs. Aldrich, whom Mark cordially detested, thought him drunk, and she was neither the first nor the last woman to be thus deceived. More penetrating women got other impressions. Geraldine Farrar was struck by his gentleness, and Lady Jebb also uses the word "gentle," though she adds "unpolished" as late as 1895, and remarks that he liked "very well to stand up and tell rather prolix stories to the whole assemblage." There can be no question that the charm was there, sometimes overwhelmingly there, even for those who had no taste for the humor.

He had always been interested in clothes. He was the glass of fashion in his pilot days, "given to patent leathers, blue serge, white duck, and fancy striped shirts," and there is a photograph of him, in his days of glory in Carson City, "in a long broadcloth cloak, a starched shirt, and polished boots." When he was thrown into the mining camps, such things were out of the question, and he went to the other extreme, taking the same pains to make himself a picturesque roughneck that he had once taken to appear a picturesque dandy. Some of this he brought with him to the East, though he later outgrew it entirely, and Katy Leary says he would spend all morning dressing for the opera at Bayreuth. The careful attention he gives to the matter of proper attire for our diplomatic representatives abroad in his paper, "Diplomatic Pay and Clothes," is more like what one would expect from a woman than from a man.

Toward the end of his life, Mark Twain came before the world as a clothes-reformer, when he laid aside the conventional dark men's suit—he had always hated it—and, save for formal evening occasions, arrayed himself thereafter exclusively in white flannel and white serge. He had always been sensitive to color combinations, in house furnishings as well as in clothes; he had often drawn the contrast between the graceful splendor of Oriental garments and the stiff, cold awkwardness of the West. "I should like to dress in a loose and flowing costume made all of silks and velvets resplendent with stunning dyes, and so would every man I have ever known; but none of us dares to venture it." He could do the next best thing; he could wear white, which was at least cheerful, even if it did fall a long way behind Oriental splendors. "He used to go," says Katy Leary, "in the beginning of summer, and sit on the steps at 21 Fifth Avenue for a little while, in his clean white suit, white shoes, and everything spotless, and he'd have a nice straw hat on his head, too. Then when he'd see one of the busses coming along, he'd just run out and stop it and climb on top and ride to the end of the route to get the fresh air. Everybody used to look at him, on top of the bus, but he didn't mind that." Katy knew. Hadn't she long ago got him to put on a warm, long nightgown by the simple expedient of decorating the new nightgowns with red, and had he not thereupon cast side his old, plain, short ones forevermore?

Mark Twain lives in the American imagination in those white clothes, but there was one garment which came his way before the end that he prized even more highly, and this was the scarlet gown that Oxford gave him with his doctor's degree. He was utterly, disarmingly simple and childlike about it. "I like the degree well enough, but I'm crazy about the clothes! I wish I could wear 'em all day and all night. Think of the gloomy garb I have to walk the streets in at home, when my whole soul cries out for gold braid, yellow and scarlet sashes, jewels and a turban!" He could not wear it all the time, but he did wear it, by request, at Clara's wedding, and it was not the only unusual garb Stormfield ever saw him in. Once, when he entertained Elizabeth Wallace there, he had a girl's pink hair ribbon nodding waggishly in his white locks all evening.

II

Sam Clemens was a delicate child, but during his mature years he was generally a well man, until late in his life, when he was wracked by bronchitis and rheumatism and, at last, the heart disease that killed him. It is surprising to find him writing Mrs. Fairbanks in 1879 that if he overworks, by writing at night, he gets into the doctor's hands; two years later he told her that he was older at forty-five than some men are at eighty, which, like the later report of his death, must have been somewhat exaggerated. In 1882 he complained to Joel Chandler Harris of malaria but made light of it, because it did not prevent his lying in bed and writing. He sometimes had trouble getting to sleep, but, as Howells says, the trouble here was not so much sleeplessness as "a reluctant sleepiness," and he seems to have needed less sleep than most men. Even in his old age, he wore out his billiard partners. "Don't you ever get tired?" H. H. Rogers asked him. And he replied, "I don't know what it is to get tired. I wish I did."

The question changes its aspect somewhat when we turn from his physical to his nervous health. When Paine was working on his biography, Joe Goodman, who had known Mark well in Virginia City, objected to his being endowed with physical vigor and activity. He had always been struck, he said, by the contrast between Mark's bodily helplessness and his mental power. It is not surprising that he should always have been a "sucker" for "remedies," all the way from osteopathy through Plasmon, the wonder food which, in 1902, had made it possible for him to eat all the "raisin-cake, plum pudding, lobster salad, candy, ice cream, & all other desirable sweet things" that he had not been able to eat for years, to various forms of mental healing.

The imaginative temperament does not, in general, conduce

to peace of mind, and in Mark Twain's case it was considerably exacerbated by the various scenes of violence and terror and horror which he witnessed in his youth—and by the stimulus of African magic also. Worst of all, perhaps, was his father's autopsy.[3] When he was twelve, a terrible epidemic of measles raged in Hannibal, and children died like flies. "At some time or other every day and every night a sudden shiver shook me to the marrow, and I said to myself, 'There, I've got it! and I shall die.'" So nervous did he become that he felt it quite impossible any longer to endure his uncertainty, with the result that he deliberately exposed himself to the disease by crawling into bed with a boy who had it, contracted it, and for days hovered on the brink of death.

It was at night that he suffered most. A somnambulist in childhood, he recovered from this tendency when he grew up, but he was never wholly free from the terror of dreams.

As we have seen, he found one of life's richest satisfactions in the sound of the human voice, and only those who are similarly constituted will understand how much this meant to him. But, alas! there was a price to pay, for there are many more unpleasant voices than lovely ones. In the West, there was a little Swede who sang away continuously at one tune until it seemed to Mark that it would be worth dying just to end the torture. In Hannibal there was a slave boy who was "the noisiest creature that ever was, perhaps." One day, Sam went raging to his mother, "and said Sandy had been singing for an hour without a single break, and I couldn't stand it, and *wouldn't* she please shut him up." The tears came into Jane Clemens's eyes as she replied, "Poor thing, when he sings it shows that he is not remembering . . . but when he is still I am afraid he is thinking . . . . He will never see his mother again; if he can sing, I must not hinder it, but be thankful for it." Sam's nerves were not very strong, but his humanity was, and Sandy's singing did not trouble him any more.

III

With regard to his diet, Mark Twain's only rule was to eat whatever he liked and as much as he liked. For breakfast he en-

[3] Wecter, *Sam Clemens of Hannibal*, 116.

joyed beefsteak and coffee—much coffee—and his food was more likely to receive his undivided attention at this meal than would be the case later in the day, when, especially if there were guests, he might very well prefer to give up eating, and march about the room, using his napkin as a flag, and deliver himself of a variety of well- or ill-considered opinions on many subjects. Lunch he rarely ate, though when Katy Leary trapped him by ordering milk and huckleberry pie, he would generally oblige her by disposing of half the pie. Pond thought him extremely irregular in lecture-tour days, and Katy complains of his fads: "Sometimes he would just leave off eating everything except one thing, and would live on that all the time. Then there was a certain kind of bread he would have to have; and he took it into his head once to live just on breakfast food, and ran all about with it. Why, he would even go to dinners and parties and carry that old breakfast food with him." The breakfast food may have been wholesome enough, but what are we to say to this? "I take only one meal a day just now. . . . It consists of four boiled eggs and coffee. I stir in a *lot* of salt and then keep on dusting and stirring in black pepper till the eggs look dirty—then they're booming with fire and energy and you can taste them all the way down and even after they get there." Once, at the home of Thomas Nast, he disposed of five plates of oysters, and there is one letter which inspires his daughter to comment that "on lecture tours he seemed to have an appetite of magnificent proportions, quite unlike his usual one." The letter reads as follows: "I ate a hearty breakfast at nine this morning. On the hotel car at 1 P.M. I took a sirloin steak and mushrooms, sweet potatoes, Irish ditto, a plate of trout, bowl of tomato soup, three cups of coffee, four pieces of apple-pie (or one complete pie), two plates of ice-cream and one orange. But I stopped then on account of the expense, although still hungry." He did not add, with Chaucer's Eagle,

Tak it in ernest or in game.

I prefer to take it "in game."

When Mark Twain first left home, his mother made him

promise neither to drink nor to "throw a card," and he seems to have kept this promise faithfully until she released him from it. Paine thought him extremely temperate during their intimacy, but it is clear that spirituous refreshment was definitely a part of his life. In the West he probably drank more; at least drinking is one of the things he was "kidded" for by his fellow journalists in the rude interchanges that were in vogue in that day and time, and there is a famous story about Mark Twain and Artemus Ward walking the rooftops of Virginia City hillsides after a gay, all-night party. Even then, however, he seems to have felt that excess was disgraceful. In 1866 he writes Will Bowen from San Francisco that he gets "tight" only once in three months now. "It sets a man back in the esteem of people whose opinions are worth having."[4] Drunkenness is often used as a source of humor in very early days, but very seldom thereafter, and H. W. Fisher quotes Mark Twain as saying, "I love a drink, but I never encourage drunkeness by harping on its alleged funny side." In his old age Mark Twain recalled once having been jailed for drunkenness, but if this is the same incident he reported in *Mark Twain's Travels with Mr. Brown*, he may have been more sinned against than sinning.[5] At one time his drinking got all mixed up with his health fads, and he got it into his head that he needed hot Scotch or champagne or ale or beer—the formula varied from time to time—to put him to sleep. In a letter written for publication in 1883,[6] he disclaimed being an expert on the effects of alcohol on thinking and writing, but he did say that though he found two glasses of champagne "the happiest inspiration for an after dinner speech," he thought wine "a clog to the pen, not an inspiration," and could not write after drinking even one glass.

He gave up drinking to please Livy upon becoming engaged

[4] See, also, the letter to Mollie Clemens, in Smith and Anderson, *Mark Twain of the "Enterprise,"* 190.

[5] See *Notebook*, 400; *Mark Twain's Travels with Mr. Brown*, Letter XVIII. Mark could, of course, have cleaned up his experience before writing the letter. But it is not safe to assume that his memory always protected him. Sometimes it made accusations that were manifestly unjust.

[6] This letter has been printed in *The Twainian*, Vol. IX, March–April, 1950, p. 1.

to her, but this reform did not stick. Much later he wrote his mother-in-law from Germany that "the children have learned how to speak German, drink beer and break the Sabbath like the natives," but he may have been teasing her. He believed that prohibition laws made liquor attractive, and there are a number of tirades against "temperance people." Mark Twain's argument that prohibition is objectionable because it is directed against the habit of drinking rather than the desire to drink, which is at the root of the difficulty, would, of course, be stronger if he himself had ever shown any serious inclination to destroy the desire. Yet he approved of the enforcement of liquor laws in New York City in 1867: "The excise has made a sort of decent place out of this once rowdy, noisy, immoral town." The absence of saloons in Hartford, and even the fact that very few men smoked on the street, seem to have been among the evidences of gentility there that pleased him. He wholeheartedly defended women temperance crusaders, even when they infringed the saloonkeeper's rights by invading his precincts and creating a disturbance there. In a country where "every ignorant whisky-drinking foreign-born savage . . . may hold office, [and] help to make the laws," while these same rights are denied to women, he can see no reason why they should be overscrupulous in the means they choose "to protect their sons from destruction by intemperance."[7]

But his particular indulgence, as all the world knows, was smoking. He began as a small boy, and he lived thereafter until the day of his death in a cloud of tobacco—"Me, who never learned to smoke, but always smoked; me, who came into the world asking for a light." In his Seventieth Birthday Speech he says that he had only two rules about the matter—never to smoke more than one cigar at a time, and never to smoke while sleeping or to refrain when awake. Both Howells and Pond were appalled by his excesses. "I do not know," wrote the novelist, who detested tobacco, "how much a man may smoke and live, but apparently

[7] Laurel O'Connor's *Drinking with Twain: Recollections of Mark Twain and His Cronies*, a pamphlet copyrighted in 1936 by Frank Edward Kelsey (no other data are given), is full of "howlers" and adds nothing to what had previously been known. As Jacob Blanck has written on his copy of the photostat copy of this item in the Houghton Library, the work had best be regarded as fiction.

he smoked as much as a man could, for he smoked incessantly."[8] Both Manuel Komroff and Robert Herrick noted that in his old age his white mustache was badly stained with tobacco.

In Mark Twain's time tobacco had not yet been unveiled as the killer it has since been shown to be, but its record was far from clear even then. Madame Caprell, the psychic who "read" for him in New Orleans in 1861, warned him against it, and promised him he would reach eighty-six if he quit smoking. In his old age he once advised Burges Johnson not to smoke, telling him that smoking was a filthy, expensive habit, but this is the only remark that he can be said ever to have made against it. He did stop for a year and a half after his marriage to please Livy, "not that I believed there was the faintest *reason* in the matter, but just as I would deprive myself of sugar in my coffee if she wished it, or quit wearing socks if she thought them immoral." His health did not improve, being already perfect, and since he never permitted himself to regret his abstinence, he "experienced no sort of inconvenience from it." One of the few out-and-out immoral utterances Mark Twain ever permitted himself on any subject was made in connection with smoking. "Why, my old boy, when they used to tell me I would shorten my life ten years by smoking, they little knew the devotee they were wasting their puerile words upon; they little knew how trivial and valueless I would regard a decade that had no smoking in it!" If he had had the extra eleven years that Madame Caprell promised him, he would have died in 1921 instead of 1910, an interesting subject for speculation. In that case he would have had to live through World War I, which he would not have enjoyed.

He professed to be unable to smoke a "good" cigar; if the cigar cost more than five cents, he could not smoke it. A pipe was no good to him until somebody else had broken it in. "I get a

---

[8] In the letter referred to in n. 5 above, Mark Twain says that he began smoking at eight, with 100 cigars a month. By the age of twenty, he had stepped up his consumption to 200 and by thirty to 300, where it remained. He adds, however, that during his summers at Quarry Farm, he sometimes smoked fifteen cigars during five hours' work, "and if my interest reaches the enthusiastic point, I smoke more. I smoke with all my might, and allow no intervals." There is a letter to Howells in which he speaks of having smoked eighteen cigars a day while sick in bed, also reading the Greville Memoirs through!

cheap man—a man who doesn't amount to much, anyhow: who would be as well, or better, dead—and pay him a dollar to break in the pipe for me. I get him to smoke the pipe for a couple of weeks, then put in a new stem, and continue operations as long as the pipe holds together." Of course this was not literally true, but in at least one newspaper office his pipe was known as "The Remains" and "The Pipe of a Thousand Smells." Coulson Kernahan tells how in England Mark Twain went about with one pocket full of stemless corncob bowls and another pocket full of stems. He gave one pipe to Kernahan, who tried to smoke it, but the result was a dry tongue and a sore throat.

Yet every Napoleon meets his Waterloo sooner or later; otherwise human pride would become insufferable, and the gods would blot us from the earth. Mark Twain, accomplished smoker, met his in the Oriental "narghili." "I took one blast at it, and it was sufficient; the smoke went in a great volume down into my stomach, my lungs, even into the uttermost parts of my frame. I exploded one mighty cough, and it was as if Vesuvius had let go."

IV

Mrs. Clemens called her husband "Youth," and there was never a more appropriate nickname. One thinks of him white-garbed and white-haired—"I am very old and very wise"—yet, in a deeper sense, he was always young, though he was often not the trusting child of the Gospels but the child who has tantrums. He skipped lightly up and down the stairs as long as he lived, and because he liked the wooden cupids and other carvings at the head of his great Italian bed, he always slept at the foot so that he might have the pleasure of looking at them. Youth was "the only thing that was worth giving to the race"; old age was an insult. Youth was also the only thing worth writing about, and he says frankly that he harks back to Hannibal days for his materials, not because life has not brought him plenty of subjects since, but because he is not enough interested in them to want to make use of them. Like Dickens, he hates leave-takings. "To part is to die a little," and he will not say good-bye to anybody if he can avoid it. They throw his picture on the screen; it has been made from a fifteen-year-old negative, without a single gray hair showing, and a great feeling of sadness comes over him. When he dies at seventy-five, Kate Leary cries, "It was a terrible, cruel thing to have him die, really, because he was too young—that is, he *felt* young, you know, and that made him young. . . ."

When youth goes in fact, he clings to its memory. When S. J. Woolf comes to do his portrait, he walks up and down the room recalling the scenes of bygone days. This done, he shows the artist his mementoes, "and how his eyes glistened as he showed the various little keepsakes which brought back the memories of dead years." When he returns to Hannibal for a visit, and is received like a king, his feelings are very nearly too much for him.

He is youthful in his eagerness and intensity: he will get up at six o'clock in the morning to make a 4:00 P.M. train. His extreme reactions of glory and despair are youthful, his proneness to moods, his extravagant praise and condemnation. His interest in curiosa and his taste for freaks are youthful also. So are his fads and rages, and he was eminently youthful in his attitude toward money. He was always "discovering" something, often something that the rest of the world had discovered long ago, not infrequently something that the rest of the world had also discovered to be worthless.

His pranks and eccentricities, his love of the *outré* and the unusual, his taste for shocking people—all this is youthful. Once a friend brought him a mechanical leap frog, and Mark got down on his hands and knees and followed the thing around the room just as a child would have done. When he stopped with the Tom Nasts, they put him up in the bedroom of their twenty-year-old daughter Julia, where the walls were completely covered with pictures, photographs, and knick-knacks—perhaps three thousand of them in all. Mark was completely fascinated. It took him an hour to get into bed and another hour to dress himself in the morning. "I would like to see Susie's room decorated in that way," he wrote Livy.

He is youthful, too, in his speculations. "A life of don't-care-a-damn in a boarding house is what I have asked for in many a secret prayer." His body roams over the world—he crossed the Atlantic fourteen times within three and a half years—and his mind ranges through the heights and depths of speculation, yet he never stays anywhere long enough to feel really at home. Partly, it was because he was always looking for something, and never quite arrived. But partly, too, it was because there were so many, many wonderful things to challenge his attention, so many objects luring him on. Helen Keller tells how when she dined at his house, he became restless during the meal and got up to walk around the table, talking, bringing flowers to her to see if she could identify them, and much besides. When she could, he would hold forth on the undeveloped powers of human beings. Then he would start the organ to discover whether she could feel the vibrations, and when he had satisfied himself on that score, he would think of something else.

His love of pageantry and his love of color suggest the boy also. He loved parades. When he was a child, he joined the Sons of Temperance, not because he cared anything about their principles but because he loved the brilliant red sash they wore. Always he must have the most brilliant colors possible. His billiard table itself must be red, not the conventional green, and when he heard that Mrs. Rogers was going to give him a new one for Christmas, he began hinting that he would like to have it right away. White he never cared for greatly, save in his own white suits. He thought the brown-skinned races much handsomer than the Caucasians, and when he had occasion to point out to his daughter Jean that white was not God's favorite color, he added that "Andrea del Sarto's pink-and-lily Madonnas revolt Him. . . . That is they *would*, but He never looks at them."

Finally, he is youthful in his inability to stand alone, his lifelong tendency to cast his burdens upon others. The most striking illustration is the way he rallies after H. H. Rogers takes over his financial affairs and orders him to stop walking the floor. Everything is going to be all right now, and there is no need for him to worry anymore. Without this tendency, Mrs. Clemens would never have obtained the literary influence that has caused some critics so much anguish.

83

V

Mark Twain himself speaks of "my vile temper & variable moods." He was absentminded and undependable in matters of schedule and likely to pass without warning from intense garrulity to silence. He misplaced borrowed books, forgot to enclose checks and clippings in the letters he had written for the purpose of sending them, and would put a manuscript he wanted to take with him in the suit he was not going to wear. Once, out walking, he threw away his sealskin cap, and did not miss it until after he had got home. Paine made a riddle about these things: Mark's mind, he thought, was like a time-table because it was subject to change without notice.

On his lecture tour with George W. Cable Mark once became so angry because he had to get up early to catch a train that he "vented his anger by squaring off with the window shutter and knocking it completely out in one round," while both Cable and Ozias Pond looked on appalled but without daring to interfere. Yet the same tour convinced Pond that "Mr. Clemens has a heart as tender as a child's; as loving as a woman's. He dreads to look upon suffering, but cannot hide the sympathy he feels for those who are affected, and although one unacquinted with him might think him almost totally indifferent to such matters, the close observer can always see the sadness in his eyes and the aching heart, when human suffering is brought within his sight."

Mark himself was of the opinion that it was because he carried an "angry" spirit within him, under his "cheerful exterior," that he could not write good satire. "I *hate* travel, and I *hate* hotels, and I *hate* the opera, and I *hate* the old masters. In truth, I don't ever seem to be in a good-enough humor with anything to satirize it. No, I want to stand up before it and curse it and foam at the mouth, or to take a club and pound it to rags and pulp." Serious crises he met with fortitude and courage, but he was always likely to go to pieces over small annoyances. Perhaps he did not try to control himself for he was very intense always, and the satisfaction he derived from "blowing off steam" must have more than compensated him for the strain involved. In any case, let him misplace his matches, let the waiter fail to bring in his bacon grilled as he liked it, let a new suit of clothes arrive which he thought did not fit him properly, let an autograph hunter fail to enclose a self-addressed envelope, and the fur would fly. It would not be fair to leave the impression that this was always the case. Once he alone, among a crowd of listeners, kept his seat during the reading of an interminable and impossible poem. "Well, that young man thought he had a divine message to deliver, and I thought he was entitled to at least one auditor, so I stayed with him." But this was rather exceptional. When he was full of malice, he once declared, he felt nearer to the Lord than at any other time. "I feel as He feels of a Saturday night when the weekly report is in and He has had a satisfactory clean-up of the human race."

The terror Mark Twain inspired on such occasions seems to have varied with the beholder. "When anger moved him," writes W. H. Rideing, "you could see his lean figure contract and his eyes ominously screw themselves into their sockets. Every fibre in him quivered, and for the moment his voice became acid and sibilant and out of tune—almost a whine. Then he would let himself out in a break, like that of a dam unable to hold the flood, in language as candid and unshrinking as the vernacular of the Elizabethans." Kate Leary, who, being Irish, loved a "scrap," was much less impressed, and so were his children. "We used to call Father the 'spitting gray kitten,'" writes Mrs. Samossoud, "because in many of his spurts of irritation he kept a soft, fuzzy quality in his demeanour that reminded us of a little kitten with its fur all ruffled. We enjoyed this spectacle, and were inclined to inspire it whenever we could. When his performance was ended, we would exclaim, 'Oh, you bad, spitting gray kitten!' and he would laugh a gay little laugh and shake his leonine head of gray curls."

The billiards to which Mark Twain devoted so much time during his last years were not exactly calculated to lessen the probability of such outbursts, and Paine describes the results with uncommon vividness:

> He was not an even-tempered player. When his game was going badly his language sometimes became violent and he was likely to

become critical of his opponent. Then reaction would set in, and remorse. He would become gentle and kindly, hurrying the length of the table to set up the balls as I knocked them into the pockets, as if to show in every way except by actual confession in words that he was sorry for what no doubt seemed to him an unworthy display of temper.

Once, when luck seemed to have quite deserted him and he was unable to make any of his favorite shots, the air became fairly charged, the lightning fierce and picturesque. Finally with a regular thunder blast he seized the cue with both hands and literally mowed the balls across the table, landing some of them on the floor. I do not recall his remarks during that performance—I was chiefly concerned in getting out of the way. Then I gathered up the balls and we went on playing as if nothing had happened, only he was very gentle and sweet, like a sunny meadow after a storm had passed by. After a little he said:

"This is a most—amusing game. When you play—badly, it— amuses *me*. And when I play badly, and lose my temper, it certainly *must*—amuse—*you*."

One of his most disarming characteristics is illustrated here— his eagerness to make amends. He did not always pour out his wrath upon others. He was quite as likely to treat the object of his anger with frigid politeness and then go off by himself to blow off steam to the four walls of his bedroom. A lady betrays him into a sharp expression. "I am sorry," he writes; "for she didn't know anything about the subject, and I did; and one should be gentle with the ignorant, for they are the chosen of God." He goes to visit his mother and sister in Fredonia; while he is there, he has a clash with a man whom he despises, and he comes away thoroughly ashamed of himself. "I would have gone to that detestably oyster-brained bore and apologized for my inexcusable rudeness to him, but that I was satisfied he was of too small a calibre to know how to receive an apology with magnanimity. . . . I came away feeling that in return for your constant and tireless efforts to secure our bodily comfort and make our visit enjoyable, I had basely repaid you by making you sad and sorehearted and leaving you so." At Victoria, B. C., he upbraids a captain for keeping a passenger boat waiting while he loads freight. After thinking it over, he sends Pond "to apologize for his unmanly abuse, and see if any possible restitution could be made," and before the voyage is over, he and the captain are the best of friends. He writes a sharp letter to William D. McCrackan, with whom he is having a controversy over Christian Science, then makes up his mind not to send it, but finds that it has already gone into the mail. With rare fineness of spirit, McCrackan returns the letter: he is sure Mark Twain does not really mean the things he has said in it—and he and Clemens are thereafter firm friends. He makes the acquaintance of Thomas Bailey Aldrich by writing him, rather sharply, demanding that he correct a misstatement in a paper he is editing, but before Aldrich has time to reply, he writes again. "I hear a good deal about doing things on the 'spur of the moment'—I invariably regret things I do on the spur of the moment. That disclaimer of mine was a case in point. I am ashamed every time I think of my bursting out before an unconcerned public with that bombastic pow-wow about burning publishers' letters and all that sort of imbecility, and about my not being an imitator, etc. Who would find out that I am a natural fool if I kept always cool and never let nature come to the surface? Nobody."

The most striking element in Mark Twain's rages was his profanity, and those of us who were born in these latter days must mourn, among other things, that we never heard Jenny Lind sing and never heard Mark Twain swear! We do have some picturesque invective in print—the epitaph for Leopold II of Belgium, for example: "Here under this gilded tomb lies rotting the body of one the smell of whose name may still offend the nostrils of men ages upon ages after all the Caesars and Washingtons and Napoleons shall have ceased to be praised or blamed and been forgotten—Leopold of Belgium." But this is not actually profanity. One of the letters to Howells quotes "quadrilateral astronomical incandescent son of a bitch," and there is a letter to an English publisher in which a proofreader who had dared to alter Mark's punctuation is called "damned bastard," "tumblebug," and, climactically, "damn half-developed foetus!" after which the writer swears off profanity as too worldly for the Sabbath. But of course the charm was not in the words themselves but in Mark's method of utterance. "To hear him denounce a thing," says Paine, "was to give one the fierce, searching delight of galvanic waves. Every characterization seemed the most perfect fit possible until he applied the next. . . . His selection of epithet was always dignified and stately, from whatever source—and it might be from the Bible or the gutter." It was the cool deliberation with which he turned himself loose that was so unusual; this comes out clearly in the report of Elizabeth Wallace, who heard him occasionally in the billiard room: "Gently, slowly, with no profane inflexions of voice, but irresistibly as though they had the headwaters of the Mississippi for their source, came this stream of unholy adjectives and choice expletives. I don't mean to imply that he indulged himself thus before promiscuous audiences. It was only when some member of the inner circle of his friends was present that he showed him this mark of confidence. . . ." In Hawaii he stuffed a little girl's ears with cotton so that she should not hear him swear, which does not sound like a man carried away with rage; he also pulled her ears to make them grow, and took her on his lap to talk about Mother Goose rimes.

Of those who heard Mark Twain swear, only Robertson Nicoll seems to have been greatly shocked—"his habitual, incessant, and disgusting profanity." The usual view is that of Katy Leary, who insists that it "never seemed really bad" to her. "It was sort of funny, and a part of him somehow. Sort of amusing it was—and gay—not like real swearing." And she tells the story of how Baby Jean was shocked one day when she heard a rough man swear in the streets, and how, when she was reminded that she had often heard her father swear, she replied, "Oh, no, Katy! You're mistaken. That wasn't swearing. That was only one of papa's *jokes!*" When Mark Twain was introduced to Charles Major, his greeting was, "I'm *damned* glad to meet you," and Major felt a warm human friendliness behind the words and was not offended at all.

It is said of Mark Twain that he cherished resentments and made an art of hatred. Pond speaks of his "fierce spirit of retaliation" toward those who had injured him, and Howells refers guardedly to two men "of whom he used to talk terrifyingly, even after they were out of the world. He went farther than Heine, who said he forgave his enemies, but not till they were dead. Clemens did not forgive his dead enemies; their death seemed to deepen their crimes, like a base evasion, or a cowardly attempt to escape; he pursued them to the grave; he would like to dig them up and take vengeance upon their clay." Probably one of these men was James Paige of the typesetting machine. "Paige and I always meet on effusively affectionate terms, and yet he knows perfectly well that if I had him in a steel trap I would shut out all human succor and watch that trap until he died."

Fifteen years after their lawsuit over the dramatization of *The Prince and the Pauper*, Clemens dictated eight virulent pages concerning Edward H. House in his *Autobiography*, and Kenneth Lynn is much impressed by his use of the revenge theme in his later works. His outburst against Bret Harte, in *Mark Twain in Eruption*.[9] is about the bitterest denunciation one American writer ever made of another—he was furious when Harte got a government appointment in Germany, and even talked about warning the Germans against him!—but he did not allow this personal animus (apparently greatly intensified by his feeling that Harte had been rude to Livy) to interfere with his estimate of Harte's work, and when Howells praised Harte after his death, in *Harper's Magazine*, Mark Twain commended him for it—"for he *was* all you have said, & although he was more & worse, there is no occasion to remember it & I am often ashamed of myself for doing it."

Even a comparatively slight thing might call forth expressions of undying hatred. The president of Vassar is not courteous to him when he lectures there. "I did not see him any more, but I detest his memory." He was rudely treated, too, or thinks he was, in Buffalo; therefore, prima donna-like, he will never lecture there again. Redpath has made a booking for him, but he must break it. "Otherwise I'll have no recourse left but to get sick." In 1876 he writes Howells, "Carlton insulted me in Feb. 1867, and so when the day arrives that sees me doing him a civility I shall feel that I am ready for Paradise, since my list of possible and impossible forgivenesses will then be complete."

[9] See, further, the numerous comments on Harte in the *Mark Twain–Howells Letters*.

When he was an old man, Mark Twain remembered that he had once bought a revolver and traveled twelve hundred miles for the express purpose of killing a man. "He was away. With nothing else to do, I *had* to stop and think—and did. Within an hour—within half of it—I was ashamed of myself—and felt unspeakably ridiculous." Nothing further is known of this incident. It may have occurred; it may simply be another example of Mark Twain's recalling what never happened.

How much of all this did Mark Twain really mean? Bernard DeVoto thought he meant most of it; to him Mark was a very vindictive man. There is some evidence on the other side. One day, on Jackass Hill, he tried to play with a goat, and the goat did not care to be played with. Mark was furious; he wanted to buy that goat so that he might have him killed; such an animal was a menace to the life of every child on Jackass Hill, and much more to the same effect. Already he had learned to dramatize, or to rationalize, his fury, to identify his own passing whims with the common weal. But since he could not immediately obtain possession of the goat, his anger passed away, and he ultimately so far forgot it as to become quite friendly with the beast, who killed no children. Then there was the cab driver, whom he prosecuted for extortion after he had overcharged Katy Leary, but after the man had been deprived of his license, and had appealed to him in behalf of his starving family (whose existence Katy frankly doubted), Mark had to make another trip to the police station to get the punishment mitigated. It is hard to believe that this was a unique case, and Howells comments on the passage about Paige and the steel trap: "So he said, but no doubt he would not have hurt them [his enemies] if he had had them living before him." His loves were real, but there was always a fantastic quality in his hates.

When Tom Sawyer finds the corpse of Injun Joe in the cave, he "was touched, for he knew by his own experience how this wretch had suffered." But I will let the last word go to that great philosopher, Huckleberry Finn. When Huck finds himself stranded on the raft with the murderers, he can at first feel only terror and horror. But soon these emotions are succeeded by others. "I begun to think how dreadful it was, even for murderers, to be in such a fix. I says to myself, there ain't no telling but I might come to be a murderer myself yet, and then how would I like it?"

What a triumph of Christian humility! What a triumph of understanding and imagination! It is Mark Twain's version of the generally misquoted and misattributed utterance of John Bradford, on seeing some criminals going to execution: "But for the grace of God there goes John Bradford."

VI

Mark Twain always considered himself a lazy man: when he found in his Suetonius a reference to one Flavius Clemens, a man widely known "for his want of energy," he wrote in the margin, "I guess this is where our line starts." "I do not like work," he says, "even when another person does it," and his best-known piece of writing tells how Tom Sawyer persuaded the other boys to do his work for him by the simple expedient of being "smart." Those associated with Mark Twain in the early days have borne no unambiguous testimony to his extreme reluctance to engage in physical labor of any kind. Part of Hawaii's never failing charm for him was the way it encouraged indolence.

But a man may dislike physical labor and still be anything but lazy in the ordinary sense of the term: indeed, it is the very excess of nervous and mental energy in some men that makes the drain and drag of an unvarying routine impossible. Mark Twain was clearly of this type. We have his own glorification of energy in an early letter to Orion: "What is a government without energy? And what is *a man* without energy? Nothing—nothing at all. What is the grandest thing in 'Paradise Lost'—the Arch-Fiend's terrible energy! . . . And to-day, if I were a heathen, I would rear a statue to energy, and fall down and worship it!" In the first flush of his success as a river pilot, he condescends to advise his older brother, a role he was never afterwards to relinquish. "I want a man to—I want *you* to—take up a line of action, and *follow* it out, in spite of the very devil."

Practice did not fall far short of precept. In literature and out of literature there was the same vast fertility; he had it in youth and he had it in age. He will get tied up in new commitments even when he is having trouble in meeting those he has already assumed. While he was working on *Roughing It,* as Paine tells us, "he discussed a scheme with Goodman for a six-hundred-page work which they were to do jointly; he planned and wrote one or two scenes for a Western play . . . ; he perfected one of his several inventions—an automatically adjusting vest-strap; he wrote a number of sketches, made an occasional business trip to New York and Hartford; prospected the latter place for a new home."

His resources were so abundant that he did not need to husband them. When he imagines Whitelaw Reid has been conducting a campaign against him in his paper, he sets to work on a grand scale to counteract that sinister influence. He works day and night himself, he employs agents both in London and in New York, and the mountain falls in labor to bring forth a mouse, until it occurs to Mrs. Clemens that it might be well to check the rumors first and make sure that there has been a conspiracy, when he finds, of course, that there has been nothing of the kind, and that all his time and energy have been thrown away. It makes no difference; neither is he in the least disturbed by it. He generates power like a dynamo; it was quite as well to be engaged in elaborate plans to blast Whitelaw Reid as it would have been to be writing reams of unmailable letters or retiring to his bedroom to swear until the air was blue.

Think of the work he did on the history game. Think of the energy that went into his social engagements—in New York—in 1894—when he was nearly sixty, and facing bankruptcy. "By half past 4 I had danced all those people down—and yet was not tired; merely breathless. I was in bed at 5, and asleep in ten minutes. Up at 9 and presently at work on this letter to you. I think I wrote until 2 or half-past. Then I walked leisurely out to Mr. Rogers's (it is called three miles but it is short of it) arriving at 3:30, but he was out—to return at 5:30—(and a person was *in,* whom I don't particularly like)—so I didn't stay, but dropped over and chatted with the Howellses until 6." Can you think of another famous author who, in the midst of a busy career, would sit down and, with his own hands, fantastically "embroider" a slipper for a little girl? Or who even while his business world was crashing around him would plan a new magazine? Less than a week before the passage of the copyright law of 1909 he came to Robert Underwood Johnson with a new plan that was ever so much better than the one they had all previously sponsored.

But there are more paradoxes than these in this energy-laziness matter. Young Sam Clemens, setting out to find his place in the world, would not seem, on first consideration, a very ambitious youngster. In 1863, when he is working on the *Enterprise*, his mother writes him that if he works hard, he may well look forward to some day holding a place on a big San Francisco daily. In his reply, he assures her that he could have such a place any time, but he does not want it. "No paper in the United States can afford to pay me what my place on the 'Enterprise' is worth. If I were not naturally a lazy, idle, good-for-nothing vagabond, I could make it pay me $20,000 a year. But I don't suppose I shall ever be any account. I lead an easy life, though, and I don't care a cent whether school keeps or not. Everybody knows me, and I fare like a prince wherever I go, be it on this side of the mountains or the other. And I am proud to say I am the most conceited ass in the Territory."

An appalling picture, no doubt, and it must have given any woman but Jane Clemens a bad moment. Jane, however, had probably already learned the truth of the principle she afterwards enunciated: all Sam's pronouncements must be discounted 90 per cent, the remaining 10 per cent being pure gold. As a matter of fact, the real reason he preferred the *Enterprise* was that it gave him a chance to do creative, humorous writing. San Francisco would have required straight reporting, which he did not like. That was just what the *Call* did require when he got there, and that was why he was unhappy. Jane remembered, too, how early he had risen above the Hannibal horizon, how he had shaken the dust of the town from his feet and set out to bustle his way in the world, and how he had made good, first as a printer, then as a pilot, and now as a newspaper man. . . .

The river may well have given her pause, and it must halt us here for a moment, and again a little later, farther along. Much has been said about Mark Twain's rackety memory. So we get the well-known story of the visitor whom he mistook for a picture

93

agent and treated accordingly, because his own pictures, which he did not recognize, had been removed from the walls for cleaning, and were lying at the stranger's feet when Mark Twain entered the drawing room, and the even more curious anecdote of how he went out, one day, to invite a neighbor to come over to play billiards, and when he reached the street, was quite unable to recognize the house in which his friend lived, so that he was obliged to go back home and get the butler to point it out to him. "More than once," writes Paine, "I have known him to relate an occurrence of the day before with a reality of circumstance that carried absolute conviction, when the details themselves were precisely reversed." If Mark Twain remembered anything in his life, one might suppose he would surely have remembered his speech at the Whittier Birthday Dinner, which cost him so much agony, yet in the last year of his life we find him telling his secretary to call up Howells to ask him "what occasion it was in Boston when he *raised Hell* about Emerson and Longfellow." And this was the man who learned the whole course of the lower Mississippi, memorized the physical features of twelve hundred miles of shifting, ever changing currents so perfectly that he could steer a boat through its tortuous recesses by day or by night!

No doubt the creative artist in Mark Twain helped him to jumble fact and fancy: he was like the too imaginative child who gets so interested in his daydreams that he cannot tell the difference between what really happened and what he himself dreamed up. But it is clear that the quality of attention entered in also. He learned the river because he gave his whole mind to it. His piloting days behind him, there was no need for giving such close attention to any other material matter, and the natural bent of his temperament inclined him to live, more and more, within himself. "It is all a matter of ability to observe things. I never observe anything now. I gave up the habit years ago." Even as a pilot, he did not learn what he did not need; never knew, for example, the names of all the parts of a steamboat. On the visual side of memory, there was some weakness, however. On one occasion, when challenged, he could not recall the color of any one of his children's eyes, and he could never recall at will the physical features of absent persons, an idiosyncrasy which became an overwhelming calamity to him after Mrs. Clemens died.

In the early days, Mark Twain's ambition may well have been impelled by the thought of the business incompetency of his father and his elder brother. Orion was greatly libeled when James O'Donnell Bennett called him the Village Idiot, but it is not necessary to rush to the other extreme, and picture him as a man whose only fault was his sensitive inability to cope with the brutal exigencies of a capitalistic civilization. As Mark himself puts it in the *Autobiography*:

> One of his characteristics was eagerness. He woke with an eagerness about some matter or other every morning; it consumed him all day; it perished in the night and he was on fire with a fresh new interest next morning before he could get his clothes on. He exploited in this way three hundred and sixty-five red-hot new eagernesses every year of his life—until he died sitting at a table with a pen in his hand, in the early morning, jotting down the conflagration for that day and preparing to enjoy the fire and smoke of it until night should extinguish it. He was then seventy-two years old. But I am forgetting another characteristic, a very pronounced one. That was his deep glooms, his despondencies, his despairs; these had their place in each and every day along with the eagernesses. Thus his day was divided—no, not divided, mottled—from sunrise to midnight with alternating brilliant sunshine and black cloud. Every day he was the most joyous and hopeful man that ever was, I think, and also every day he was the most miserable man that ever was.

There is a large, fortuitous element in success; full many a flower is born to blush unseen; and Mark Twain knew this well. He dramatized it in "Luck," in "Edward Mills and George Benton," in the early fables of the Good and Bad Little Boys. If he had not happened to possess genius, would he have been another Orion? Not quite, for he had a practical energy, determination, and, in some aspects at least, common sense which Orion lacked. But he would have come a good deal closer to Orion than he came. "Clemens," says Paine, "proposed almost as many things to Howells as his brother Orion proposed to him."

If there were times when Mark Twain refused to emulate the Horatio Alger hero, it was not so much laziness that impelled him as his love of freedom, of personal independence. The standardization of life and thought which has proceeded to such appalling lengths in our own time was already beginning in his, and with the tradition of the Old South behind him, he resisted it with all his might. It was not only that he was born "different" and could not be pushed into a mold; he would not if he could, but resisted on principle. For example, he was naturally a good speller, but, though he makes endless fun of Mrs. Clemens for her fantastic spelling, he takes no pride in his own prowess. "Before the spelling-book came with its arbitrary forms, men unconsciously revealed shades of their characters, and also added enlightening shades of expression to what they wrote by their spelling, and so it is possible that the spelling-book has been a doubtful benevolence to us."[10] If a rule did not seem reasonable to him, he would break it, and if you told him he must not do something, he would be sure to do it, as when, in Washington, he discussed the precise aspect of the copyright law he had been warned to avoid. With the Old South behind him and the new industrial North ahead of him, Mark Twain, as a young man on the make, was an apostle of "rugged individualism," but he was to be appalled by "ruthless individualism" in many of its aspects before he finished. Huck Finn is not quite a creature of fancy in his final phase in *Tom Sawyer*, when he finds his money and his new position in life such a burden that he only wishes he could throw it all away and go back to the days of comfortable poverty, when he had no obligation except to be himself.

In connection with this matter of Mark Twain in his go-getter aspect, it is interesting finally to glance at the minor controversy which has developed during recent years about his piloting. Though Horace Bixby had nothing but good things to say about his former pupil when Paine interviewed him in 1908, he is reported to have said upon a later occasion that though Sam knew

[10] One of Mark's very few errors in spelling was made in connection with the name of the inventor James Paige, of the infernal (typesetting) machine. He always spelled it "Page."

the river well, he was a failure as a pilot because he was a coward.[11] If a coward is one who shirks a dangerous task because he fears it, this is obviously nonsense. Mark Twain went through with the business of piloting, and there was never a serious accident on any boat he piloted. Moreover his reputation was good enough so that Bixby himself twice took him as his partner.

What it may have cost him to achieve this is another matter. Knowing as we do how fully he possessed—or was possessed by— what Henry James was to call "the imagination of disaster," and what a capacity he had for blaming himself for every evil that had afflicted this earth since the Fall of Man, one can hardly believe that he could have carried the pilot's burdens without paying a price.[12] One may even doubt that he could have continued to carry them very long, or that so sensitive a man was ever meant to carry them. But this is not equivalent to saying that Mark Twain was a coward. It means rather that he had not got his feet stuck in Neanderthal days.

The question comes up in other aspects also. Mark Twain's Civil War record will be discussed later. He has been accused of attacking bravely, even insolently, and then backing down when he is challenged, and there are those who profess to be greatly shocked by his writing penetrating social criticism during his later days but failing to publish it. Miss Effie Mack writes suggestively of the days when he was amusing himself by learning to fence: "Mark nearly always contested with the foils and became quite an expert in his 'stoccado, imbrocata, passada,' and 'montanto.' In attack it was said that 'he was fiery and particularly dangerous for the reason one could not watch his eyes.' He habitually half-closed his eyes; at times, it was remarked, they resembled those of an eagle with an inner lid. In defense he was not so good, and would nearly always give ground when hotly pressed."

11 The evidence is summed up by Dudley R. Hutcheson, "Mark Twain as a Pilot," *American Literature*, Vol. XII (1940), 353-55. For a sensible discussion, see DeLancey Ferguson, *Mark Twain, Man and Legend*, 53-55.

12 "Mark Twain's Piloting," an item from the St. Louis *Republican*, June 13, 1875, reprinted in *Missouri Historical Society Bulletin*, Vol. XIII (1956-57), 403-405, gives the reminiscences of the first engineer on the *Alexander Scott* when Mark Twain was a cub, and describes a trick played on him. If the account is accurate, it shows that he was very nervous about fire at this time.

It is true that Mark Twain sometimes backed down,[13] true, too, that he sometimes withheld what he considered dangerous stuff from publication. But if the reader does not already know that he spoke out bravely concerning a wider range of abuses than probably any other writer of his time, he will discover just that before he has finished the volume in hand. "To the Person Sitting in Darkness" caused the *Army and Navy Journal* to brand him a traitor. And who else ever dared to attack a popular American military hero in the hour of his glory, as Mark Twain attacked General Frederick Funston?

Steve Gillis says Mark Twain didn't "scare a cent" at the time of the famous fake robbery hoax in Western days, but he was very angry when he learned afterwards that a hoax had been played on him. Ozias Pond tells an amusing story of what happened when he and Mark were in a train accident in Illinois. Most of the passengers, including Mark, rushed for the doors, but Pond and Cable both remained in their seats. "Mark said later he thought the train was going into the river, and he would rather fall on top of the train than have the train fall on him. He said that he knew he would be all right if he got into the river, as it was perfectly familiar to him, and he could pilot us all to safety." As for the duel he is supposed to have narrowly avoided fighting, just before leaving Virginia City, most modern readers will be most impressed, not by his avoiding it, which was the only sensible thing he did, but by the really unpardonable journalistic arrogance and brashness which brought him to the brink. It was not a coward who refused to leave the plague-stricken ship on which he was bound for New York in 1866–67, at Key West, as he might have done, nor who insisted upon staying with the cholera-stricken Dan Slote in the Holy Land, when the more pious pilgrims decided to go on without him. "Gentlemen," said Mark, "I understand that you are going to leave Dan Slote here alone. I'll be God-damned if I do."

[13] See Webster, *Mark Twain, Business Man*, 143, 214–15, and cf. Charles E. Shain, "The Journal of the *Quaker City* Captain," *New England Quarterly*, Vol. XXVIII (1955), 388–94.

VII

For all that he hated going to school, no man ever had more faith in education than Mark Twain. He had educated himself, largely, through miscellaneous reading, and he believed in this method as far as it goes; when he was told that the passage of the copyright law might make the classics more expensive for people in humble circumstances, he began to wonder whether he had done wrong in supporting it. But reading alone was not enough, for he did not, like so many "self-made men," glorify his limitations. "The self-made man," he says, "seldom knows anything accurately, and he does not know a tenth as much as he could have known if he had worked under teachers; and besides, he brags, and is the means of fooling other thoughtless people into going and doing as he himself has done." Wherever he goes, he is interested in the schools, and rejoices when he finds them prosperous. It is true that his comments are sometimes a bit naïve, as when he remarks of the graduate of the German *Gymnasium* that he has "an education . . . so extensive and complete, that the most a university can do for it is to perfect some of its profounder specialties." But there are moments of penetration also.

He is impressed, and even oppressed, by the vast scope and variety of learning. When he is brought into the society of learned men on terms of equality, he is flattered. "I was at breakfast lately," he writes in 1894, "where people of seven separate nationalities sat and the seven languages were going all the time. At my side sat a charming gentleman who was a delightful and active talker, and interesting. He talked glibly to those folks in all those seven languages—and still had a language to spare! I wanted to kill him—for very envy." It was a lovely sort of envy. Mrs. Fields has a priceless phrase for him—"this growing man of forty." But he did not stop at forty; even on the *Equator* tour, we find him reading scientific books, "to improve the mind." He even tends, rather romantically, I fear, to identify learning with virtue. "Learning goes usually with uprightness, broad views, and humanity."

What of his own learning?

We may begin with history, in which field much of his most

absorbed reading was done. It was history which first awakened his intellectual curiosity; perhaps he even had some dim prescience of what the future held for him that day when, according to the story he liked to tell, the wind brought a stray sheet from the story of the life of Joan of Arc across his path.

About Roman, French, and English history particularly, he knew a good deal. But his sense of the romance of the past was always stronger than his knowledge:

> Here is a crumbling wall that was old when Columbus discovered America; was old when Peter the Hermit roused the knightly men of the Middle Ages to arm for the first Crusade; was old when Charlemagne and his paladins beleaguered enchanted castles and battled with giants and genii in the fabled days of the olden time; was old when Christ and his disciples walked the earth; stood where it stands to-day when the lips of Memnon were vocal, and men bought and sold in the streets of ancient Thebes!

What gave the past its charm for him was "a haunting sense of the myriads of human lives that had blossomed, and withered, and perished here, repeating and repeating and repeating, century after century, and age after age, the barren and meaningless process." Even India, whose past he knew so little about, cast this spell upon him. On the other hand, "the deserts of Australia and the ice-barrens of Greenland have no speech, for they have no venerable history; with nothing to tell of man and his vanities, his fleeting glories and his miseries, they have nothing wherewith to spiritualize their ugliness and veil it with a charm."

This is a poet's response to the past, or a mystic's, rather than a scholar's, and though Mark Twain's knowledge of history was not inconsiderable, I think the imaginative appeal always dominated. His sense of continuity was stronger than his sense of change. Consequently, he tends to judge the past by the standards of the present, and whatever does not square with his own code is condemned. Consider his argument at the close of *Is Shakespeare Dead?* where he tries to prove that if Shakespeare had written the plays attributed to him, he must have been much better known in his own time, and that, specifically, his death must have attracted more attention than we have any reason to suppose was the case. In establishing this conclusion, he relies on a comparison between Shakespeare and himself, entirely disregarding all the differences between his own America and sixteenth-seventeenth-century England, between the craft of authorship in the two periods and the attitude of the public toward authors.

Recent investigations[14] have shown that Mark Twain read more science than he was formerly given credit for. For his time, his layman's knowledge in this field was more than respectable. The stars began to fascinate him in his pilot days, and in later years the immense distances suggested by the studies of the more advanced astronomers stimulated his imagination. He tried to compute the astronomical light year, and he makes considerable use of astronomical data in *Captain Stormfield's Visit to Heaven*. He liked collecting geological specimens: in 1870 he and Joe Goodman tried to classify fossils found at Quarry Farm; much later he invited Rollin D. Salisbury to Stormfield to study the geological formations there. His emphasis in later years upon the importance of training may have been influenced by his study of Darwin. It is now reasonable to believe that he got his knowledge of fingerprinting from Sir Francis Galton and not from the palmist Cheiro, as was formerly believed.[15] As for the application of science in technology, for all the fascination which gadgets held for Mark Twain—once, at least, he equated the inventor with the poet—he certainly did not swallow mechanical civilization uncritically nor place his faith in it, and anybody who believes that a

14 See, especially, H. H. Waggoner, "Science in the Thought of Mark Twain," *American Literature*, Vol. VIII (1937) 357–70, and two articles by Sherwood Cummings: "Mark Twain's Social Darwinism," *Huntington Library Quarterly*, Vol. XX (1956–57), 163–75, and "Science and Mark Twain's Theory of Fiction," *Philological Quarterly*, Vol. XXXVII (1958), 26–33. I cannot, however, accept Professor Cummings' view that Darwin destroyed Mark Twain's social idealism and made him less the champion of the underdog. He may have regarded the kind of world he had to live in during his later years as, under scientific determinism, inevitable, but his heart did not acquiesce in it; if it had, there would have been no occasion for his pessimism. Some of the boldest denunciations of social evil date from his last years.

15 See Anne P. Wigger, "The Source of the Fingerprint Material in Mark Twain's *Pudd'nhead Wilson and Those Extraordinary Twins*," *American Literature*, Vol. XXVIII (1956–57), 517–20.

nation can be saved by technology might do worse than ponder the melancholy close of *A Connecticut Yankee*.[16]

On mathematics, Mark Twain is a bit contradictory. He assures us that he detests mathematics, yet few things give him more pleasure than to play with statistics. The light-year calculation was his most spectacular achievement in this field and about as useful as most of them. It is interesting to know that, on one occasion, when he applied his gift for ciphering to the study of his household expenses, he was utterly betrayed. "When I came down in the morning a gray and aged wreck, and went over the figures again, I found that in some unaccountable way . . . I had multiplied the totals by 2. By God I dropped 75 years on the floor where I stood."

If, under any circumstances, we can think of Mark Twain as a scholar, philology must have been his field. Syntax and grammar, structure and word order—these things fascinated him always. The connotations, the overtones of words fascinated his imagination, and there is one passage on the technical aspects of style which indicates that he must have been greatly interested in Edith Rickert's attempt to analyze our reactions to various types of rhythm and structure. The same interests show in his study of foreign languages. French he began as far back as his pilot days, and his two essays on Italian show both keenness and imagination. But German was, after English, the language to which he devoted most attention, and in spite of all his denunciation of its awkward immobility, German was the foreign language he knew and loved best. There were times when, in their determination to conquer the language, all the Clemenses used more German than English. Mark Twain tried public speaking in German; he translated a good deal of material from German into English, and one story, at least, from English into German. His translation of "*Die Lorelei*" is a very good one. The very amusing discussion of "The Awful German Language" in the appendix to *A Tramp Abroad* is said to have delighted Kaiser Wilhelm II.

[16] See Allen Guttmann, "Mark Twain's *Connecticut Yankee*: Affirmation of the Vernacular Tradition," *New England Quarterly*, Vol. XXXIII (1960), 232–37, and cf. Bellamy, *Mark Twain as a Literary Artist*, 314.

Mark Twain showed considerable conscience about documentation. He could burlesque the citation of authorities when he chose; he could make an elaborate parade of mock-learning; but he also knew how to get things right, and when he departed from historic fact, he liked to indicate the fact and explain his reasons, as he did in *The Prince and the Pauper*. There is a good deal of documentation in this book, especially when one remembers that it was intended for children; and there are footnotes, corrections, citations, and the like, all through the book on Christian Science. In *Joan of Arc*, he explains carefully in advance just how he plans to use the records of the trial.

What, finally, can we say of Mark Twain's thinking? Since he was not systematically trained, it goes without saying that he sometimes generalizes from insufficient data. He was also sometimes carried away by emotion. Once, he had a marvelous idea for a play. "I was enchanted with the felicity of the conception—I might say intoxicated with it. It seemed to me that no idea was ever so exquisite, so beautiful, so freighted with wonderful possibilities. I believed that when I should get it fittingly dressed out in the right dramatic clothes it would not only delight the world, but astonish it. Then came a stealthy, searching, disagreeable little chill; what if the idea was not so new, after all?" So he asked James Hammond Trumbull about it. "His answer covered six pages. . . . The theft of my idea had been committed two hundred and sixty-eight times. The latest instance mentioned was English, and not yet three years old; the earliest had electrified China eight hundred years before Christ." And he adds, "I did not write the play."

Yet he had thought the idea out, and since he was not indebted to his predecessors, he was just as original as he would have been if they had never existed. There are many other instances in his thinking of which exactly the same thing might be said. He delighted in the use of his mind. It was not a great mind; the minds of creative artists seldom are. But it was a thoroughly good mind and an interesting mind and an eager one. Within the limitations that circumscribed him, he loved to think things through. "What is it that confers the noblest delight?" he asks.

"What is that which swells a man's breast with pride above that which any other experience can bring to him? Discovery! To know that you are walking where none others have walked; that you are beholding what human eye has not seen before; that you are breathing a virgin atmosphere." In a world as old as this one, it is difficult to achieve such an ideal, but at least one may strive toward it. Mark Twain's conclusions did not always have absolute value, but they were valuable for him, or as he puts it in connection with one theme that long interested him, "I am not playing with Christian Science and its founder, I am examining them; and I am doing it because of the interest I feel in the inquiry. My results may seem inadequate to the reader, but they have for me clarified a muddle and brought a sort of order out of a chaos, and so I value them." Can a great scholar say much more?

VIII

Like his friend William Dean Howells, Mark Twain feared romance. Romance was a specious gilding, a false light thrown over life, an attempt to live by illusion instead of facing the truth. The Yankee sees himself as "the champion of hard unsentimental common-sense and reason." It is not only that the romantic fritters away his energy in fruitless maunderings, that he lives with shadows and unfits himself for playing a part in real life. Romance is vicious. It paints black white, and upsets men's moral judgments. Romance casts a deceptive haze over Abelard's criminal passion, and the world is led to revere what it ought to detest. In "A Curious Experience" we have a case-study of a boy who has fed his imagination on the cheap romanticism of dime novels until the real world and the world of the imagination have become hopelessly confused. Daydreaming utterly ruins the moral backbone of the hero and heroine of "The $30,000 Bequest" also, and there is hope that Sally Sellers may become a happy and useful young woman only when she shall have put her dreams behind her. Romanticism is a moral question, then, but it is much more than a matter of individual morality. Social progress is impossible until the cobwebs of musty sentimentality have been rudely dispersed, until men's eyes are strong enough to see things as they are.

So Mark Twain comes out as an aggressive modernist; he is convinced that the age in which he is living is far and away the greatest that the world has known. "The valuable part . . . of what we call civilization" did not exist when Queen Victoria was born. Gutenberg, Watt, Arkwright, Whitney, Morse, Stephenson, and Bell are "the creators of the world—after God." There was no knowledge in the past: Tom Sawyer laments that he is obliged to consort with "a passel of low-down animals that don't know no more than the head boss of a university did three or four hundred years ago." There were, even, no gentlemen in Europe before the nineteenth century. "A poet has said, 'Better fifty years of England than all the cycles of Cathay.' But I say better one decade of this period than the 900 years of Methuselah. There is more done now in a year than he ever saw in all his life." When Mark Twain praises the civilization of ancient Egypt, it is simply because he believes Egypt anticipated certain modern discoveries.

It was on this basis that he gloried in material progress. Telephones and typesetters and writing-machines induced an ecstatic mood. He was the first man in the history of the world to install a telephone in his private residence, and one of the first to use the fountain pen. He was the first author of distinction to employ the typewriter. "At 12:20 this afternoon a line of movable types was spaced and justified by machinery, for the first time in the history of the world! And I was there to see."

It was not enough to keep up with the present; he must anticipate the future. He made fingerprinting an element in *Pudd'n-head Wilson*, at a time when fingerprinting was a new thing—"virgin ground," he calls it—"absolutely *fresh*." As early as the late seventies, he himself made a balloon ascension, and *Tom Sawyer Abroad* prophesies modern developments in aviation.

Here, then, is ammunition for those who see Mark Twain as a go-getter at heart. When he goes to Italy, he damns the old masters but lavishes his praise on the railways: "These things win me more than Italy's hundred galleries of priceless art treasures, because I can understand the one and am not competent to appreciate the other." Could anything be more stupid than to find no knowledge, no civilization in the Middle Ages, nothing that has value for our lives today? Could anything be more insensitive than the absurd assessment of French culture at the beginning of the essay on Paul Bourget? And could anything be more barbarous than the letter to Whitman on his seventieth birthday, in which the poet was congratulated at having lived in an age which, among other benefactions, had given to the world "the amazing, infinitely varied and innumerable products of coal-tar"?

But here, again, the paradox. People do not denounce romanticism, or anything else, without having felt its power. Mark Twain dreamed typesetters and other mechanical contrivances, as his father had dreamed the Tennessee land before him, but he did not approach these things as a materially minded, practical man. "The castle-building habit," he writes feelingly in "The $30,000 Bequest," "the day-dreaming habit—how it grows! what a luxury it becomes; how we fly to its enchantments at every idle moment, how we revel in them, steep our souls in them, intoxicate ourselves with their beguiling fantasies—oh yes, and how soon and how easily our dream-life and our material life become so intermingled and so fused together that we can't quite tell which is which, any more." And there is an observation in *The Gilded Age* that has much force in this connection: "One never ceases to make a hero of one's self (in private), during life, but only alters the style of his heroism from time to time as the drifting years belittle certain gods of his admiration and raise up others in their stead that seem greater."

There is some justification for his antiromanticism, then, in Mark Twain's consciousness of his own weakness: when he fights romance, he is fighting the Sellers side of himself and of his family. There is some justification also in the kind of romantic literature in vogue, especially in the South, during his own early life, in the juvenile literature of the time, in the kind of travel books he himself burlesqued in *The Innocents Abroad*.

Only, of course, this is not the whole story. For Mark Twain did not, by any means, entirely kill the romancer in himself, and such writers as S. B. Liljegren paint a very one-sided picture of him. The superb rhetoric of his description of Palestine brooding in sackcloth and ashes, of distant lands under the spell of the darkness of night are fresh in all our minds. His love of legendry is familiar also, and though he was not an Irishman, he was quite capable of imagining, not too seriously, that he had seen the little people scampering away through the forest. For if romance can corrupt, he knew too that romance can ennoble. The effect of Tom Canty's reading on his own mind, at the beginning of *The Prince and the Pauper*, is a perfect illustration of Oscar Wilde's saying that art does not imitate life any more than life imitates art, and it will be remembered that Mark Twain always appreciated the power of the theater's romance to transfigure the lives of children, "the power," as Jane Addams once expressed it, "of even a mimic stage to afford to the young a magic space in which lives may be lived in efflorescence, where manners may be courtly and elaborate without exciting ridicule, where the sequence of events is impressive and comprehensible." There is considerable verisimilitude in "The $30,000 Bequest," in "The Man That Corrupted Hadleyburg," and even in *The Prince and the Pauper* itself, but, in each case, even as in Shakespeare's romances, the situation rests upon an initial, inherent improbability, or even absurdity, which is the element of "given," and which must be accepted. Howells believed his friend fundamentally romantic, and DeVoto spoke of the *Joan of Arc* as his "capitulation to romance." Yet it might reasonably be argued that Mark Twain was no more romantic about Joan of Arc than DeVoto himself was about Huckleberry Finn; as John Steinbeck has remarked, the story of Joan of Arc could not have happened—only it did. Even *The Mysterious Stranger*, devastating as it is, is drenched in romantic illusion, and the people who berated Harper and Brothers for first giving it to the world in a fairy-tale format did not aim their weapons very skillfully. Whatever incongruity may exist here, Mark Twain himself was fundamentally responsible for.

Mark Twain's much-criticized letter to Whitman was written in 1889. Let us look at another letter, this one to Twichell, and written in 1905:

> Well, the 19th century made progress—the first progress after "ages and ages"—colossal progress. In what? Materialities. Pro-

digious acquisitions were made in those things which add to the comfort of many and make life harder for as many more. But the addition to righteousness? Is it discoverable? I think not. The materialities were not invented in the interest of righteousness; that there is more righteousness in the world because of them than there was before, is hardly demonstrable, I think. In Europe and America there is a vast change (due to them) in ideals—do you admire it? All Europe and all America are feverishly scrambling for money. Money is the supreme ideal—all others take tenth place with the great bulk of the nations named. Money-lust has always existed, but not in the history of the world was it ever a craze, a madness until your time and mine. This lust has rotted these nations; it has made them hard, sordid, ungentle, dishonest, oppressive.

So he learned after all then. Learned that science, too, is a false god, learned what some of us had to wait for the war to find out, that he had been leaning on a broken reed, that materialities cannot solve the problem of human life. The typesetters were working perfectly now, and men had wings at last. For what? For this?—the world of 1905, which was the world of 1914 in the making? Poor Mark Twain! He who had believed so passionately. And yet they twit him for his "pessimism"!

CHAPTER FIVE: *God's Fool*

I

"AH, WELL, I AM A GREAT AND SUBLIME FOOL. But then I am God's fool, and all His works must be contemplated with respect."

There are contradictions in Mark Twain's attitude toward himself, as in everything else about him. He uses self-vaunting and self-depreciation alike as elements in his humor. On the one hand, he is not satisfied with mere ignorance—he must claim idiocy, utter selfishness, and complete savagery; on the other hand, he advertises for obituaries, compares himself to the Czar and the Pacific Ocean, and when a new planet appears in the skies, he is sure it is going to be named for him. As a Mississippi pilot, the opportunity came to him to establish his right to be considered a person with some business in the world, under circumstances that appealed powerfully to his always dramatic temperament, for the pilot was cock o' the walk, in the river towns as well as on the boat itself. It is clear that Mark took advantage of his opportunity to swagger a bit before those who had hitherto manifested a tendency to patronize him, and the fact that, at the same time, he became the principal support of his family naturally tended to strengthen his conviction that he was a pretty good fellow. From then on, he always occupied the center of a steadily widening stage, and he always felt perfectly at home on it, no matter how many spotlights played upon him. When he went to Washington, at the time of the copyright hearings, Paine tried to take him into the dining room at the Willard Hotel in an inconspicuous, round-about way, but he would have none of that; they must go back and travel the full length of Peacock Alley, making the most spectacu-lar and ostentatious entrance possible. "When I appear clothed in white, a startling accent in the midst of a sombre multitude in midwinter, the most conspicuous object there, I am not ashamed, not ill at ease, but serene and content, because my conspicuous-ness is not of an offensive sort; it is not an insult and cannot affront any eye nor affront anybody's sense of propriety." He definitely plans a record for posterity, wonders who may be reading his let-ters and looking over his photographs in the years to come. When S. J. Woolf comes to paint him, he wants the picture to be as handsome as possible, explains how he wears his hair, keeps the artist waiting while he goes upstairs to brush it, so that it may look just right. He was a celebrity; he knew he was a celebrity; he could see no point in pretending that he was not. "I am afraid my talk-ing bothers you," he tells Woolf. "I guess you are one of the few people who would be willing to pay me to keep quiet."

All this is too natural to be offensive. Take his love of com-pliments, his basking in the light of praise. He quotes the kind things people say about him, repeats them, rolls them on his tongue, "I can live for two months on a good compliment." As he himself says, he values his Oxford degree because it reassures him as to his value. But it is not only the great whose praise de-lights him. "We despise no source that can pay us a pleasing at-tention—there is no source that is humble enough for that." He compels a boor in a railway carriage to move his parcel from the seat beside him so that a lady may sit down. The lady thanks him, saying, "It is not often that one has so distinguished a defender." And Mark is delighted. "She knew me; she knew me!" he exclaims to his companion. But more precious than praise is straight human affection. "I can stand considerable petting," he says. Or, as he puts it more touchingly, when his neighbors welcome him at Stormfield, "I wonder why they all go to so much trouble for me. I never go to any trouble for anybody."

For, in the last analysis—the Czar and the Pacific Ocean notwithstanding—Mark Twain was not an arrogant man. He had a man's proper pride; he resents a slur or a libel; he dislikes being dependent or beholden; he will form his own judgments, wisely or unwisely, will not accept opinions ready-made, not even from those who are wiser than he. Twice, in Berlin, he was mistaken for the historian Mommsen. "We have the same hair," he says, "but on examination it was found the brains were different." When he was a young man he met Anson Burlingame and was encouraged by him. "You have great ability," said Burlingame; "I believe you have genius. What you need now is the refinement of association. Seek companionship among men of superior intellect and character. Never affiliate with inferiors; always climb." He accepted the advice and followed it, and Burlingame ever after had a place all his own in his heart.

If he was modest about his art and his knowledge, he was also modest about his character. To be sure, he can tell his sister that his character never gives him any concern. "I never sit up with it when it seems to be sick, never bother about it in any way. I have always approved & admired it, I still approve & admire it, I strenuously desire & do steadfastly believe that my relatives and friends approve & admire it, I know God approves & admires it—& there's an end." But look at his "Salutatory" in the Buffalo *Express*. He is not going to hurt the paper deliberately or intentionally. He will not be slangy or vulgar. He will avoid profanity even when discussing rent and taxes. And he will write poetry only if he should feel spiteful toward the subscribers. "We are all inconsistent," he confides to his notebook. "We are offended and resent it when people do not respect us; and yet no man, deep down in the privacy of his heart, has any considerable respect for *himself*." He could never be sure that he would not let himself and others down. "I am *bound* to wander out of the straight path & do outrageous things occasionally, & believe I have a genuinely bad heart anyhow—but in the course of time I will get some of the badness out of it or break it."

The publishers want to use his picture as a frontispiece for *The Innocents Abroad,* but he will not hear of it: he hates "the effrontery of shoving the pictures of nobodies under people's noses that way, after the fashion of quacks & negro minstrels." He would like to speak to General Pope, when he sees him at the Grand Army reunion in Chicago, but he lacks the courage, "thinking it might be presumptuous to tackle a man so high up in military history." Charles Eliot Norton learns that Darwin is in the habit of reading himself to sleep with Mark Twain's books every night, and he passes the word on with some diffidence, not quite sure whether Clemens will accept it as a compliment. But he does. "I do regard it as a very great compliment and a very high honor that that great mind, laboring for the whole human race, should rest itself on my books. I am proud that he should rest himself to sleep with them." His friends wish to name a day for him at the St. Louis fair, but he will not have it: such honors are not for the living. "So long as we remain alive we are not safe from doing things which . . . can wreck our repute and extinguish our friendships."

How abject Mark Twain is in his apology to Oliver Wendell Holmes after having plagiarized from him unconsciously, and how he humbles himself before Holmes, Emerson, and Longfellow after he has, as he now believes, insulted them at the Whittier Birthday Dinner! He was sure that he was never worthy of his wife and daughters. Susy was quite "above my duller comprehension. I merely knew that she was my superior in fineness of mind, in the delicacy and subtlety of her intellect, but to fully measure her I was not competent." He can be delightfully playful about all this, as when, in the recently published fragment, "The Autobiography of Belshazzar,"[1] he makes the cat say of the family, "They were quite creditable people, as people go, except the man. He was well meaning, but a kind of ass. In his looks he was quite ordinary, but did not know it; and he was clumsy with his hands and wobbly in his gait, and drawled his words, and was lazy, and unreliable and meddlesome, but had a good head of hair." But there was no

[1] In *Concerning Cats.*

whimsy whatever in the letter he wrote Clara from Bermuda, two months to the day before he died, about his unworthiness and his inability to understand her love for him, or the love Jean had given him, and his boundless gratitude for such love. He was sure, too, that he had never treated Mrs. Clemens as she deserved. "I have known few meaner men than I am." In 1899, when he was already world famous, "Mother" Fairbanks, who had held his heart in fee since taking him on as her cub in *Quaker City* days, died. "I am grateful to know that I was one who for a generation held an unchallenged place in her favor," he wrote her son and daughter. "I was never what she thought me, but was glad to seem to her to be it. She was always good to me, & I always loved her."

II

None of this means, however, that Mark Twain was not the king-figure in any group in which he moved, nor that he did not relish that position, and in later years accept it as a matter of course. He was called "the King," and he behaved like a king. "By long habit," he writes in *Life on the Mississippi*, "pilots came to put all their wishes in the form of commands. It 'gravels' me, to this day, to put my will in the weak shape of a request, instead of launching it in the crisp language of an order." Once, in Europe, he admitted having been spoiled by ten years of petting in England and America, and Paine makes it clear that he was not often contradicted during his later years. Perhaps the suggestion of royalty is strongest in Helen Keller's account of the time he read *Eve's Diary* for her and a small company. At the end, she was weeping openly, and the others were trying to choke back their tears. Mark Twain sat enthroned, monarch of his little world. He put on his Oxford robes for Helen Keller also. "He seemed pleased that I was impressed. He drew me towards him and kissed me on the brow, as a cardinal or pope or a feudal monarch might have kissed a little child."

We have all been told that Mark Twain was a wonderful conversationalist, but he seems to have preferred monologues to real conversation. "With no more inspiration than a 'yes' or a 'no' from one of us to prove he had our attention," writes Mrs. Samossoud, "Father could lead, fill, and finish the conversation all by himself." Susy was sharper when she wrote, "He doesn't like to go to church at all, why I never understood, until just now, he told us the other day that he couldn't bear to hear anyone talk but himself, but that he could listen to himself talk for hours without getting tired, of course he said this in joke, but I've no doubt it was founded on truth." Once he himself stated that he would like to read his work for Shakespeare, Milton, and Bunyan when he got to heaven; only he knew they would not let him. There is a record of his excusing himself from a group on one occasion when a stupid, chattering woman monopolized the company and prevented him from talking, and it cannot be claimed that he was really generous in the matter of Cable's position on the program, relative time consumed, etc., during the reading tour they did together.[2] Robert Underwood Johnson reports of a meeting with Mark Twain, Mrs. Fields, and Sarah Orne Jewett in Venice, that "the great humorist did most of the talking, the others only putting in a few words now and then by way of keeping him going." When Clara made her concert debut, he apparently wanted to lead her out upon the stage, but the management did not approve of this, though he did take a "call" with her at the end.

There is egotism in all this, of course, but there is much more of eagerness, enthusiasm, appetence for life. Mark Twain had such unusual ability to put his whole soul in whatever he happened to be doing that, with the best will in the world, he could not avoid seeming to dominate less vivid people. This appears in the improvised passages he added to the play in which he acted; it appears in Calvin Higbie's delightful account of the Aurora dance;[3] it appears in his extensive preoccupation, in letters and writings alike, with what had happened to him personally. These things were real to him; they were vital; they filled his mind; he was hardly more self-conscious in speaking of them than a child is when it prattles on about the concerns of its own little world. Mark Twain's world was much vaster than the child's but it was

[2] See Arlin Turner, *Mark Twain and George W. Cable*, 93, 97, 101, 103, 119, 134, and cf. Guy A. Cardwell, "Mark Twain's 'Row' with George Cable," *Modern Language Quarterly*, Vol. XIII (1952), 363–71.

[3] Cf. Paine, *Mark Twain: A Biography*, I, 195.

hardly less personalized, and when abstract matters entered upon it, he infused personal emotion into them, too.

If he is to blame here in any important particular, the charge must proceed somewhat along this line: that sometimes he became so deeply interested in his own ideas—and especially in the "philosophy" he developed during his later years—that he expatiated upon them without giving very much attention to the tastes and comforts of those who were obliged to listen to him. He had to have an audience. He had lived in the spotlight so long that now he must do his very thinking aloud, and if there had been no human beings to listen to him, he would have preached to the birds, as St. Francis did. Before the death of his wife, he had come to realize this failing, and, as was his habit, he heaped exaggerated abuse upon his head. "I WISH—I WISH—but it is too late. I drove you to sorrow and heart-break just to hear myself talk. If ever I do it again when you get well I hope the punishment will fall upon me the guilty, not upon you the innocent."

Like many men of marked individuality, he did not always allow as carefully as he might have done for the rights of others, or perhaps it might be fairer to say that he did not always sufficiently realize how much the habits and desires of others might differ from his own. "I have known him to sit for hours in a smoking car on a cold day," writes J. B. Pond, "smoking his pipe and reading his German book with the window wide open." When Pond remonstrated in behalf of the other passengers, Mark blustered a bit and tried to justify himself, but he closed the window. "Whenever he had been a few days with us," W. D. Howells tells us, "the whole house had to be aired, for he smoked all over it from breakfast to bedtime. He always went to bed with a cigar in his mouth, and, sometimes, mindful of my fire insurance, I went up and took it away, still burning, after he had fallen asleep."

In such matters, Mark Twain seems to have accepted himself as he was, and expected others to accept him also. If it was in his power to change, he apparently did not care to take the trouble. "I love you," he writes his sister Pamela, "& I am sorry for every time I have ever hurt you; but God Almighty knows I should keep on hurting you just the same, if I were around; for I am built so, being made merely in the image of God, but not otherwise resembling him enough to be mistaken for him by anybody but a very near-sighted person." Yet he could be exquisitely, even quixotically, courteous, as he was when, while he was living in Riverdale, Norman Hapgood invited him to come into New York to see Duse. On the night set there was a terrific storm. At the end of the first act, Mark Twain appeared at the theater. "It was impossible to reach you, by telephone," he said, "or in time by telegraph; so I have come to explain that Mrs. Clemens is so unwell this evening that I ought not to be away." And thereupon he went back to Riverdale, through the storm.

CHAPTER SIX: *The Damned Human Race*

I

THEORETICALLY, MARK TWAIN IS the Devil's Advocate in the case of the Universe versus Humanity; no man ever poured fiercer scorn upon his own kind. He is willing to admit that he himself rests under this self-pronounced condemnation, for "what a man sees in the human race is merely himself in the deep and honest privacy of his own heart." Let us hope not, in Mark Twain's case. His heart would have to be very black, upon that basis. "Man is a museum of diseases, a home of impurities; he comes to-day and is gone to-morrow; he begins as dirt and departs as stench." Of all animals, he is least adapted for life on this planet, and if he was made for any purpose at all, it must have been for the support and entertainment of the microbes. Probably he was not made intentionally at all, but worked himself up from the primeval slime, through some unhappy accident, much to the surprise and grief of the Creator. In any event, the evolutionary process failed when he came on the scene, for his is the only bad heart in the whole animal kingdom; he alone is capable of malice, drunkenness, vindictiveness, and when he is not cruel by nature, he is a mere stupid sheep. "Damn these human beings; if I had invented them I would go hide my head in a bag." What can be said of such a race, save that it would be better dead? "Often it does seem such a pity that Noah and his party did not miss the boat." And he wondered whether it might not be possible to exterminate the race by means of some device which should withdraw all the oxygen from the air for a period of two minutes.

So much for humanity in the abstract, but when he comes to the individual, there is an altogether different story to tell. The capacities of mankind in general were contemptible, yet as late as the time of the autobiographical dictations, he declared it to be his experience of life that there were few hardhearted persons. He told his notebook that the medical profession was the noblest of all professions because it saved life and stifled pain. "Next comes the pulpit, which solaces mental distress; soothes the sorrows of the soul. These two are the great professions, the noble professions. The gap between them and the next is wide—an abyss." It might be a contemptible race, but even a contemptible creature must be cared for when he is in need. "He would listen, no matter what you wanted to say," Katy Leary tells us, "just like he would listen to a little child's story, and help you. He was never too tired or busy to hear what you had to say." An afflicted woman writes to him, asking for his autograph and a picture. He mislays her letter, and when he finds it again, it is not enough to send the picture; he must also write a letter, explaining carefully and in detail why he delayed so long. A boy writes, boy-fashion, to invite him to dinner; he replies courteously, explaining that, since he is in mourning, he is not dining out just now, for he knows well, as he expresses it in another connection, that it is "a glorious thing to be a boy's idol, for it is the only worship one can swear to as genuine." In New Zealand, an old man is taken ill during one of his lectures. He stops talking, and goes back stage to offer assistance, nor will he resume until the man has recovered. A storm comes up when an artist is visiting him, painting his portrait; when the man is about to leave, he insists on lending him overshoes. He will not miss them, he says, for he is old enough now to be able to refuse any invitation on the ground of bad weather. When young authors come to him, he gives them his time and his thought, encourages them as much as he conscientiously can, and if he is really impressed by them, he is not averse to making a personal effort toward bringing their work before the public.

The truth is that he was drawn powerfully in two directions at once: he admired noble deeds and aspirations, and he thoroughly detested mean ones. He could not accept pain, as Miss Bellamy seems to think he ought to have accepted it, nor yet as it was accepted by Calvinists who acquiesced in the damnation of the greater part of the human race, or those Christians who accept every hideous calamity, even if it was man-made, as "God's will." Apparently Miss Bellamy thinks that he ought to have accepted evil also. "As a moralist, Mark Twain too often fails to sense the eternal paradox of man, the great truth that out of the conflict of good and evil there emerges the greatest of human achievements, man's ethical character." Because he could not do this, she finds his sympathy for humanity "deep and intense" but not "broad." If he had been less sensitive to fineness of spirit, if the standard he had set up for the human animal had not been quite so high, perhaps he would not have minded it so much when people behaved disgracefully. This dual aspect has never been better expressed than in the piece he wrote about the murdered Empress of Austria: "She was so blameless, the Empress; and so beautiful, in mind and heart, in person and spirit; and whether with a crown upon her head or without it and nameless, a grace to the human race, and almost a justification of its creation; *would* be, indeed, but that the animal that struck her down, re-establishes the doubt." There you have it.[1] It was "the damned human race," yet

[1] Since he is often accused of sentimentalism, it should be noted that Mark Twain never joined hands with soft-headed people who attempted to save dangerous criminals (cf. his attitude toward Injun Joe in *Tom Sawyer*, chapter XXXIII). See his sarcastic letter in the New York *Tribune*, March 7, 1873 (reprinted in *The Twainian*, Fourteenth Year, March–April, 1955, pp. 2–3), about the brutal murderer William Foster. "I freely confess that it was the most natural thing in the world for such an organism to get drunk and insult a stranger and then beat his brains out with a carhook because he did not seem to admire it. Such is Foster— and to think we came so near losing him! How do we know but that he is the Second Advent?" The last sentence is, no doubt, a gibe against the clergymen who had come to the murderer's defense. Foster was hanged.

after all, it had produced Anson Burlingame and Henry H. Rogers and John Hay and Dr. John Brown—and Livy Clemens—and Joan of Arc.[2]

It was impossible to avoid admiring such people, and he was aware that there were others like them whom he personally had not had the good fortune to know. When a deed of unselfish heroism was reported to him, he would walk the floor, his eyes filled with tears: "What noble generosity! By gosh! that's a fine man for you!" So it comes about that, for all the blasting pessimism of his generalizations, practically speaking his books exemplify a high standard of moral idealism. He admires King Arthur risking his life in the smallpox hut; he admires Huck Finn refusing the surrender of Nigger Jim, though he expects to be damned for his refusal;[3] even in the devastating *Mysterious Stranger* we have Margaret and Wilhelm Meidling and the good priest, side by side with Satan's fierce denunciation of the human nature which, in the last analysis, they must share. What Albert Schweitzer calls "reverence for life" possessed Mark Twain. His deterministic philosophy being what it finally was, he knew he had no right either to praise man or to blame him, yet he went right on doing it just the same. In 1872 he wrote a letter to the Royal Humane Society of London, recommending that the captain of the *Batavia* and the volunteer rescue crew be awarded the Society's medal for rescuing nine men from the wrecked *Charles Ward*. A little later,

[2] Mark Twain admired a great many people besides those who became his special saints. "I am sorry enough to ever miss any moment of [Joseph] Jefferson," he writes Howells, "for some day I am going to need his influence when he is an archangel." I am greatly surprised by the occasional passages in which he expresses admiration for Napoleon. In one he even brackets him with Joan of Arc, which I should think he would consider almost blasphemous—as I do. See *Notebook*, 241; cf. *Love Letters*, 235.

[3] Without knowing it, Huck is following what Quakers call the "Inner Light." See the especially perspicacious remarks on Huck in this aspect by Edgar M. Branch, *The Literary Apprenticeship of Mark Twain*, 202, 205. Mark Twain defended lies told to save other people pain and in the public interest but barred those told to injure someone else or to benefit oneself. The most detailed examination of his own truthfulness is in Paul Fatout's article, "Mark Twain, Litigant," *American Literature*, Vol. XXXI (1959), 30–45, which deals with his lawsuit with Edward H. House over the dramatization of *The Prince and the Pauper*. Mark Twain comes through the ordeal very well. See the story "Was It Heaven? or Hell?" in *The $30,000 Bequest*; re-enacted in part in Mark's own household, as related in Paine's Biography, III, chapter CXXVI.

he attracted considerable attention by advocating rafts as more practical, and more likely to save lives at sea, than the conventional lifeboats. Like many a man, he was bigger than his philosophy, and Gamaliel Bradford sums it up well when he writes, "No man ever more abused the human heart, or railed at the hollowness of human affection, and no man ever had more friends or loved more."

II

Though he says he was never completely without reserves except to two people during his lifetime—his wife and his brother Henry—Mark Twain wanted friends, and needed them. He hated solitude, could not bear to be left alone. Had he lived in Eden, he was sure he would have greeted the Serpent as "a welcome change —anything for society." He pretty nearly did this the night he spent in a New York jail.[4] Even in grief the consciousness of human sympathy was precious. It was in some ways unfortunate that so sensitive a man should have been so dependent upon human contacts, for, though as Huckleberry Finn observes, "the more you join with people in their joys and sorrows, the more nearer and dearer they come to be to you," it is also true that the more you open your heart to them, the better chance they have to hurt you. Mark Twain experienced some broken friendships—with Bret Harte and with Dan Slote—but he was certainly very fortunate in the loyalty and understanding he received from such noble men as Joseph H. Twichell and William Dean Howells, and though he said some ungenerous things about George W. Cable, he and Cable did not do badly by each other, when you consider how antithetical their temperaments were, and what a strain traveling and appearing together must have been for them. There is one brutal letter to Will Bowen, but we do not have the evidence to decide whether Mark is simply blowing off steam here, or whether he is deliberately hurting his friend for that friend's good.[5] He has been accused of imposing upon Howells—"But

[4] See *Mark Twain's Travels with Mr. Brown*, letter XVIII.
[5] See *Mark Twain's Letters to Will Bowen*, 23–25. Cf. letter to J. H. Burrough, in DeVoto, ed., *The Portable Mark Twain*, 749–52. The letter to Burrough

mind, if this is going to be too much trouble to you,—go ahead &
do it, all the same"—but, though this may sometimes seem to be
the case, the relationship was less one-sided than many persons
suppose, and I get the impression that Howells was decidedly nobody's fool, and well able to look out for himself. Howells cost
Mark Twain money by, at the last moment, capriciously withdrawing a play they had both put a good deal of work into, but
though Mark spoke his mind, there was never any question of the
disagreement disturbing their friendship.[6] Neither was Mark offended when Howells missed his chance to write an introduction
to his friend's collected works because the publisher refused to
pay him the extravagant sum of $1,500 for it. Some critics find
Mark Twain patronizing toward his brother Orion, but it is difficult to see what else he could have done, Orion being what he
was. Toward Henry Ward Beecher, before and after the famous
trial, he seems to have gone through every possible variety of feeling—once he wanted to "cut" Beecher's sister, Isabella Hooker,
because she believed him guilty, and again he himself had very
serious doubts about Beecher's innocence—but he never failed in
essential humanity and understanding, any more than Whittier
did. Nobody has ever doubted that Mark Twain had great charm
in social life, despite all his capacity for gaucherie, and his quick
sympathy is well suggested by Helen Keller: "He knew with keen
and sure intuition many things about me; how it felt to be blind
and not to be able to keep up with the swift ones—things that
others learned slowly or not at all. He never embarrassed me by
saying how terrible it is not to see, or how dull life must be, lived
always in the dark."[7]

It may be well to look at his social life in its more general
aspects. In his teens, he appears to have been shy, but he became
a social lion at least as early as the Carson City days, and after
marriage and fame, there were naturally many social opportuni-
ties. One observer testifies: "The Clemens house was the only one

suggests that Mark Twain had more self-control than he is generally given credit for,
or else that his conscience troubled him, and he was trying to justify himself.

[6] See *Mark Twain–Howells Letters*, especially II, 558–63.

[7] See, also, *Mark Twain's Travels with Mr. Brown*, letter XXI.

I have ever known where there was never any *preoccupation* in the evenings, and where visitors were always welcome." As late as the turn of the century, we hear of one week when guests were entertained at seventeen out of the twenty-one meals and on three out of the seven evenings.

Of course he could be bored, or, rather, he could be enraged. "All the old cats in Christendom seem to have chosen this particular day to visit here. . . . Miss S. (whom I delight to hate) called first, and she was no sooner gone than Mrs. B. (whom to hate is an unspeakable luxury) came. When I get sight of either of these women I am 'done' for that day. When they both come in one evening I degenerate into pure lunacy." Yet congeniality far outweighed annoyance. Katy Leary describes his sessions with Howells: "Well, you couldn't hear a thing from the Billiard Room but peals of laughter from them two men when he was visiting here. Oh, how they'd laugh!" Chauncey M. Depew says that Mark Twain was very uneven as a conversationalist. "Sometimes he would be the life of the occasion and make it one long to be remembered but generally he contributed nothing. At this dinner, whenever he showed the slightest sign of making a remark, there was dead silence, but the remark did not come." I should not think it would—in the dead silence; Mark Twain always had difficulty in doing what he knew he was expected to do. But on the whole his personality would seem to have been quite impressive enough without his reputation. Bernard Shaw says that when he visited Adelphi Terrace, the parlor maid did not know him from Adam, yet she admitted him without question and unannounced.

Clemens had no great interest in most of the games and sports with which many men reinforce their social lives. Physically he was much too fond of his ease to be attracted to sports. According to Steve Gillis, he objected to tenpins as too strenuous for anybody except a drayman or a coalheaver, and Jervis Langdon says that when Mark went rowing with him, he settled himself comfortably among the cushions in the rear seat, declaring that he loved rowing above all other exercise but that unfortunately he could not ride backwards! Even in childhood, only swimming and skating seem to have attracted him very much. He did a little fencing in his Virginia City days. In Hartford and, at the end, in Bermuda, he used to go to baseball games. He once went to see Corbett box, and was impressed by the fine form he displayed. Neither golf nor yachting interested him. Though he did a good deal of horseback riding in Hawaii (extraordinarily badly, it seems),[8] he cared nothing for horseflesh. His bicycling was simply inspired by his curiosity about new machinery. He always preferred walking to riding, and told Dan Beard he intended to do his traveling on his own "hind legs." In Hartford days, he and Twichell used to love to hike to Talcott Mountain, five miles away. Once they started to hike to Boston but did not get far beyond Westford, Massachusetts. When he was a boy, his uncle and his cousins sometimes took young Sam out hunting, but he soon decided he could find no pleasure in killing dumb creatures, and as a man he regarded all blood sports with horror. He once went to a cockfight but had to leave before it was over, and the bullfight was, in his eyes, completely indefensible.

Indoor amusements pleased him more, but except for billiards, which, at the end, became a kind of religion, they did not take a very deep hold on him either. He danced in his youth, and sometimes in later life also. He played poker and euchre, in mining-camp days and later with Henry Rogers, and the Whittier Birthday Speech uses a good many poker terms; not understanding these, Emerson necessarily missed a good deal of the fun. In Hartford he played whist. But he was no gambler, and he was likely to prefer solitaire or hearts. I find some mention of chess but none of checkers. "Father," writes Mrs. Samossoud, "was like a little child in his capacity for getting angry over cards. Continuous bad luck would start those little twitching muscles under his eyes that signified a growing storm, and then suddenly followed an avalanche of cards on the table and Father would sing out: 'By the humping jumping —— who can play with a hand like that? Look at those cards! Just look at them! Products of the devil and his ancestors." But better than any card game he enjoyed charades, for they brought his dramatic gift into play, and he liked nothing

[8] See Frear, *Mark Twain in Hawaii,* 37–39, 42.

better than to devise curious methods to help his children learn their lessons, as may be seen best of all in the history game.

Of course, he did not always follow the accepted rules of social behavior. In the early days he disregarded them because he did not know them; later, sometimes, because he did not think them important. Once, at a dinner given in his honor, he pushed back his chair midway through the meal, declared he had had enough, called for a cigar, and walked up and down the room talking while the other guests finished their meal. Laurence Hutton tells, too, how Mark once walked in on a dinner to Sir Henry Irving, to which he had not been invited, because it was not known that he was to be in the city. "He had arrived from Hartford late in the afternoon, had discovered from the gossip at the Club that the Huttons were having 'a rather unusual dinner-party,' was told who were to be present, and decided that it was too good a thing to lose. So he dressed hurriedly, walked in without ceremony just as the feast began, drew up a chair by the side of his hostess, helped himself to her oysters, and for the rest of the evening was the life of the party."

III

Though the shortcomings of women have always been one of the principal themes of the professional humorist, Mark Twain is very rarely cynical in this regard. There is one speech on "Woman" which verges on ribaldry, and when he went to Washington in behalf of better copyright laws, he stated as one of the reasons why he needed money the fact that he had reared his daughters as young ladies, and that therefore they didn't know anything and couldn't do anything. *The Washoe Giant* has some coarse but amusing burlesques of women's fashion reporting.[9] *Eve's Diary* makes fun of woman's social proclivities, her passion for hanging ornaments on her person, and her disposition to interfere with the things men like to do.

All this is nothing compared to the many passages in which Mark Twain expresses his respect and regard for women. When

9 *The Washoe Giant in San Francisco*, 32–44.

he encountered a man who lacked such respect, he always felt that he had learned nothing about women but a great deal about the man. So he hated Strindberg for the unpleasant women encountered in his plays, "a dead give-away on the author's part, for a writer who sees no good in women confesses that he was found out by the sex he wars on." He loathed and scorned the Neapolitans who jeered an old actress on the *Quaker City* tour, and his animus against Bret Harte was increased by what he considered his cruel treatment of his wife. He was especially impressed by women's courage in the painful business of childbirth. "I do admire Katharine's courage. I hope I shall never have a baby, for I know I should dread it so that every one would be ashamed of me." He declares bluntly that the average woman is superior to the average man: his notion of the form that superiority was likely to take is shown very clearly in "The $30,000 Bequest," where both husband and wife make fools of themselves as they dispose of their imaginary fortunes, but the woman's dreams are on a far higher level than the man's. Indeed when Mark Twain denounces the human race, it is generally to be understood that he is denouncing only the male half of it. There is an interesting passage in his autobiography in which he declares that the whole population of the United States is now financially rotten, but immediately adds that, of course, he does not mean to include the women. Did all this begin, one cannot but wonder, because, as a child, Mark Twain sympathized so much more with his mother than he did with his father?

Some of Mark Twain's contemporaries professed great respect for women, at the same time opposing what were called women's "rights." In the sixties, indeed, he himself opposed woman suffrage because he did not want to see women contending in the marketplace with men. But as early as 1875 he championed it before Hartford's Monday Evening Club. In a public address of 1901, he declared unequivocally, "I should like to see the time come when women shall help make the laws. I should like to see that whip-lash, the ballot, in the hands of women. As for this city's government, I don't want to say much, except that it is a shame—

a shame; but if I should live twenty-five years longer—and there is no reason why I shouldn't—I think I'll see women handle the ballot. If women had the ballot today, the state of things in this town would not exist."

Children he always loved: it is significant that when he wishes to describe a group of beautiful women he should say, "They fasten one's eyes like a magnet—or a baby—or a wood-fire in the twilighted room." "The darling mispronunciations of childhood!" cries the Connecticut Yankee—"dear me, there's no music can touch it," and there can be no doubt that here, as in the preceding section describing the serious illness of his child, he is speaking for Mark Twain.

In his writings, Mark Twain succeeds much better with boys than with girls. The little heroine of "The Death Disk" is an impossible creature, and though the young Joan of Arc is much better, there are weaknesses even here. In life, however, he seems distinctly to have preferred girls. He always knew how to charm a boy. Max Eastman was overwhelmed "at the princely grace of his greeting. . . . I might have been the Lord Mayor instead of a scared child." And Manuel Komroff, who met him after playing the leader of the mob in a production of *The Prince and the Pauper*, thought him "the nicest man in the whole world." But after his own girls had grown up or died, he turned to other little girls for solace, as if through them he wished to recapture the past. Dorothy Quick and Elizabeth Wallace have written about him so well in this aspect that it would be futile to try to compete with them. He had his "Aquarium," made up of "Angel Fish" (girls in their early teens), and he found much pleasure in the Juggernaut Club, which consisted of a number of little girls, each from a different country, he himself, the only male member, being designated the Chief Servant. Even in the busy Hartford days, there was a club of little girls who used to meet with him every Saturday morning. "Girls are charming creatures," he declared in his old age. "I shall have to be twice seventy years old before I change my mind as to that."

IV

Of Mark Twain's servants, the shrewd Katy Leary is by far the best known. He watched over her and guarded her like a dragon, though she may not always have appreciated it when he sent her admirers home at ten o'clock and locked up the house. That there were no limits to her devotion to him, her whole book eloquently testifies, but she knew his peculiarities too, played up to him when necessary, and well understood how to evade directions she did not care to carry out. He seems never to have been unreasonable with her except when he would mislay one of his manuscripts and then accuse her of having burned it, which could always be counted upon to lead to grand high passages between them, but he had certain services which she must perform in his behalf, and if she failed, there was the devil to pay. "He always had three sets of cuff buttons and shirt buttons fixed, so there'd always be a shirt ready for him. My goodness! I used to have to fix three shirts at the same time, because if he found one shirt that didn't have the proper cuff buttons in, he'd tear it up." Katy wouldn't have that, for she thought him far too extravagant already, and when he told her a shirt was worn out and she must throw it away, she would mend it instead and put it back in his drawer, and Mark would go on wearing it without ever knowing the difference.

In the Orient, Mark Twain loathed the jinricksha because he could not feel it right that one man should draw another about. No doubt he showed remnants of the Southern racial attitude when he decided to employ a colored butler because he did not feel comfortable giving orders to a white man, but George was never much troubled by orders, much less indeed than nine persons out of ten would have felt a proper regard for discipline and decorum required. And when the coachman, Patrick Mc-Aleer, died, Clemens acted as pallbearer, in company with his own gardener, and, in a public address, lauded Patrick as the ideal gentleman.

People who worked for Mark Twain in other capacities were less fortunate, however. His relations with publishers were stormy.

Except for Harpers, it was his view that they all cheated him, or managed his affairs with an ineptitude bordering upon idiocy; even his friend Dan Slote, who manufactured the "Mark Twain Scrap Book" for him, fell under the ban at last. Charles L. Webster's son has now documented the unfairness of many of the charges against Webster.[10] Directive followed directive, and, as likely as not, today's directive would completely contradict yesterday's. Moreover, Webster was not only required to conduct a publishing company; every five or six minutes, he was expected to drop everything he was doing to investigate the possibility of suing some villain or another, or to run miscellaneous errands in connection with Mark's multitudinous ideas and inventions. Even Mrs. Clemens contributed her share to the confusion, for whenever she wanted a clock from Tiffany's, or a new fender, or some dining-room chairs, or a sofa, Webster must get them for her. The demands made of Pond in connection with the Cable reading tour were often unreasonable also.[11] Yet always, in the midst of the unreasonableness, there are flashes of rare sensitiveness and consideration. He wants Charley Webster to get rid of a magazine for which he has not renewed his subscription but which the publishers persist in sending him. "I do not want to have to refuse to receive the publication from the post-man, for that is an offense which I don't wish to offer to anybody."

V

Probably no man ever loved animals better than Mark Twain, and—as everybody knows—his favorite animal was the cat. He began to love cats as a boy, though, as the painkiller incident in *Tom Sawyer* shows, there were times when his sense of mischief got the better of his affections,[12] and he liked to recall how, one Sunday morning, he had seen a cat walk into some flypapers placed

10 In Samuel C. Webster, *Mark Twain, Business Man.*
11 See Kjell Ekström, "Extracts from a Diary Kept by Ozias W. Pond during the Clemens-Cable Tour of Readings in 1885," *Archiv für das Studium der neueren Sprachen*, Vol. CLXXXVIII (1951), 109–13.
12 Mark Twain said, in his autobiographical dictations, that he gave Perry Davis's Pain-Killer to Peter the cat, during a cholera scare. See *North American Review*, Vol. CLXXXIII (1906), 841–42.

close to the pulpit, "saw her struggle and fall down, more and more unreconciled, more and more mutely profane." He ate with cats, and slept with cats. "Next to a wife whom I idolise, give me a cat." When Jean is born, Susy and Clara could not worship her more if she were a cat. His own opinion as to the merits of the Tiger in the House, he summed up categorically: "They are the cleanest, cunningest, and most intelligent things I know, outside the girl you love, of course." Or, as Susy puts it, in her own charming way, "The difference between papa and mama is, that mama loves morals and papa loves cats."

It might be expected that such a man as Mark Twain would invent ingenious names for his cats. He does not disappoint us. Four kittens at Quarry Farm were named Sour Mash, Apollinaris, Zoroaster, and Blatherskite. He chose the names, he said, to give the children practice in pronunciation, and when all four animals died young, he was sure their names had killed them. When he came to spend a summer at Dublin, New Hampshire, he simply could not consider getting along without a cat, but he could not disregard the question of what would happen to the animal when he was no longer there to care for it. He solved the problem triumphantly by renting a cat instead of adopting one, renting two, in fact—Sackcloth and Ashes—and paying enough to insure their care after he should have returned home in the autumn. In a man as absent-minded, as careless in matters of detail, as Mark Twain was, one could hardly ask for more than this. "Once," writes Paine, "as he was about to enter the screen-door that led to the hall, two of the kittens ran up in front of him and stood waiting. With grave politeness he opened the door, made a low bow, and stepped back and said: 'Walk in, gentlemen. I always gives precedence to royalty.' And the kittens marched in, tails in air."

Danbury and Tammany were the great favorites in Stormfield days. "Mark Twain might be preoccupied and indifferent to the comings and goings of other members of the household; but no matter what he was doing, let Danbury appear in the offing and he was observed and greeted with due deference, and complimented and made comfortable. Clemens would arise from the table and carry certain choice food out on the terrace to Tammany, and be satisfied with almost no acknowledgment by way of appreciation." And how fine and tender is his own story of the kitten on the billiard table.

> If I can find a photograph of my "Tammany" and her kittens, I will enclose it in this. One of them likes to be crammed into a corner-pocket of the billiard-table—which he fits as snugly as does a finger in a glove and then he watches the game (and obstructs it) by the hour, and spoils many a shot by putting out his paw and changing the direction of a passing ball. Whenever a ball is in his arms, or so close to him that it cannot be played upon without risk of hurting him, the player is privileged to remove it to anyone of the 3 spots that chances to be vacant.

After Tammany's death, he lauded her to Louise Paine as "the most beautiful cat on this western bulge of the globe, and perhaps the most gifted. She leaves behind her," he added, "inconsolable, two children by her first marriage—Billiards and Babylon; and three grandchildren by her second—Amanda, Annanci and Sind-bad." He requested that each M.A. (Member of the Aquarium) "wear black head ribbons during one hour on the 30th of this month—Tammany's birthday."[13]

Sometimes the family cunningly played on Mark Twain's love of cats, as when they rented an apartment in an undesirable neighborhood in Berlin without consulting him. "The women took that apartment in Slumland over my head, and lured me to approve of their choice by having two purring cats on the hearth when I first saw the place." Mrs. Samossoud tells us that if, as a child, she had occasion to disturb him at work, and had any reason to feel doubtful concerning her reception, she always took a kitten with her in her arms.

Dogs were quite another story. His great sensitiveness to sound made their barking very unpleasant to him, and he sometimes declared he wished he could exterminate them all. Like many persons who have learned to appreciate the independent spirit of the

---

[13] See Louise Paine Moore, "Mark Twain as I Knew Him," Twainian, Eighteenth Year, Jan.–Feb., 1959, pp. 3–4.

cat, he disliked the dog's servility, and he shared O. Henry's opinion about people who escort dogs about the street at the end of a string. Yet the Clemenses kept dogs, and there are some tender passages in Mark Twain's writings concerning them. After Mrs. Clemens's death, he wished "I could see a dog that I knew in the old times! & could put my arms around his neck & tell him all, everything, & ease my heart." There is no tenderer dog story in literature than "A Dog's Tale"—written as an anti-vivisection tract—and one of the most touching passages in "The Death of Jean" relates how he and his daughter's dog were drawn together in their common grief.

Actually, Mark Twain did not know how to be unkind to any animal. As for vivisection specifically, he declared that his opposition was unaffected by the question of whether or not it benefited the human race. "The pain which it inflicts upon unconsenting animals is the basis of my enmity toward it, and it is to me sufficient justification of the enormity without looking further." He continues: "It is so distinctly a matter of feeling with me, and is so strong and so deeply rooted in my make and constitution, that I am sure I could not see even a vivisector vivisected with anything more than a sort of qualified satisfaction." When Edmund Yates visited Mark Twain, he found in the greenhouse a cage containing a pair of California quail: Mark had bought them from a boy in order to save them, and when spring came, he planned to set them free. In 1904 there is a characteristic entry in his notebook. He is staying at Tyringham, in very unpleasant weather. "We built a fire in my room. Then clawed the logs out and threw water, remembering there was a brood of swallows in the chimney. The tragedy was averted." When he was abroad with Twichell, he would never permit the drivers to whip their horses. "Never mind that! We are going fast enough. We are in no hurry." Not even snakes and bats were excluded from his sympathies, though, according to Clara, once when, in his Hartford house, a snake crawled out from the conservatory, he handled it very gingerly with the fire-tongs. He detested flies and spiders.

Like many lovers of animals, Mark Twain refuses to believe that they cannot think, or that they do not converse with one another. He thinks of them as individuals, and describes their individual characteristics so that they almost seem human. I find no indication that he ever read the folk epic of *Reynard the Fox,* or even the two beautiful English poems which it inspired—"The Nonne Preestes Tale" and Spenser's "Mother Hubberds Tale"— but he would have relished these masterpieces, in which human and animal characteristics are so ingeniously mingled, and animals are used so cleverly for satirical commentary on human nature and institutions. He did not live long enough to meet George Herriman's "Krazy Kat"—"the most tender and most foolish of creatures, a gentle monster of our new mythology," as Gilbert Seldes called him—nor, of course, the vastly ingenious and variegated menagerie of Disney.

With Mark Twain, the emphasis of such satire must always have been rightly pointed, for—let there be no mistake about it— he was completely, and quite seriously, convinced that man is the least admirable figure in the animal kingdom. "Man isn't even handsome, as compared with the birds; and as for style, look at the Bengal tiger—the ideal of grace, physical perfection, and majesty. Think of the lion and the tiger and the leopard, and then think of man—that poor thing!—the animal of the wig, the ear-trumpet, the glass eye, the porcelain teeth, the wooden leg, the trepanned skull, the silver wind-pipe, a creature that is mended and patched all over from top to bottom." Test his character, and he shows no more attractively: what animal would be guilty of the refined useless cruelties that human beings inflict upon one another? "Many a time, when I have seen a man abusing a horse, I have wished I knew that horse's language, so that I could whisper in his ear, 'Fool, you are master here, if you but knew it. Launch out with your heels!'" Again he tells us that "if man could be crossed with the cat it would improve man, but it would deteriorate the cat." Man's inferiority to the other animals is most seriously argued in *The Mysterious Stranger,* where Satan comments feelingly on the calculated gall human beings manifest when they describe hideously cruel acts as "brutal." They are not brutal, but peculiarly human! Epigrammatically the whole thing is summed up in the words of Pudd'nhead Wilson: "If you pick up a starving dog and make him prosperous, he will not bite you. This is the principal difference between a dog and a man."

There is something very touching about Mark Twain's attitude toward animals at the end of his life: as his pessimism grew upon him, as he became more and more disgusted with the damned human race, he turned to them for comfort. They delivered him from the domination of the Moral Sense, for, like the angels, they never sinned and therefore are sure of heaven. Here, in his own way, he suggests Cowper, who needed refuge, to be sure, not so much from other men as from himself, Cowper, who loved his hares and his cats so tenderly, and who could write: "The season has been most unfavorable to animal life; and I, who am merely animal, have suffered much by it." And again, he recalls Swift, who came, at last, in his utopia, to the land ruled by horses, with vicious, degraded human creatures subordinated to their proper place. When, in *The Prince and The Pauper,* young royalty is cast out by men, he finds comfort in a calf thrown in his way, and Clarence suggests to the Yankee—here is the closest parallel with Swift—that since mankind apparently will not consent to be deprived of the gewgaws of royalty, a race of cats to rule us would be the best.

CHAPTER SEVEN: *The Root of Evil*

I

THERE IS HIGH AUTHORITY for the statement that the love of money is the root of all evil, but life and morals are both much less simple than most of us would like to have them, and in actual experience we find that a good deal of evil is inspired by the lack of money. Mark Twain was quite familiar with this Janus-faced aspect of the money problem, as these entries in his notebook show:

> *Saturday, January 3, 1903:* The offspring of riches: Pride, vanity, ostentation, arrogance, tyranny.
> *Sunday, January 4, 1903:* The offspring of poverty: Greed, sordidness, envy, hate, malice, cruelty, meanness, lying, shirking, cheating, stealing, murder.

There was no cant in his own attitude toward money. He saw a particularly ugly aspect of money lust in his Western mining camp days, and, as he grew older, he was saddened by much uglier manifestations of it in the increasing commercialism of modern society. He considered Jay Gould one of the worst calamities that had ever befallen the Republic. He wavered on Rockefeller, and after Henry H. Rogers had saved him from financial disaster there was nothing more he could say about Standard Oil.

He came out of a household which knew poverty. He had a most worthy but impractical father, and an equally worthy and impractical brother. He did not want to be like them. He made up his mind to push out into the great world of active humanity, as they had never done it, to get a share of the good things of life, not only for himself but for his family also. As pilot, he came into a large salary, which he spent freely and generously. From piloting he went on to prospecting, then, through the antechamber of his newspaper days, to the *Innocents* tour, to the lecture platform, to his prosperity as a man of letters, to his many adventures in business and in speculation. For money, dangerous as it is, is "a good and strong friend," and when business fails, he is haunted by the fear of poverty.

II

He considered the economic aspects of literature carefully. In his early days, he agreed to write some letters for the Keokuk *Post* at five dollars each. After writing the first, he asked seven dollars and a half for the second, which was granted. With the third, he pushed the price up to ten dollars, and the publishers refused. Mark was born with the writing urge in his bones, but he had no intention of writing for nothing. When the American Publishing Company suggested that he make a book out of his *Quaker City* letters, he made this quite clear. "But I had my mind made up to *one* thing," he explained to his mother—"I wasn't going to touch a book unless there was money in it. I told them so."

This is no exceptional note. He would like to sell *Tom Sawyer* to the *Atlantic*, but he does not think that magazine could pay him what he can get elsewhere, and he is not disposed to sacrifice cash for glory. "You see I take a vile, mercenary view of things— but then my household expenses are something almost ghastly." Elsewhere he asks of a publishing venture: "Why should we assist our fellowman for mere love of God?" When it comes to *Pudd'n-*

head Wilson, you would think he was selling cordwood or pota-toes. "Now, then what is she worth? The amount of matter is but 3,000 words short of the American Claimant, for which the syndi-cate paid $12,500. There was nothing new in that story, but the fingerprints in this one is virgin-ground—absolutely *fresh*, and mighty curious and interesting to everybody." When John T. Ray-mond is on tour with the *Gilded Age* play, he sends an agent with the company to count the receipts and make sure the author is not cheated. He pays Cable a flat salary on their joint reading-tour, keeping the lion's share of the profits for himself. Even Howells is offered one-third, not one-half, on a proposed collaboration. Only with *Joan of Arc* is this consideration neglected. "Possibly the book may not sell, but that is nothing—it was written for love."

When he died, his estate, despite his not-so-distant bank-ruptcy, was valued at about $600,000. This was not all from roy-alties, for H. H. Rogers had played the market cannily in his behalf. But it was not a bad showing for a barefoot boy from Hannibal. He had bargained well with publishers, on the whole, disastrous as his other financial transactions had been. The terms of his final contract with Harper, arranged by Rogers, were very generous. The publishers were to pay royalties on a minimum of 50,000 volumes a year, and every time they left an advertisement for his books out of *Harper's Magazine*, it was to cost them $200.

III

By nature, Mark Twain was extravagant. In his pilot days, "a ten dollar dinner at a Fresh restaurant—breathe it not unto Ma!" was enough of an event so that he had to write home about it, but he soon came to the place where his indulgences, though of a dif-ferent character, cost a great deal more than that. As early as 1868, when he goes to California to persuade the *Alta* people to release his travel letters for book publication, one stateroom is not enough for him; he must have two. When he is married, his bride tells him not to worry about finances, for they can live on a very mod-erate sum, and he comments significantly, "I know very well that she can . . . but am not so sure about myself." Careful computation of costs was not for him. He ordered clothes and household accessories by the dozens, by the hundreds; when he decided to wear white clothes, he immediately ordered fourteen suits, so that he would always have seven for each week—seven at the cleaners' and seven at home. Take the mere detail of barbering. While he was in Hartford, the barber used to come to the house every morning to shave him, for which service he paid a dollar and a half a shave, or about ten times what a shave then cost in the barber shop. Nook Farm people apparently had a tendency to live beyond their means. The house on Farmington Avenue cost $122,000 in 1874; in the year 1881 alone, $30,000 were swallowed up in "improvements," including $12,000—a highwayman's price—for an adjoining strip of land, where building was threatened. The Clemenses employed six servants, at a combined salary of about $1,650 a year, and entertained lavishly. Even during his last years at Stormfield, when his family was shrunken, he was spending fifty dollars a day, though it is only fair to add that some of this was due to the fact that he was being robbed by a trusted subordinate, and that when Paine took charge the expense was considerably reduced.[1]

I am not forgetting that there were times when Mark Twain and his family went to Europe to live because they could not afford to remain in America. But even then they did not live like paupers. In 1898, in Vienna, they paid $600 a month for "4 bedrooms, a dining-room, a drawing-room, 3 bath-rooms and 3 Vorzimmers, (and food)" at the best hotel in the city. A few years later, he paid $2,000 a year for the Villa Quarto in Florence. No wonder Mrs. Clemens found it necessary to remind him, during one financial crisis, when, with his excited imagination, he saw them all settled in the poorhouse, that even if it came to the worst, they would still have $6,000 a year, plus what he could earn with his pen. I have known Americans who managed to get along with that much. And, indeed, those who have really suffered financial disaster do not traipse off to Europe to live in hotels; they move to a third- or fourth-class neighborhood in the city—or to the country.

Mark Twain was also, of course, very generous toward others

[1] E. Hudson Long, *Mark Twain Handbook*, 253; Caroline T. Harnsberger, *Mark Twain: Family Man*, 254–55.

with his money. William Gillette (at the beginning of his career), Karl Gerhardt the sculptor, Helen Keller—here are only a few of the many he helped, most of them quite unknown to fame. "Irving Underhill wants to pay me $500—owing seven years," he writes in his notebook. "Cannot allow it. He has had a hard time." In Hartford, too, there were lavish Christmas baskets and many appearances for charity.

It must not be supposed that because Mrs. Clemens came out of a family whose household expenses ran to $40,000 a year, she was primarily responsible for the lavish scale of Mark's living. His financial position, at the time he won her, was not impressive, and there was no question of his trying to support her, as the saying is, in the style to which she was accustomed. He even dramatizes his poverty—a bit unnecessarily it would seem, in the light of some of his other expenditures: "I gave her only a plain gold engagement ring, when fashion imperatively demands a two-hundred dollar diamond one, and told her it was typical of her future lot—namely, that she would have to flourish on substantials rather than luxuries." When they were prosperous, she wore beautiful clothes, but Mark seldom noticed a new gown until after she had been wearing it for six months. If she ever tried to curb his extravagances, I have found no trace of it, but her own tastes were simpler than his, and had her inclinations ruled, they would have lived more simply than they did. Opinion in some quarters to the contrary notwithstanding, it is quite clear that he, not she, was the dominant partner in their marriage.

Mrs. Clemens comes in for special consideration in connection with Mark Twain's business failure, which, it should be remembered, carried away her fortune as well as his own. It was difficult for her to accept the idea that her husband was actually bankrupt. "I have a perfect *horror* and heartsickness over it," she wrote her sister. "I cannot get away from the feeling that business failure means disgrace." But was this because she was a conventional child of the Gilded Age, or was it merely because she was honest? It is not necessary to give Livy full credit for her husband's determination to pay one hundred cents on the dollar instead of the fifty with which he might have escaped. If it had not been for the kindness and financial sagacity of H. H. Rogers, they would have lost everything; it was Rogers who made it possible for Mark Twain to have his cake and eat it too, to satisfy all the obligations of honor and still enjoy a comfortable old age.[2] Mark Twain did not need his wife to teach him to be an honest man. If he had ever needed such teaching, he had got it from his father long ago. But it is certainly to her credit that she stood by him as she did. He could not help knowing that she was desperately hurt and grieved, but he knew too that the one thing that would kill her would be for him to weaken. "I seem to see you grieving and ashamed, and dreading to look people in the face," he writes, but he rejoiced in her courage and loyalty.

IV

But the thing that really wrecked Mark Twain financially was not his extravagance but his investments. All through his mature life, he had the gambling fever in a highly aggravated form. He did not gamble with cards, but he was never able to resist a speculation, though being, as he says, a man who was never able to understand even a contract, he should have been the last man to be tempted by speculation. Pudd'nhead Wilson's advice in the matter is of unimpeachable wisdom: "There are two times in a man's life when he should not speculate: when he can afford it, and when he can't." One wonders how Mark Twain himself managed to escape both conditions. In the single year 1881 he invested no less than $46,000, mainly in abortive projects. It was exciting entertainment while it lasted, though clearly the most expensive he could buy. "I was always taking little chances . . . — a thing which I did not greatly mind because I was always careful to risk only such amounts as I could easily afford to lose." It was more than Carnegie could have afforded to risk; otherwise he would never have become Carnegie. Among the world-revolutionizing inventions Mark Twain sponsored were a steam generator, a steam pulley, a new method of marine telegraphy, a new engraving process, a patent cash register, and a spiral hat pin.[3] When he died,

[2] DeLancey Ferguson, *Mark Twain, Man and Legend,* 259.

the appraisers of his estate found only $8,000 of his investments in bonds. Among his assets were 375 shares of capital stock in the Plasmon Milk Products Company. These were appraised at $100 for the lot.

In other words, as he puts it, "all through my life I have been the easy prey of the cheap adventurer." Only once does he seem to have been cautious, and this was when he might have had any number of shares in Alexander Graham Bell's telephone, virtually upon his own terms.

He was a literary man who somehow, unfortunately, got it into his head that he was also a man of business. Of course, to those lacking in such ability, it must seem something of a miracle that a man should be able to put a book together, and make something to exist where nothing was before. But once you had done it— shucks! it was nothing. He knew a trick worth two of that. Over there, on the other side of the fence, were those astonishing businessmen. Business was not what it had used to be. It was expanding, developing, running out in infinite ramifications. It needed men of imagination, as much as writing did. If you were in business, you could feel power under your hands—you were the force that made things go—you even made these damned kings crawl in the dirt beneath your feet. "Unconsciously, we all have a standard by which we measure other men, and if we examine closely we find that this standard is a very simple one, and is this: we admire them, we envy them, for great qualities which we ourselves lack." When he finds in himself even a little ability along this line, he swells up like a pouter pigeon; no purely literary achievement could for a moment be compared with it. He plans to take the manuscript of *The Gilded Age* to England, so as to print simultaneously on both sides of the Atlantic, and foil the pirates: "Some people think I have no head for business, but this is a lie."

He had, to be sure, one great triumph as a businessman. As a publisher, he got the Grant Memoirs away from the Century Company by offering unheard-of terms and backing up his faith with a check for $25,000 advance royalties. Here, again, the specu-

³ See George Hiram Brownell, "Mark Twain's Inventions," *Twainian*, N.S. Vol. III, Jan., 1944, pp. 1–5.

lative element appealed to him strongly; he saw a long chance, and he took it, and this time he was fully justified. (He was also very generous, for he admired Grant and wanted to help his family.) The sales of the book reached his most sanguine expectations and ultimately earned some $425,000 in royalties for the Grant estate. This was during the period when, in his own words, he was frightened at the proportions of his own prosperity. "It seems to me that whatever I touch turns to gold." But even then he was out of his orbit; he was doing what he had no business to do, planing against the grain of the wood. "Life has come to be a very serious matter with me. I have a badgered, harassed feeling, a good part of my time." In his heart he knew—or he soon learned—that he had no place in business—and the conviction gained upon him as time went on. "I am terribly tired of business. I am by nature and disposition unfit for it, & I want to get out of it." When the crash came, there was a part of him—deep down inside—that was glad. "Now and then a good and dear Joe Twichell or Susy Warner condoles with me and says 'Cheer up—don't be downhearted,' and some other friend says, 'I am glad and surprised to see how cheerful you are and how bravely you stand it'—and none of them suspect what a burden has been lifted from me and how blithe I am inside."

V

It will be seen, then, that there was a visionary quality in Mark Twain's adventures with money, and only when this element appeared to stimulate his imagination was he greatly interested. Howells was, therefore, perfectly justified when he wrote, "He was never a man who cared anything about money except as a dream, and he wanted more and more of it to fill out the spaces of this dream." And this is why I said, at the beginning of this book, that Mark Twain appeared as Colonel Sellers. In *Roughing It* he tells of the pipe dreams that came to him when, in his mining days, he and Calvin Higbie once thought that they had struck it rich. The account is not factual, but Higbie himself gives us all the collaboration we need so far as Mark's temperament is concerned: "He was determined . . . to have a marble mansion several stories high with ample grounds, fine horses and carriages, and a pack of hounds. He was very emphatic about the hounds, and a steam yacht he could steer himself. We talked all night long in this strain."

Paine commented on the Sellers elements in Mark Twain's attitude toward the Paige typesetter. "He immediately began to calculate the number of millions he would be worth presently when the machine was completed and announced to the waiting world. He covered pages with figures that never ran short of millions, and frequently approached the billion mark. Colonel Sellers in his happiest moments never dreamed more lavishly. He obtained a list of all the newspapers in the United States and in Europe, and he counted up the machines that would be required by each." The Mergenthaler machine made those millions, and at one time Mark Twain could have had a half-interest in the Mergenthaler machine by merging his interests with those of its sponsors; he came that close.[4] In any event, the typesetter was not the boldest of his ideas, but only the most disastrous; in 1885 he asked Leland Stanford about the possibility of building a railroad from Constantinople to the Persian Gulf. The same Sellers-quality entered into his publishing schemes, especially the bad ones, like the life of the Pope, which was published in serene disregard of the fairly self-evident fact that the Irish immigrants who, in those days, made up the bulk of the Church in America, did not buy books. Once, with Howells, he projected a fearful thing to be known as "Memorable Murders," and, writes his partner in crime,

[4] Tom Burnam, "Mark Twain and the Paige Typesetter: A Background for Despair," *Western Humanities Review*, Vol. VI (1951–52), 29–36, is right in seeing poetry and not merely greed of gold in Mark Twain's adventures with the Paige machine, though I think he becomes too metaphysical in his interpretation of it. I cannot agree that "Twain did not want the typesetter to be finished and turned over to the capitalists he was ostensibly seeking; for in so doing he would be forced out of the world of mechanics which he loved because it enabled him to create, as any artist creates, his own microcosm, his own order out of chaos." This may have been true of Paige, but not, I am sure, of Mark Twain. It was Paige who was forever tearing the machine apart to "perfect" something or other, just when it seemed ready to be marketed. On one occasion he did this just when the New York *Herald* was on the point of accepting it. It must be admitted that Mark showed the patience of a saint in permitting Paige to do these things, but his financial and mechanical ignorance and inexperience are more convincing explanations of his conduct than any of the considerations advanced by Mr. Burnam.

"by the time we reached Boston we were rolling in wealth so deep that we could hardly walk home."

But perhaps the Sellers-quality comes out best in his late interest in the carpet-pattern machine of the great Polish inventor, Jan Sczezepanik. Here, if anywhere, he shows himself completely incorrigible, for the burned child dreads the fire, and he is just recovering from the Paige disaster. Yet he is off again, asking an option on world rights and covering pages with figures summing up the enormous profits that are to accrue. Fortunately Rogers was about to prick the bubble of his enthusiasm, or he might, within the limitations of his means, have gone through the Paige fiasco all over again.

It can hardly be necessary to point out that at no time did the visionary aspect of Mark Twain's schemes interfere with a most scrupulous honesty on his part. What he had promised he performed to the letter. When Frank Harris praised Bret Harte, Mark denounced him and told a story about how he had cheated his publishers. "I told the publishers," he said, "that they ought to have put him in prison. A man should be honest, above everything." Harris complained that writers were underpaid anyway, but Mark Twain was unmoved. They did not need to write unless they wanted to, he argued; "they could make shoes or do manual labor of some kind." But the best story in this connection relates to the occasion when a New York paper offered to pay $100 to any charity he might name in return for a fifteen-minute interview on a subject he did not wish to discuss. "The refusal worried him during the rest of the afternoon," says S. J. Woolf, who was in the house that day, "and before I left he gave me a note to mail to a certain hospital, enclosing a check as contribution to its 'conscience fund.'"

CHAPTER EIGHT: *Literature and Love*

I

SAMUEL L. CLEMENS WAS ONE OF THOSE favored men who taste all the sweets of love with none of its bitter cruelties. There was in his life no Dark Flower, as Galsworthy calls it, no night-blooming cereus, permeating his imagination with strange, exotic odors, inflaming his imagination, maddening his senses, so that at last a man cannot tell which predominates—the pleasure or the pain. "Would I had never seen her!" cries Antony. But the wise Enobarbus replies, "O, sir, you had then left unseen a wonderful piece of work, which not to have been blest withal would have discredited your travel." That cry finds no echo in the life of Mark Twain, nor did he ever have cause to share the grief of the Wife of Bath, as expressed in the words which, as John Livinston Lowes once remarked, sum up "half the passion and pain of the world":

Allas! allas! that evere love was synne!

It was not "synne" for him. He grew a White Rose in his own garden, and his feet were never tempted beyond the happy pale.

But he was thirty-four when he married, and he certainly did not need to wait until then to learn that there are two kinds of people in the world. There were Laura Hawkins (who became Becky Thatcher) and others from Hannibal days on,[1] but there is no evidence of any serious entanglement. He admired girls everywhere he went; even on Jackass Hill there were the Carrington youngsters, who were nicknamed the "Chapparral Quails." Indeed, he never ceased to do this. On the Cable tour in the eighties, he wrote Livy about having gone tobogganing with college girls at Toronto, and when he took Susy to college in 1890, he had the time of his life dancing with the Bryn Mawr girls. But it seems always to have been youth and innocence that attracted him. In his Nevada days they used to make fun of him because he went out with a little girl in short dresses; he said she would grow up soon enough to suit him. But one night he forgot his obligation to her, and at the end of the evening he and her parents found her, in her finery, weeping upon her bed. She accepted his apologies but would never go out with him again. If any of Mark's early flames left a lasting impression, it must have been Laura Dake. Twenty-seven years after parting from her, he noted the anniversary in his notebook, and, though he had known her only three days, between boats in New Orleans, he could still sufficiently identify her to himself as "L."

Mississippi steamboats and Western mining camps were prostitute-ridden in Mark Twain's time; here, one would think, he could hardly have avoided contact with a less innocent kind of girl. In 1949 Dixon Wecter placed his authority behind the view that "almost incredible as it appears, the known facts suggest that he entered into marriage as a virgin of thirty-four."[2] Though this opinion has been greeted in some quarters with incredulity, and even with something approaching indignation, Wecter may well have been right, for Mark Twain was always, under his "bark," an extremely fastidious man; even Howells noted that, sympathetic as he was, he never put his hands on anybody. Alexander Jones[3]

---

[1] See Dixon Wecter, *Sam Clemens of Hannibal*, 181–85.
[2] *The Love Letters of Mark Twain*, 3–4.
[3] "Mark Twain and Sexuality," *PMLA*, Vol. LXXI (1956), 595–616.

and Louis J. Budd[4] have usefully mustered most of the considerations which might be urged in rebuttal of Wecter's view, but except for Jones's citation of one statement in the *Notebook*—"The course of free love never runs smooth. I suppose we have all tried it."—there is nothing that is worth much as evidence. When Jane Clemens visited her son on the river in 1860, she "was delighted with her trip, but she was disgusted with the girls for allowing me to embrace and kiss them—and she was horrified at the Schottische as performed by Miss Castle and myself." One suspects that he was teasing "Ma." He himself was teased for his drinking in the West, as we have seen, but not for running after women,[5] and it is difficult to believe that this angle would not have been explored if he had been vulnerable. The statement that he was once enamored of Ina Coolbrith, though several times made, seems without foundation, and I get the impression that though Adah Isaacs Menken (then the wife of Orpheus C. Kerr) interested him in Virginia City, he was also very wary of her. It is true that the Langdons were considerably agitated about Mark Twain's Western past when he became Livy's suitor, but from the correspondence we have, it is impossible to tell what any of the parties involved thought they were talking about. This was the one period of his life when Mark was trying to work up an orthodox Christian conviction of sin—"I now claim that I am a Christian"—and, even aside from this consideration, his devilish conscience was never, at any period, able to make a reasonable distinction between a crime and a peccadillo. Yet even Mark wrote his prospective father-in-law, "I think that much of my conduct on the Pacific Coast was not of a character to recommend me to the respectful regard of a high eastern civilization, but it was not considered blameworthy there, perhaps." Coming from a man with his genius

[4] "Mark Twain Plays the Bachelor," *Western Humanities Review*, Vol. XI (1957), 157–67.

[5] There is one exception. Serious charges against Mark Twain are implied by Albert S. Evans ("Fitz Smythe"), his journalistic opponent in San Francisco days, but, for reasons too complicated to discuss here, it is doubtful that any weight should be given to this. See H. N. Smith and Frederick Anderson, eds., *Mark Twain: San Francisco Correspondent*, 38–40, noting also the editors' comments.

as a self-tormentor, and with what he had at stake at the time, this does not sound like the voice of a heavily burdened conscience.

Confronting sexual irregularity in literature or in life (he uses it in his own fiction even less than Howells did), Mark Twain can generally be counted upon for the "correct" reaction, and this is the more interesting because he is generally so uninterested in correctness in other aspects. Pompeiian frescoes shocked him, and his description of Titian's *Venus Reposing* in *A Tramp Abroad* is almost hysterical. When he witnesses the can-can, he places his hands before his face, "for very shame"; he is almost equally shocked by the hula-hula. He gets a good deal of fun, for literary purposes at least, out of the girls who bathed naked in Hawaii, and I am sure he enjoyed seeing them, but he is distressed over the low sexual standards which prevailed there in the old days, and he praises the missionaries for helping to raise them. When he speaks of Boccaccio in his *Autobiography*, he cannot resist the opportunity to take a fling at his "improper tales," and the Yankee is much impressed by the improprieties of Elizabethan and eighteenth-century literature. He criticizes Swift, Zola, and Flaubert on this same score, and he refused to allow Kemble to illustrate the camp-meeting scenes in *Huckleberry Finn*. Toward Lancelot and Guinevere, Petrarch and Laura, and Abelard and Heloise, he is heavily moralistic, always judging the man much more severely than the woman.[6] In *Life on the Mississippi*, he uses the pious formula "they sinned" to indicate sexual intercourse outside of marriage. In one letter, he seems to accept masturbation as natural and harmless in youth, but when he is discussing Rousseau, it becomes shameful. Venereal diseases are "loathesome diseases." His Fenimore Cooper paper accepts, as one of the axioms of criticism, the author's obligation to discourage vice and inculcate virtue. In an early essay, he speaks of the Byron scandal as not susceptible of burlesque, "because the central feature of it, incest, was a 'situation' so tremendous and so imposing that the happiest available resources of burlesque seemed tame and cheap in its presence.

[6] In the French historian Michelet, Mark Twain once found the doubtful statement that Joan of Arc never menstruated. In the margin he wrote this touching and innocent comment: "The higher life absorbed her & suppressed her physical (sexual) development."

Burlesque could invent nothing to transcend incest, except by enlisting two crimes, neither of which is mentioned among women and children, and one of which is only mentioned in rare books of the law, and there as 'the crime without a name'—a term with a shudder in it."[7] DeVoto thinks the fancy-women helped to "civilize" the frontier, but Mark never sentimentalized either prostitutes or criminals; neither did he take up a scornful or "holier-than-thou" attitude toward them. When he got to New York as a young man, he was impressed by the effort that the Midnight Mission was making to reclaim girls of the street, and the night he was thrown into contact with some of these girls in jail, he seems to have treated them with genuine humanity and consideration, but he was so horrified by their moral and spiritual condition that in his heart he thought they would be better off dead. When Lecky comments on the success of the church in guarding the chastity of female slaves, Mark Twain notes in the margin that this is better than the Protestant church of America was able to do in the South. He was delighted when he reached Hartford to find that unescorted ladies could attend evening concerts there with perfect propriety and that girls could walk on the streets after dark in perfect safety. Mark Twain himself once presided over a "shotgun wedding" involving one of his servant-girls, which seems to have turned out well enough, though the girl in question was no more pregnant than he was. He wrote a story about this incident and read it to the Twichells, offending Harmony, who was too polite to tell him, with the result that he read it again, next day, to a literary society whose members shared her reaction. He was not superior or uncomprehending toward Gorky, when the latter's American mission was blasted by the untimely revelation that he was traveling with a lady who was not legally his wife, but there was no doubt in his mind that Gorky's usefulness to the cause was, for the time being, ended.

[7] If Paul Baender is right in identifying certain Buffalo *Express* editorials as the work of Mark Twain, he was himself capable of treating incest both seriously and humorously. This, however, is not surprising, nor does it indicate any basic frivolity toward moral problems. Mark Twain sometimes wrote humorously of his relations with his wife, but nobody supposes that therefore he was not serious in his love and admiration for her. See "Mark Twain and the Byron Scandal," *American Literature*, Vol. XXX (1958–59), 467–85.

In a more formal way, Mark Twain's puritanism—and his respect for women—come out in two very specialized articles. The first, and much the more important, is "In Defence of Harriet Shelley," which was occasioned by Edward Dowden's attempt to whitewash the poet at the expense of his first wife. "The charge insinuated by these odious slanders is one of the most difficult of all offenses to prove; it is also one which no man has a right to mention even in a whisper about any woman, living or dead, unless he knows it to be true, and not even then unless he can also *prove* it to be true." "In Defence of Harriet Shelley" is so hot that it still burns the paper on which it is printed; it is also just about the best example we have of Mark Twain's ability to sift and weigh historical evidence. But it will not do to dismiss it as an amusing piece of invective or a touching example of Mark Twain's "Southern chivalry," for the late Professor Newman Ivey White, than whom there is no higher authority on Shelley, could find no fault in Mark's reasoning.

The other item is an explosive little piece, "Why Not Abolish It?" which appeared without fanfare in *Harper's Weekly* in 1903 and has never been reprinted from it. The "it" that Mark proposes to abolish is the word "consent" in its legal sense in seduction cases. "Consent" is not adduced as a palliating circumstance in connection with murder or arson; why should it appear here? "I should say simply that commerce *with a spinster*, of whatever age or condition, should be punished by two years of solitary confinement or five years at hard labor; and let the man take his choice." Himself he would prefer an even heavier penalty; the monster ought, reasonably, to be flayed alive, but he knows that that is more than could be reasonably hoped for. No more savage piece of sexual puritanism has ever found its way into print.

II

But what, then, of Mark Twain's bawdry—the published 1601 and such unpublished items as the speech on "The Science of Onanism" and the Yale Library verses on the subject of lost virility? What of the testimony of Howells, Robert Underwood Johnson, and others concerning the Rabelaisianism of his conversation. "He had," wrote Howells, "the Southwestern, the Lincolnian, the Elizabethan breadth of parlance, which I suppose one ought not to call coarse without calling one's self prudish; and I was often hiding away in discreet holes and corners the letters in which he had loosed his bold fancy to stoop on rank suggestion; I could not bear to burn them, and I could not, after the first reading, quite bear to look at them."

If Howells received such letters, he must finally have burned them, for the whole Mark Twain–Howells extant correspondence has now been published, and while there are some few indelicacies included, I doubt that any reader has been shocked. The most impure suggestion in Mark Twain's published writings is in an 1874 speech on "Cats and Candy," where, speaking of Jim Wolfe, he remarks, "He and I slept together—virtuously." By all means the funniest is in a *Golden Era* sketch of 1866, where a mother is made to say, "You Sal, you hussy, git up f'm thar this minit, and take some exercise! for the land's sake, ain't you got no sense at all?—settin' thar on that cold rock and you jes' ben married last night, and your pores all open!"

This is much funnier than anything in 1601, though, in saying so, I realize that I am again running the risk of offending Mr. Franklin J. Meine, who apparently considers 1601 the greatest thing in all literature. I ran afoul of Mr. Meine in my first edition by calling 1601, not censoriously but descriptively, the most famous piece of pornography in American literature. Mr. Meine insists that it is not pornographic, but he does not say what it is.[8] There are, nevertheless, touches of pornography in it, but, being always ready to receive instruction from experts, I am quite willing to admit, after twenty-five years, that it is more scatological than pornographic, and I am reliably informed that the same is, in general, true of the other pieces. As to why, being, as nobody doubts he was, a "moral" man, Mark Twain found it necessary to write such things, I am not sure that any explanation can completely cover the case, but, by the same token, I am not sure that any explanation is necessary. The suppression theory will not get us far, except as every man who lives in society is, in a sense, suffer-

[8] See his edition of 1601, 27–28.

ing from sexual suppression; in any event, this has nothing to do specifically with the conventions of the Gilded Age. Chaucer was not a "Victorian American," but, so far as bawdry is concerned, Chaucer and Mark Twain would have understood each other very well. And, for that matter, "Victorian American" males characteristically relished their bawdry on stag occasions, quite as much —perhaps even more—than their descendants do today. "Things called indecent or obscene," says Santayana, "are inextricably woven into the texture of human existence; there can be no completely honest comedy without them." And Mark Twain was a humorist.

But did Mark Twain ever express anti-puritan or non-puritan ideas in sexual matters, not humorously but seriously? Yes, for Mark Twain was almost consistently inconsistent, and there are few subjects upon which he cannot be heard on both sides. In his *Notebook* he makes fun of man's inconsistency in leaving out of his idea of heaven, sexual intercourse, the thing he cares most for on earth. Among his unpublished papers there is a long discussion of copulation, dwelling upon the delight which women find in it. In 1884 he condoned the Cleveland scandal. "To see grown men, apparently in their right mind, seriously arguing against a bachelor's fitness for President because he has had private intercourse with a consenting widow! . . . *Isn't* human nature the most consummate sham & lie that was ever invented?" Once, commenting on a piece by Bernard Shaw, he declared that "it is not immoral to create the human species—with or without ceremony; nature intended exactly these things." And, most startling of all, he once argued (in his *Notebook*) that "clean women subject to rigid inspection" ought to be provided for British soldiers in India.

Yet the anti-puritanism of these passages is weakened by their context, and the contrast between what he says here and what he has previously said in other connections is less sharp than it might seem. He wanted Cleveland to be elected because he opposed Blaine for immoralities of a non-sexual character, much more likely to affect his performance in the White House adversely than Cleveland's fault could possibly affect his. Context is particularly important in the Shaw passage;[9] Mark Twain is not saying that fornication is "right"; for the moment, he has simply realized the immoral (or non-moral) character of life itself. And the most shocking piece of all—the one about the British army—is actually the one in which he comes closest to the piece on Harriet Shelley and to "Why Not Abolish It?" What is happening as things now are, is that "those 70,000 young men go home and marry fresh young English girls and transmit a heritage of disease to their children and grandchildren." Again, it was not a question of whether it was right for them to fornicate. There was no need to discuss that. It was simply that, not being a babe in the woods, he knew that most of them *would* fornicate. Once more, he was out to protect women and girls. For all that, I can imagine that, in another mood, Mark Twain might have been greatly shocked by his own suggestion, or would have been, in any event, if somebody else had made it.

Mark Twain also enjoyed nakedness, and this, like so much else about him, goes back to his youth in what some of his interpreters think was a painfully prudish environment. Shame and modesty did not trouble Hannibal boys when they were off by themselves together, or, as Huck Finn puts it, "Clothes is well enough in school, and in towns, and at balls, too, but they ain't no sense in them where there ain't no civilization nor other kinds of bothers and fussiness around." Huck and Jim wear no clothes on the raft—"we was always naked, day and night, whenever the mosquitoes would let us—the new clothes Buck's folks made for me was too good to be comfortable, and besides I didn't go much on clothes, nohow." Not even Thomas Hart Benton has illustrated the book correctly from this point of view.

But it is not merely that clothes are uncomfortable. Tom Sawyer and his comrades clearly recognize the play function of nakedness:

> After breakfast they went whooping and prancing out on the bar, and chased each other round and round, shedding clothes as they went, until they were naked, and then continued to frolic far away up the shoal water of the bar, against the stiff current, which

[9] Paine, *Mark Twain: A Biography*, III, 1335.

later tripped their legs from under them from time to time, and
greatly increased the fun. . . . When they were well exhausted, they
would run out and sprawl on the hot, dry sand. . . . Finally it occurred to them that their naked skin represented flesh-colored
"tights" very fairly; so they drew a ring in the sand and had a circus.

Another day, they decided to play Indian:

so it was not long before they were stripped, and striped from head
to heel with black mud, like so many zebras—all of them chiefs, of
course—and then they went tearing through the woods to attack
an English settlement.

That was boyhood. Adult America could not give Mark Twain
much in the way of nakedness—not much, that is, beyond the
privilege of denouncing the obscene practice of placing fig-leaves
over the genitalia of works of sculpture. "The statue that advertises its modesty with a fig-leaf brings its modesty under sus-
picion." But he traveled, and his travels carried him into benighted
countries, where the simple natives had not yet learned that God
is indecent. This strange point of view he encountered in the
Hawaiian Islands, where the children ran about as God made
them, "clothed in nothing but sunshine—a very neat fitting and
picturesque apparel indeed." On the astonished eyes of the "Innocents" more startling scenes sometimes burst: "A girl apparently
thirteen years of age came along the great thoroughfare dressed
like Eve before the fall"—nor was it uncommon to come upon
men bathing "stark-naked," in full view of the road, and "making
no attempt at concealment." But "an hour's acquaintance with
this cheerful custom reconciled the pilgrims to it, and then it
ceased to occasion remark." In Germany he saw naked children
again, and in Colombo, when he was "following the equator," he
commented particularly on one little boy who "had nothing on
but a twine string round his waist, but in my memory the frank
honesty of his costume still stands out in pleasant contrast with
the odious flummery in which the little Sunday School dowdies
were masquerading."

Alexander Jones seems to regard Mark Twain's interest in

nakedness as evidence of his sexuality. To me, on the other hand, he seems to have succeeded as well as any post-Edenic man can be expected to succeed in differentiating between innocent naked-ness and guilty nakedness, that is between unveiling which is free of shame because it is free of guilt and that which is undertaken deliberately, as in *The Black Crook* and other stage spectacles which shocked Mark Twain when he went to New York, for the purpose of rousing lust, or which is associated with a desire to cor-rupt. And since bare bodies were much less frequently seen then than they are now, this was a greater achievement for Mark Twain than it would be for us. He was never a nudist, even in the limited degree to which Whitman and Benjamin Franklin were nudists, but there are two notes among his memoranda which go as far as any nudist could ask:

MODESTY ANTEDATES CLOTHES
& will be resumed when clothes are no more.

MODESTY DIED
when clothes were born.

III

As has already been noted, Sam Clemens fell in love with Olivia Langdon even before they met. Many young men have fallen in love with a picture; fewer have found the original so alluring as they had hoped; fewer still have been able to write as Mark Twain did, late in life: "It is forty years ago. From that day to this she has never been out of my mind."

He was full of reverence and tenderness for her, in the first precious days of their engagement. "These several times today this face has amazed me with its sweetness and I have felt so thank-ful that God has given into my charge the dear office of chasing the shadows away and coaxing the sunshine to play about it al-ways." She seems altogether too good for him, too pure for the world which they both inhabit. "Oh, Livy darling, I could just worship that picture, it is so beautiful . . . . But its beauty startles me—it somehow makes me afraid. It makes me feel a sort of awe

—and affects me like a superstition. For it is more than human, Livy—it is an angel-beauty—something not of earth—something above the earth and its grossness."

This was, it may be said, a sentimental engagement mood. But Mark Twain never felt otherwise to the end of his life. He had found the pearl of great price, and all the honors and triumphs that life was to bring him were dust in comparison. The beautiful letter he wrote his wife on her thirtieth birthday, the article he sent to *The Christian Union*, without permitting her to see it, "to save it from getting edited into the stove," his public tribute to her in the sixty-seventh birthday speech—all these things speak with a single voice. He had loved quickly, eagerly, boyishly, but it was no mere "love of the eyes" that had enthralled him. "Love," he wrote in one of his notebooks, "seems the swiftest but is the slowest of all growths. No man and woman really know what perfect love is until they have been married a quarter of a century." And the Yankee's love for Sandy is clearly autobiographical: "People talk about beautiful friendships between two persons of the same sex. What is the best of that sort, as compared with the friendship of man and wife, where the best impulses and highest ideals of both are the same? There is no place for comparison between the two friendships; the one is earthly, the other divine."[10]

She brought him great happiness, and, in the end, she brought him great pain, for, as we all know, the only way to avoid pain is never to care for anyone. "Last night at 9.20 I entered Mrs. Clemens's room to say the usual goodnight—and she was dead— tho' no one knew it. . . . I bent over and looked in her face, and I think I spoke—I was surprised and troubled that she did not notice me. Then we understood, and our hearts broke. How poor we are to-day!" So, with quiet dignity, he announces her death to

10 The marriage of the Clemenses was a complete union of body, mind, and spirit. I cannot at all agree with Alexander E. Jones that Mark Twain had a sense of guilt in connection with sex, even in his relations with Livy. There is not the slightest reason for supposing that either party ever felt anything of the kind. If any man ever learned that marriage is both a physical and a spiritual relationship, the two elements being blended in a perfect whole which excludes all thought of shame, that man was Mark Twain. Mrs. Clemens's health being what it was, however, there must have been many periods when a physical relationship between them was impossible.

Howells. And he adds simply, "I am tired and old; I wish I were with Livy."

He never recovered. When he went to Washington with Paine, to speak for the copyright bill, "he was light-spirited and gay; but recalling Mrs. Clemens saddened him, perhaps, for he was silent as we drove to the hotel, and after he was in bed, he said with a weary despair which even the words do not convey: 'If I had been there a minute earlier, it is possible—it is possible that she might have died in my arms. Sometimes I think that perhaps there was an instant—a single instant—when she realized that she was dying and that I was not there." And sadder still is the letter he wrote, two years before his death, to a friend about to be married:

June 5, '08

Dear Father Fitz-Simon,—Marriage—yes, it *is* the supreme felicity of life, I concede it. And it is also the supreme tragedy of life. The deeper the love the surer the tragedy. And the more disconsolating when it comes.

And so I congratulate you. Not perfunctorily, not lukewarmly, but with a fervency and fire that no word in the dictionary is strong enough to convey. And in the same breath and with the same depth of sincerity, I grieve for you. Not for both of you and not for the one that shall go first, but for the one that is fated to be left behind. For that one there is no recompense—For that one no recompense is possible.

There are times—thousands of times—when I can expose the half of my mind, and conceal the other half, but in the matter of the tragedy of marriage I feel too deeply for that, and I have to bleed it all out or shut it all in. And so you must consider what I have been through, and am passing through and be charitable with me.

Make the most of the sunshine! I hope it will last long—ever so long.

I do not really want to be present; yet for friendship's sake and because I honor you so, I would be there if I could.

Most sincerely your friend,
S. L. CLEMENS

157

IV

Such, then, was their marriage, from his point of view. What, now, of hers. She was not a professional writer, and only a few of her letters have been printed, but her attitude is clear. Unlike her husband, she was demonstrative in love, poured out kisses, caresses, and endearments with a prodigality which astonished, delighted, and bewildered him. When J. R. Clemens announced his engagement, she wrote to him: "I feel entirely with Browning when he says, 'Love is best.' Surely it is far and away the best, there is nothing that in the very least approaches it." One day, Clara asked her whether if father died, she would die too. "Unfortunately, no" was her reply. But I don't know that anything is more impressive as revealing her attitude toward her husband than her question when Mark Twain once confessed that, though intellectually he did not believe in hell, emotionally he was still often afraid that he was going there. "Why, Youth," she exclaimed, "who, then, can be saved?"

The judgments of third parties are never worth much where marriage is concerned, but there can be no harm in glancing toward them in passing. Her husband was of the opinion that Mrs. Clemens possessed the most perfect character he had ever come in contact with, and there are others who practically reaffirm this judgment. "She was in a way," wrote Howells, "the loveliest person I have ever seen, the gentlest, the kindest, without a touch of weakness; she united wonderful tact with wonderful truth." After her death, when Mark wrote him how she had kept his letter about Susy in her New Testament, he replied, "You know how it must humiliate a man in his unworthiness to have anything of his so consecrated. She hallowed what she touched, far beyond priests." J. B. Pond accompanied the Clemenses, on the world lecture tour, as far as Victoria, B. C. "The more I see of this lady," he declares, "the greater and more wonderful she appears to me. There are few women who could manage and absolutely rule such a nature as 'Mark's.' She knows the gentle and smooth way over every obstruction he meets, and makes everything lovely."

It is clear that Mrs. Clemens's goodness was not motivated by weakness; she was never one of those distressing persons who are always perfectly good because they lack the spunk to be anything else. Her daughter tells us that she "could blaze out at times if occasion warranted," and Mark Twain himself refers to her as "that turbulent spirit." Absurdly overconscientious as he was, he accused himself, especially during his later years, of having been a bad husband, and in the last talk he had with her, he begged her to forgive him for all the tears he had brought into her life. Every man needs to beg forgiveness of the woman who is so generous as to live with him and put up with him, but Mark Twain was one of the best of husbands. Yet, for all his kindliness, he must have been, in his own way, as difficult a man to live with as was Lincoln. As Mrs. Samossoud puts it:

> I used to marvel at my father's ability to sit at the table and pour out uninterruptedly a flow of words expressing his feelings on matters intimately connected with himself, in the presence often of comparative strangers, who were wide-eyed with interest and surprise. Yet this was but one side of the medal, for he could be forbiddingly reserved and locked away from the most vivacious attempts of visitors to enter his personality ever so tiny a distance. He was a constant surprise in his various moods, which dropped unheralded upon him, creating day or night for those about him by his twinkling eyes or his clouded brows. How he would be affected by this or that no one could ever foresee.

His absent-mindedness and capacity for self-absorption also caused difficulties. He always held himself responsible for the death of his son Langdon, by diphtheria, having carelessly exposed the baby during a sleigh ride on a cold winter day. "I was not qualified for any such responsibility as that. Some one should have gone who had at least the rudiments of a mind." That this really caused Langdon's death is, of course, debatable; it may even be one of the self-incriminating things Mark Twain had a habit of remembering which never happened. But there is also the story of his taking Clara out for a ride in her baby carriage, and then, forgetting his responsibility, releasing the handle suddenly on an incline, so that the carriage ran away from him and spilled the child out by the roadside. These are not helpful things for a husband and father to do, nor can Mrs. Clemens have particularly enjoyed the Sunday morning when, annoyed at finding a button missing from his shirt, he threw shirts, collars, and ties out the bathroom window, decorating the shrubbery with them for the benefit of persons passing on their way to church. Fortunately Mrs. Clemens had a sense of humor, and on this occasion she made no protest whatever, simply lying quietly and peacefully in her bed and repeating all his swear-words in order, as he had uttered them. "Livy," he said, "it would pain me to think that when I swear it sounds like that. You got the words right, Livy, but you don't know the tune."

That he was ever consciously inconsiderate of her, I do not believe. Unconsciously, he must often have been, for, as Katy Leary observes, that is "the way with men—even the best of them." "It was remarkable," writes Mrs. Samossoud, with characteristic frankness and honesty, "that two people like my father and mother, possessing highly sensitive and emotional natures, managed so to live that in my memory *few discords stand out* and those of but a superficial nature." And again she says of her father, "He *almost never* permitted his wrath to rise toward my mother."[11] There is a good deal to be read between the lines of Mrs. Clemens's remark, upon taking to her sickbed upon one occasion, that at least she would not now have to hear quite so much about "the damned human race," and it may be that the otherwise puzzling restrictions upon his intercourse with her when she was ill, other members of the family apparently seeing her much more freely, were due to a feeling that, even with the best intentions, he could not be trusted not to upset her. There is one remarkable letter from her to him during the last years of her life in which she makes an all-out effort to save him from what she obviously considers some of the debilitating aspects of his thinking:

> I am absolutely wretched today on account of your state of mind —your state of intellect. Why don't you let the better side of you work? Your present attitude will do more harm than good. You go

11 Italics mine.

too far, much too far in all you say, & if you write in the same way as you have in this letter people forget the cause for it & remember only the hateful manner in which it was said. *Do* darling change your mental attitude, *try to change* it. The trouble is you don't want to. When you asked me to try mental science I tried it & I keep trying it. Where is the mind that wrote the Prince & P. Jeanne d'Arc, The Yankee &c &c &c. Bring it back! You can if you will— if you wish to. Think of the side I know, the sweet dear, tender side—that I love so. Why not show this more to the world? Does it help the world always to rail at it? There is great & noble work being done, why not sometimes recognize that? Why always dwell on the evil until those who live beside you are crushed to the earth & you seem almost like a monomaniac. Oh! I love you so & wish you would listen & take heed.

V

Mark Twain's attitude toward children in general being what it was, it can only be for the sake of the record that one should find it necessary to set down the fact that he loved his own. While they were small, he frolicked with them, played with them, took part in amateur theatricals, and rejoiced when they abused him and tyrannized over him, and was never bored when they insisted that he tell them very long improvised stories. When Grace King visited the Hartford home, she was surprised and charmed at the freedom the children were permitted, "Susy and Clara taking the lead in their bright, girlish way, expressing themselves boldly, without fear of criticism or correction, making keen remarks on the people they knew or had met." Discipline was entirely in the hands of Mrs. Clemens, who seems to have combined absolute firmness with complete gentleness and justice.[12] Mark Twain himself was far too volatile to be good for anything as a disciplinarian. On the other hand, he was capable of playing tricks on the chil-

[12] In his letter in *The Christian Union*, July 16, 1885 (reprinted in *The Twainian*, N.S. Vol. III, May, 1944, pp. 1-4), Mark Twain said he would not attempt to discipline a child, knowing that his wife was quite capable of handling the matter, while he would only make an ass of himself. Mrs. Clemens spanked when it was necessary, a good, honest spanking, which hurt. But the spanking was never given in anger or temper. There was always a cooling-off period between the promise and its fulfilment. "By that time both parties are calm, and the one is judicial, the other receptive." Before the child left her, reconciliation had always taken place.

dren, as when he got Clara to believe that the calf Jumbo was going to grow up into a pony, and on the other hand, he permitted her to keep squirrels in her room, without the knowledge of her mother, even though they gnawed the woodwork to pieces. Once, when he heard Jean praying for a goat, he rushed out and got her one. When the children were ill, he was nearly beside himself, nor did he shirk his share in nursing them; Mrs. Fields tells one story that might be straight out of the biography of Mrs. McWilliams.[13] It would be difficult to carry solicitude much further than Mark himself carries it in an 1877 letter to J. R. Clemens: "We should all greatly like to make the Richmond excursion Sunday, but Clara has had a fall in the gymnasium and we are afraid to have her go, and so the rest of us will have to stay at home and keep her company."

Susy was undoubtedly his favorite, as how could she help being when she was so much like him? Charming, and gifted even apart from her beautiful voice, she was volatile and impractical in the extreme, and her inability to remain at Bryn Mawr, for homesickness, even through her freshman year, seems as abnormal as her family's refusal to celebrate Christmas and other anniversaries after she had gone.[14] Terrible as Susy's dying was, it was not entirely her father's pessimism which led him to observe that by the time she was twenty-four, such a girl had seen the best of life. Jean, at first much less intense, manifested a "sudden and unaccountable" personality change as early as 1892, though the illness which caused this was not definitely diagnosed as epilepsy until four years later. It is touching to find Mark Twain, on one occasion, giving her the same good advice about her temperament and behavior that we have seen his wife giving him. Perhaps he and

[13] M. A. DeWolfe Howe, ed., *Memories of a Hostess* (Atlantic Monthly Press, 1922), 255.

[14] For Susy's personality, see Caroline T. Harnsberger, *Mark Twain, Family Man*, and *The Love Letters of Mark Twain*, 315–16. If Mrs. Charles M. Andrews was right in her assessment of the situation, it was Susy's separation from her father, rather than her mother, that caused the mischief; see *Mark Twain–Howells Letters*, II, 636. It is possible that Mark Twain overdramatizes the change in the household after Susy's death; the record is not without suggestions of life going on in a normal way. Mark Twain had a great capacity for suffering, but he also showed an admirable ability to recover from the blows life dealt him.

Jean came closest to each other in Stormfield days, and in "The Death of Jean" he made a record of their love for each other which all the world may read—and has read. The middle daughter, Clara, had some of her father's temperament, too, the first two syllables of it at least—and he loved her for it: "a very dear little ash-cat, but has claws." After she had grown up, there was a good deal of friendly sparring between them; Paine found it "always a delight to see them together when one could be just out of range of the cross-fire." "You must know Clara better," her father once wrote Mrs. Rogers; "she is one of the very finest and completest and most satisfactory characters I have ever met."

In 1886 Clemens wrote Howells of a "thunder-stroke" which had fallen upon him "out of the most unsuspected of skies"; he had "found that all their lives my children have been afraid of me! have stood all their days in uneasy dread of my sharp tongue & uncertain temper." It would be easy to dismiss this as another example of Mark's melodramatic gift for self-accusation. The Clemens children were certainly neither unloved nor inhibited; Clara grown up called him not only a "bad, spitting gray kitten" but "Dearest little Marcus" and "a cunning little man." For all that, he was too mercurial for his children to feel quite at ease with when their mother was not present, and when they were small, they tried to avoid being left alone with him. "I have to go down to breakfast, now," writes Susy, in one letter to Clara, "and I don't enjoy this one bit, altho Papa hasn't stormed yet. Still I feel constrained and he pierces me thru with his eyes as if he were determined to see whether I am embarrassed or not."

Above all, Mark Twain's sense of propriety where his daughters were concerned was such as to make Mrs. Grundy look like a young hussy. The girls were educated at home; when, at fourteen, Clara attempted to attend Hartford Public High School, she found adjustment as difficult, in her own way, as Susy did at Bryn Mawr. They did not even go to Sunday School; Jean could only remember having been to church once—"when Clara was crucified," i.e., christened. In Paris, Clara once flashed the blue card of the S.P.C.A. to stop a driver from beating his horse; one might have expected that her father would have wanted to give her a medal; on the contrary, he was furious because she had made a spectacle of herself. Once he cut the decorations off her hat because he saw some men looking at them, and once, when her mother was away, he literally locked her up in her room to keep her away from an undesirable suitor.[15] And though he was determined that she should be chaperoned till she was married, he would entrust her care, with fine recklessness, to anybody, for though he had no belief whatever in human decency in the abstract, he instinctively trusted many individuals he knew nothing whatever about. All in all, he was a fascinating father, and a passionately loving one, but one could not quite set him up as a model for other fathers to follow.

VI

It is time now to turn to Mrs. Clemens's much-discussed editorship of her husband's work.[16] Of the fact there can be no ques-

[15] See the fantastic letter Clemens wrote Clara after he thought she had been guilty of a social indiscretion, in Harnsberger, *Mark Twain, Family Man*, 140–41, and compare Susy's wonderful addendum on p. 142: "you know that even in *Carmen* when she is drinking healths with the officers in the second act she has her aunts there present as chaperones."

[16] In *The Ordeal of Mark Twain* (1920), Van Wyck Brooks presented Mrs. Clemens as the "simple Delilah" who, allying herself with the wicked forces of Puritanism and capitalism, and aided and abetted by William Dean Howells, enslaved the soul of Mark Twain and broke his courage, made him a humorist instead of the great satirist he was intended to be, plunged him at last into complete pessimism and despair, and thus robbed American literature of its king-figure. Mr. Brooks did not study Mark Twain in this volume; he simply used him as a stick to beat down all the tendencies of which he disapproved in modern American life. That Brooks himself still holds these views seems extremely doubtful; there is no hint of such belief in his *Howells: His Life and World* (Dutton, 1959). Bernard DeVoto made an all-out attack on Brooks in *Mark Twain's America*; in "Mark Twain's Elmira" (*Heroes I Have Known*), Max Eastman showed, out of personal knowledge, that neither the Langdons nor their city were anything like what Mr. Brooks supposed. See, further, DeVoto's article, "Mark Twain and the Genteel Tradition," *Harvard Graduates' Magazine*, Vol. XL (1931–32), 155–63, and two articles by DeLancey Ferguson, "The Case for Mark Twain's Wife," *University of Toronto Quarterly*, Vol. IX (1939), 9–21, and "Huck Finn Aborning," *Colophon*, N.S. Vol. III (1938), 171–80. In 1938, writing in apparently complete ignorance of all Mark Twain criticism, Edgar Lee Masters rehashed, coarsened, and vulgarized the Brooks thesis in the worst book ever written about Mark Twain, and very nearly the worst book ever written about anybody: *Mark Twain, A Portrait*; see my review, *New York Times Book Review*, May 8, 1938. It is unfortunate that, though Mr. Brooks's thesis has never been accepted by anybody who knows anything about

tion. She is "a hard critic to content," and his stuff "generally gets considerable damning with faint praise out of her." It was his habit to read to her in the evening whatever he had written during the day, or to leave his manuscripts beside her bed for her approval. When she is ill, she suggests that he send them to Stedman or to Howells. Later Clara sometimes serves as her deputy. Occasionally she extends her supervision over letters, illustrations, and interviews. Mark once gave Hamlin Garland an interview, but made him promise not to print it without Mrs. Clemens's consent, and this was not forthcoming. "Ever since we have been married," Clemens told F. M. White, "I have been dependent on my wife to go over and revise my manuscript. . . . Not but that I can do the spelling and grammar alone—if I have a spelling-book and a grammar with me—but I don't always know just where to draw the line in matters of taste. Mrs. Clemens has kept a lot of things from getting into print that might have given me a reputation I wouldn't care to have, and that I wouldn't have known any better than to have published."

Mrs. Clemens's influence being indisputable, how did she use it? Against burlesque, against extravagance, against blasphemy and irreverence of all kinds, whether it shocked her personally or whether she merely thought it might prove shocking to others. She believed in her husband's work. In her eyes, it was no mere method of making a living; neither was it a pretty toy with which he amused himself when he had nothing better to do. She believed that he had great gifts, but she also believed that he was quite definitely in need of guidance to bring out the best that was in him. "You see, the thing that gravels her is that I am so persistently glorified as a mere buffoon, as if that entirely covered my case—which she denies with venom." When he was on tour with Pond, she suggested that too many humorous selections in his programs tired an audience with laughter. Accordingly, he worked in a few serious pieces, and Pond thought the result distinctly an improvement. When he wrote a wild piece of burlesque like "The Undertaker's Love Story," and came down happily to

---

Mark Twain, it still maintains a hold over persons who are more interested in theories about literature than they are interested in literature.

read it to the family, under the pathetic delusion that it was good, it was she who saved him from printing it.

His paper on the idea of God, which seems sensible and reverent enough today, she would not permit him to print, and she could not even hear him mention his "Gospel," now known as *What Is Man?*, without a shudder. Paine gives some of her comments on the manuscript of *Following the Equator*, together with Mark Twain's annotations on them.

Page 597. I hate to say it, but it seems to me that you go too minutely into particulars in describing the feats of the aboriginals. I felt it in the boomerang-throwing.

Boomering has been furnished with a special train—that is, I've turned it into "Appendix." Will that answer?

Page 1002. I don't like the "shady-principled cat that has a family in every port."
Then I'll modify him just a little.

Page 1020. 9th line from the top. I think some other word would be better than "stench." You have used that pretty often.
But can't I get it in anywhere? You've knocked it out every time. Out it goes again. And yet "stench" is a noble, good word.

Page 1038. I hate to have your father pictured as lashing a slave boy.
It's out and my father is whitewashed.

Page 1050. 2d line from the bottom. Change breech-clout. It's a word you love and I abominate. I would take that and "offal" out of the language.
You are steadily weakening the English tongue, Livy.

Page 1095. Perhaps you don't care, but whoever told you that the Prince's green stones were rubies told an untruth. They were superb emeralds. Those strings of pearls and emeralds were famous all over Bombay.
All right, I'll make them emeralds, but it loses force. Green rubies is a fresh thing. And besides it was one of the Prince's own staff liars that told me.[17]

VII

But it was not only Mark Twain that Livy edited; she also edited Samuel L. Clemens. Here she possessed a distinct advantage, for if he would submit to her control in the professional aspect of his life, where she was certainly no expert, how much more completely would she be able to dominate him in his social relations, a field where she was so much better versed than he. At home, partly as a result of her early invalidism, she had been treated like a princess. Her lover, coming out of a more austere environment, could not but wonder at it, much as he reverenced her and believed her to deserve such homage. "Her father and mother and brother embrace and pet her constantly, precisely as if she were a sweetheart, instead of a blood relation." Once they were married, she assumed full control of their domestic establishment, and so long as her always delicate health permitted her to be up and about, she managed things completely to her own satisfaction, and without any suggestions or criticisms from her husband. Let us run briefly down the years:

> 1875: I mean to try to go down the Mississippi river in May or June. . . . But there's nothing certain about it—except that at the last moment Livy will put her foot on it.

17 Paul J. Carter, Jr., "Olivia Clemens Edits *Following the Equator*," *American Literature*, Vol. XXX (1958–59), 194–209, studies *all* Mrs. Clemens's comments on this manuscript. He finds that though she sometimes weakened Mark Twain's language, "she was usually more concerned about the accuracy and readability of the manuscript." Furthermore, "the tone of Mark's comments on Livy's suggestions reveals his awareness of the value of her services, while his refusal to accept some of her changes shows that he was not always submissive and certainly never cowed." It is interesting that in the last instance quoted above, Paine bowdlerized Livy's own language, changing "a lie" to "an untruth." Mr. Carter also quotes some coarse and unpleasant expressions which Mrs. Clemens did not question. In "Some Evasions of Censorship in *Following the Equator*," *American Literature*, Vol. XXIX (1957–58), Durant da Ponte suggests that Mark Twain's reference to *lingam* got by because Mrs. Clemens did not understand the phallic meaning of the word, and that her husband "put one over" on her and the public, "taking obvious delight in seeing how far he could go." But since the passages in question specifically identify the *lingam* with "priapus-worship," it seems very doubtful that either Livy or the public can either have been or been expected to be so stupid as Mr. da Ponte assumes. There is, however, a distinct difference between using a technical term to indicate an expression of sexuality in an historic context and using such modern words as "offal" and "breech-clout" to which Mrs. Clemens did object.

1882: I cannot come, because I am not Boss here, and nothing but dynamite can move Mrs. Clemens away from home in the winter season.

1891: I'm going to do whatever the others desire, with leave to change their mind without prejudice, whenever they want to.

1895: According to Mrs. Clemens's present plans—subject to modification, of course—we sail in May.

1901: If Livy will let me I will have my say.

1903: Livy is coming along . . . and, in the matter of superintending everything and everybody has resumed business at the old stand.

It never occurred to him that he could have any life apart from her. "This is a secret," he writes Howells, "to be known to nobody but you." And he immediately adds: "(of course I comprehend that Mrs. Howells is part of you)."

He tells us, generally and in detail, just how she handled her problems:

I was always heedless. I was born heedless, and therefore I was constantly, and quite unconsciously, committing breaches of the minor proprieties, which brought upon me humiliations which ought to have humiliated me, but didn't, because I didn't know anything had happened. But Livy knew; and so the humiliations fell to her share, poor child, who had not earned them and did not deserve them. She always said I was the most difficult child she had. She was very sensitive about me. It distressed her to see me do heedless things, which could bring me under criticism, and so she was always watchful and alert to protect me from the kind of transgressions which I have been speaking of.

They visit the Howellses, and when they get home again, she enumerates for him carefully all the errors he has made:

I "caught it" for letting Mrs. Howells bother and bother about her coffee when it was "a good deal better than we get at home." I "caught it" for interrupting Mrs. C. at the last moment and losing her the opportunity to urge you not to forget to send her that MS when the printers are done with it. I "caught it" once more for personating that drunken Col. James. I "caught it" for mentioning that Mr. Longfellow's picture was slightly damaged; and when . . . I confessed, shamefacedly, that I had privately suggested to you that we hadn't any *frames*, and that if you wouldn't mind hinting to Mr. Houghton, &c., &c., &c., the Madam was simply speechless. . . .

When he was in New York without her, trying to avoid his financial crash, she wrote from Paris, urging him not to go out too much and not to be rude to Mr. Rogers. "You must not think I am ever rude with Mr. Rogers," he writes back without a trace of resentment, "I am not. He is not common clay, but fine—fine and delicate—and that sort do not call out the coarsenesses that are in my sort." As soon as they were old enough, the children seem to have assisted Mrs. Clemens. Susy once told Henry Fisher that "Pa . . . was an awful man before Mamma took him in hand and married him." The children had a name for the address she would give him after a dinner party—"dusting off papa," they called it— and they helped her with a series of signals devised at Mark Twain's own suggestion, so that they might inform him at any point just what particular crime he then happened to be committing.

VIII

It amused Mark Twain upon occasion to describe his wife as a fearsome Amazonian virago. "George was the first person she stumbled on in the hall, so she took it out of George. I was glad of that, because it saved the babies." And again: "My wife was afraid to write you—so I said with simplicity, 'I will give you the language—and ideas.' Through the infinite grace of God there has not been such another insurrection in the family before as followed this."

The point of such statements was their complete absurdity. (Howells was fond of making similar jokes about his gentle invalid wife.) Mark Twain's trusted correspondents understood this, and enjoyed the fun. Unfortunately his erudite critics have not always understood.

Mrs. Clemens understood her husband and had the gift of making him feel that all the suggestions she made were for his good. Nothing could be further from the truth than to imagine that she made Mark Twain live in an atmosphere of nagging. Her love was the greatest blessing of her husband's life; her displeasure was the thing he wanted primarily to avoid. "In her mouth," he writes, "that word 'disapprove' was as blighting and withering and devastating as another person's damn." She gives him a letter to mail to Mrs. Howells. She ought to have known better, for of course he mislays it. But he remembers its contents; so he writes to Mrs. Howells himself. She must not tell Livy what happened, but "just answer her the same as if you had got it."

Mrs. Clemens believed in freedom of thought and expression even for husbands. As Katy Leary records:

> He'd say hard, severe things about religion, and Mrs. Clemens, although she hated to hear him talk that way, said she'd made up her mind when they first married, that her husband was going to be *free* to *say* anything and everything that he wanted to—no matter what it was; that he wasn't ever going to dread her criticizing him—there was never going to be any "curtain lectures" or nothing like that; that his home was going to be a place where he could say and do what he wanted. It struck me as kind of wonderful for her to think all that out when she was just a young wife. It showed how much she loved him and what a lot of common sense she had and how she never believed in interfering with other people's rights—even if they was her husband's.

Publishing that kind of thing was different; when she acted as a restraining influence here, she felt that she was protecting her husband as well as the public. Nobody doubts that Mark Twain needed guidance. Often, when Mrs. Clemens seems to dominate, she is only doing what needs to be done, what, to be sure, the husband, not the wife, ought to do; only Mark Twain would never have done it. He speaks of "her plans" in a letter to Mrs. Howells, "hers, mind you, for I never have anything quite so definite as a plan." From our point of view (which is of course irrelevant), of course Mrs. Clemens sometimes overstressed the importance of the conventionalities. But no blame attaches to her for seeking to discipline and to regularize Mark Twain. If such regulation is subversive of genius and destroys it, then genius ought always to live unwed.

Of course again, he was sometimes annoyed or evasive. Once he developed a wild fantasy of which she did not approve. Himself he thought it entirely too good to lose; so he laboriously translated it into German, with the idea of printing it without her knowledge, but his conscience (or his final realization that the thing was not worth printing, or impossible to print) got the better of him, and the work never appeared. On one occasion at least, he exercised uncommon tact of his own: "When I started to write this note my wife came up and stood looking over my shoulder. Women always want to know what is going on. Said she: 'Should not that read in the third person?' I conceded that it should, put aside what I was writing, and commenced over again. That seemed to satisfy her, and so she sat down and let me proceed. I then—finished my first note—and so sent what I intended." I doubt that he did such things very often, though he must have written a good deal, first and last, that he knew she would not approve of. Once, at the home of Mr. and Mrs. James T. Fields, he spoke of the autobiography he intended to write. "His wife," writes Mrs. Fields, "laughingly said she should look it over and leave out objectionable passages. 'No,' he said, very earnestly, almost sternly, '*you* are not to edit it—it is to appear as it is written, with the whole tale told as truly as I can tell it." And as for *What Is Man?* her influence kept him from printing it during her lifetime, but the force of her disapproval did not modify his opinion of it, and he seems to have talked it freely.

Generally, however, he encouraged her. "Do you know, Sue," he once remarked to her sister, "whenever I have failed to follow the advice of Livy to change this or that sentence or eliminate a page, I have always come to regret it, because in the end my better taste in thoughts and their expression rises up and says: 'You should have done as she said; she was right.' " Even in matters of style, he thought her nearly infallible. "I am notorious," he writes her, "but you are great—that is the difference between us. . . . You had a sentence in your letter that all the culture and all the genius and all the practice in the world could not improve. It was admirable." He even seems to have been anxious that she should not overlook anything. When he read *Tom Sawyer* to her, she made no objection to Huck's "they comb me all to hell." Neither did Howells when he read it. Nevertheless it worried Mark Twain himself, and so we find him writing to Howells to ask him whether he thinks it had better come out.

At Quarry Farm, Mrs. Clemens would sit on the porch, pencil in hand, reading aloud from her husband's manuscripts, and whenever she came to "a particularly satisfactory passage," she would strike it out. Mark Twain's humor, which spared nothing and nobody else, could not always spare his editor either. Aided and abetted by the children, he often "interlarded remarks of a studied and felicitously atrocious character purposely to . . . see the pencil do its fatal work. I often joined my supplications to the children's for mercy, and strung the argument out and pretended to be in earnest. They were deceived, and so was their mother. It was three against one, and most unfair. But it was very delightful, and I could not resist the temptation. Now and then we gained the victory and there was much rejoicing. Then I privately struck the passage out myself."

"Then I privately struck the passage out myself." We have already seen how he behaved about Huck's "they combed me all to hell." This—and the publishing mores of the time—is the justification for Mrs. Clemens, and Howells, and the other persons, clear back to Mrs. Fairbanks and Joe Goodman, to whom Mark Twain turned when, for one reason or another, Livy or Howells could not function. Criticism of Howells has been quite as unfair as criticism of Mrs. Clemens herself; he was, in some aspects, less prudish and proper than Mark Twain himself. If Livy had not edited Mark Twain, his publishers and editors would have done so, would, indeed, have been compelled to do so. Compare the book *Huckleberry Finn* with the serialized version in *The*

Century Magazine, and you will perceive that compared to the enlightened Richard Watson Gilder, Mrs. Clemens was a liberal editor indeed.[18]

Even when we come to the more disputed questions, it is still possible to make a very strong case for Mrs. Clemens. She sensed the merit of *The Mysterious Stranger,* but she feared its influence. "It is perfectly horrible," she said — "and perfectly beautiful!" Concerning *What Is Man?* there can be no question at all. For Olivia Langdon, Mark Twain was not primarily the Great American Writer; he was the man she loved, and this is quite what he ought to have been. And in this instance she was abundantly justified by the effect the work had upon its creator. "Since I wrote my Bible (last year)—which Mrs. Clemens loathes, and shudders over, and will not listen to the last half nor allow me to print any part of it, Man is not to me the respect-worthy person he was before; and so I have lost my pride in him, and can't write gaily nor praisefully about him any more."

If Mark Twain was a suppressed genius, he died without ever finding it out. It is true that Mrs. Clemens did not completely understand his work in all its aspects, did not fully appreciate the superiority of *Huckleberry Finn* to *Joan of Arc* and *The Prince and the Pauper,* for example. But that is no discredit to her. Nobody else in her time did either. Mark Twain himself did not. In the minor, but very necessary, aspects of literary creation, she was of inestimable value to him. In the larger matters, there is not the slightest evidence that her influence was very important. He did attack the missionaries; he did write *Huckleberry Finn;* he did formulate his philosophy of determinism. There was too much vitality in him for him to permit himself to be pushed very far away from his native bent; his qualities and his limitations alike were such that he could never have been the conventional man of letters under any circumstances. What he would have been like had he married another woman, we shall never know. But it would have been very unreasonable to expect any woman of his time to do more for him than Olivia Langdon did. Very few could have done so much.

[18] See Arthur L. Scott, "The *Century Magazine* Edits *Huckleberry Finn,*" *American Literature,* Vol. XXVII (1955–56), 356–62.

CHAPTER NINE: *Charts of Salvation*

I

IN HIS LATER YEARS, Mark Twain loved to think of himself as a philosopher; there was nothing he enjoyed more than to expound what he thought of as the original and highly ingenious world-view he had worked out for himself. A very different world-view had been presented to him in his early days, however, and this was the Christian religion, as interpreted in the form of popular Mid-western Calvinism of the early nineteenth century. To be sure, the Calvinism of Hannibal, Missouri in general and of the Clemens family in particular has often been grossly exaggerated by writers who understand neither Hannibal nor Calvinism very well. Eighteenth-century rationalism was an influence in the community; Mark's father and uncle were unbelievers, and neither Orion nor Pamela grew up as a model of orthodoxy.[1] The Calvinistic pattern was there, nevertheless, and its influence upon

[1] See Alexander E. Jones, "Heterodox Thought in Mark Twain's Hannibal," *Arkansas Historical Quarterly*, Vol. X (1951), 244–57. Cf. Webster, *Mark Twain, Business Man*, 41, 226.

Mark Twain was profound and, as we shall see, in some aspects permanent.

How much of it he "believed" it would be hard to say. As an American, and a provincial midwestern American at that, he knew no "church" in the sense in which many Europeans use that term. What he did know was a succession of clergymen, many of them of the ranting persuasion, not particularly intelligent, each contradicting half of what the others stand for, yet all agreed that this world is a vale of tears, in which God intends us to be thoroughly miserable, and that He will roast us in hell if we manage somehow to evade the miseries which, in His merciful wisdom, he designed for us here. "What a man wants with religion in these breadless times," Mark wrote Orion in 1860, "surpasses my comprehension," and when he met, and became engaged to, Olivia Langdon, and came closest to making a real connection with organized Christianity, he looked back upon his early life as distinctly non-Christian in its character. Yet there are many passages in *The Innocents Abroad* which have obviously been written from the view of a believer, and these do not stand alone among Mark's early writings. As a San Francisco newspaperman, he investigated spiritualistic phenomena from the vantage-point of (as he elsewhere expresses it) a "Brevet Presbyterian," and when he got to New York, he "did" the churches as industriously as he "did" the theaters. He went through the great plant of the American Bible Society and reported on it for *Alta California* as sympathetically as any believer could have done it. "Their highest price Bible, a splendid affair, in morocco, on exquisite paper, beautiful letterpress and gilt edges, is sold at $14—worth $40 if anybody else published it. And they will sell you a complete Bible, well bound in sheep, for forty-five cents. Therefore, why need men be ignorant of the Word?" In "The Cathedral" James Russell Lowell tells us that, though he says his prayers habitually, morning and evening, he has "truly prayed" only three times in his life,

> *Thrice, stirred below my conscious self, have felt*
> *That perfect disenthralment which is God.*

What Mark Twain's early prayer habits may have been I do not know, or whether he ever experienced what Lowell has here described, but I do know that there was at least one occasion when he prayed with passion, and this was when Henry was blown up with the *Pennsylvania.*

He did not, in general, care for Sunday School as a boy, though there was one Methodist Sunday School teacher—"Richmond, the stone mason"—whom he loved for his kindliness. "I was under Mr. Richmond's spiritual care, every now and then, for two or three years." As a man, he was famous for making friends with clergymen. When, as a result of having published the life of Pope Leo XIII, Charles L. Webster had an audience with His Holiness, Mark wrote him that he feared he himself would be tongue-tied "in the presence of the head of two or three hundred millions of subjects, whose empire girdles the globe, & whose commands find obedience somewhere in all the lands & among all the peoples of the earth." The cardinals and archbishops were nearer his "size," and he would like "to swap courtesies" with them "first rate." In 1866 he had written, "I am thick as thieves with the Rev. Stebbins, and I am laying for the Rev. Scudder and the Rev. Dr. Stone. I am running on preachers now, altogether. I find them gay." Even in Nevada he formed a close association with an Episcopalian, Franklin Rising, who died young. Looking back upon their friendship afterwards, he wrote, "I used to try to teach him how to preach in order to get at the better natures of the rough population about him, and he used to try hard to learn—for I knew them and he did not; he was refined and sensitive and not intended for such a people as that." It is interesting, too, that one of his clerical acquaintances in San Francisco should have been Emily Dickinson's friend, Charles Wadsworth.

Late in life, Mark Twain denounced the missionaries in China, but this denunciation was not based upon either religious convictions or their absence. Rightly or wrongly, he thought that missionaries were being used, and were letting themselves be used, as tools of imperialist aggression. It is true that by this time he was doubtful not only of the practicability and the usefulness but even of the morality of the missionary effort to create what he calls "religious deserters" in other lands—"I have no sympathy with such things & take no interest in them," he wrote one correspondent—but this was not the primary consideration. In the early days, in Hawaii, he had been much friendlier to the missionaries—and, surprisingly for one of his background—especially toward the Catholic missionaries, and though it would be an overstatement to say that he never criticized them, he did pay them several warm tributes. "Missionaries have made honest men out of the nation of thieves; instituted marriage; created homes; lifted woman to same rights and privileges enjoyed elsewhere; abolished infanticide; abolished intemperance; diminished licentiousness; given equal laws, whereby chief's power of life and death over his subjects is taken away; in a great measure abolished idolatry; have well educated the people."[2]

One religious, or semi-religious, affiliation Mark Twain did make during his early life: in 1861, in St. Louis, he became a Freemason. At first his interest seems to have been keen. He apparently dropped Masonry when he went west, but he was reinstated in Polar Star Lodge in 1867. Two years later he applied for a demit, and there is no record of his having ever affiliated with any other lodge. Since Masonic beliefs are, or were at this period, distinctly deistic, an interest in Freemasonry on Mark Twain's part might well have drawn him away from a formal church affiliation. This in itself would not, however, explain much, for we should still need to ask what it was that caused him to accept Masonic beliefs and reject his inherited Calvinism.[3]

II

Falling in love is, in a sense, a religious experience, and perhaps we should not be surprised to find Mark Twain sounding the religious note strongly when love comes into his life. The letters

[2] The fullest consideration of this matter is in W. F. Frear, *Mark Twain in Hawaii*, chapter IX.

[3] See Alexander E. Jones, "Mark Twain and Freemasonry," *American Literature*, Vol. XXVI (1954-55), 363-73, a full and authoritative account of what is known about this matter. Professor Jones stresses the resemblances between Mark Twain's thinking and that of Albert Pike, *Morals and Dogma of the Ancient and Accepted Scottish Rite of Freemasonry* (1871).

of the engagement period are distinctly evangelical in thought and expression. "Don't be sad, Livy, we'll model our home after the old home, and make the Spirit of Love lord over all the realm. Smile again, Livy, and be of good heart. Turn towards the Cross and be comforted—I turn with you—What would you more? The peace of God shall rest upon us, and all will be well." He reads the Bible and prays every night before going to sleep, and he reads sermons also and writes to Livy about them.

At this time he intended to unite with the church as soon as he should have a settled home. To the best of my knowledge, he never did so, though he did hold a pew at the Asylum Hill Congregational Church in Hartford. How often he occupied it, I do not know. He once told Howells that he went to church although it nearly killed him; his daughter says he only went under compulsion. I suspect he went more often during the earlier years, but there was no sudden, dramatic break, such as Paine places during a walk Mark took with Twichell in the Black Forest—"Joe, I'm going to make a confession. I don't believe in your religion at all. I've been living a lie straight along whenever I pretended to." Nor is it true that, during their later years, Mark Twain and Twichell never discussed religious matters. Mark was a member of the Asylum Hill group as long as he lived in Hartford, his intimacy with Twichell endured until his own death, and both men always felt free to say whatever was in their hearts. Twichell even speaks of their having prayed together. Mark and Livy did read the Bible together, and, as a newly married man, Mark said grace before meat, much to the astonishment of visitors like Joe Goodman, to whom Mark is supposed to have confided that the practice meant nothing to him but he did it to please Livy. In any case, he clearly found it uncongenial, and it was soon given up.

It is generally believed that when Mark gave up religion, Livy did too, and we have such stories as her telling him that if he were lost, she wanted to be lost with him, and that once, when in a time of stress, he said to her, "Livy, if it comforts you to lean on the Christian faith, do so," she replied, "I can't, Youth. I haven't any." This is supposed to have cut Mark to the quick and added to the weight upon an already overburdened conscience, so that he went through the rest of his life reproaching himself for having robbed her of her faith. To Mark's capacity for self-reproach I set no limits, but I suspect that what happened was considerably less dramatic.

A good many people write and think about Mark Twain as if he were a settled apostate. Actually, he was not. He never doubted God, and though the Spirit That Denies certainly had a hold upon him in some aspects, he was a seeker and a searcher all his life.

It is true that there is an 1885 letter to Charles Warren Stoddard, whom Mark Twain considered the purest man he had ever known, in which he says that he himself has derived the same comfort from "absolute unbelief" that Stoddard himself has found in the absolute certainties of the Catholic Church. "I look back with the same shuddering horror upon the days when I believed I believed, as you do upon the days when you were afraid you did not believe." This is a very significant letter. It testifies eloquently to Mark Twain's need of certainty, and probably also to the terrors he experienced during his early life, when, like Tom Sawyer, he read God's personal wrath against him into every disturbance of nature, but if there is any comfort to be derived from "absolute unbelief," he never achieved it, and there are thousands of utterances to prove that he did not.

Mrs. Clemens, though troubled at times by her own religious coldness,[4] must, I am sure, have achieved it much less. The same people who think of Mark, in his old age, as a raging atheist often think of her, in her youth, as the most rabid and bigoted of fundamentalists; again, the major premise is wrong, and now that Max Eastman has taught us what the Langdons were really like, and what their remarkable pastor, Thomas K. Beecher, was like, there is no longer any excuse for anybody entertaining it. Jervis Langdon was a rich man, but he was about as untypical a rich man as ever lived, and if there have not been many truer Christians than Thomas K. Beecher, there has certainly never been a more unconventional one in ecclesiastical life. Moreover, we have his own word for it that, liberal as he was in his interpretations of religion,

[4] See Wecter, *The Love Letters of Mark Twain*, 167–68.

Mrs. Langdon, Olivia's mother, did not hesitate to reject even her pastor's views whenever her own inner light impelled her to do so.[5] There was nothing in Livy's later life with Mark that should cause her to "revolt" against anything that Beecher or the Langdons had taught her, or make her feel that she had "outgrown" it. Henry van Dyke tells us that Mark often spoke to him about his wife's religious faith. We know that, as long as she lived, she cherished, "in her worn old Testament," the letter of comfort that Howells wrote her when Susy died. Certainly she brought up her children in religious faith and ways. When she died, her husband chose to have engraved upon the stone that marks her grave:

Gott sei dir gnädig, O meine Wonne!

Yet I must admit freely that, in a sense, these considerations make Mark's religious apostasy, such as it was, more, not less, difficult to understand. The man had a religious temperament; he certainly had the moral constitution of a Christian. Why, then, did he stand apart?

If the clergymen he knew had been men of narrow hearts and minds, this would be easy to understand. If they had, even, all been extreme evangelicals, it would not be too difficult to understand. "A religion that comes of thought, and study, and deliberate conviction, sticks best," says Mark Twain. He did not approve even of D. L. Moody, though if he had known that great-hearted man personally, he might perhaps have found him as hard to resist as Joseph H. Twichell, whose companionship, he said, "stands first after Livy's." The Moody type of religious expression he could never have been expected to relish however.

But Twichell was no revivalist, nor Calvinist neither; nor was Thomas K. Beecher, nor, for that matter, his brother, Henry Ward, whatever other shortcomings he may have had. Ecclesiastically and theologically, Twichell was a disciple of Horace Bushnell, whom Mark Twain himself called "that greatest clergyman that the last century has produced," Bushnell, who saved us all from degrading and mechanical interpretations of Christ's atone-

[5] Max Eastman, *Heroes I Have Known*, 128.

ment, and destroyed the old belief that God Himself could not forgive a debt until it had been paid, even if He had to pay it to Himself, and for whom Calvary was simply the supreme manifestation of God's love, a demonstration, rather than a declaration, that there was no price too great for God to pay to win man back to Himself. One would suppose that a man with such a capacity for loving as Mark Twain possessed would be, of all men, the one most likely to be fired by such an idea. Why did it not take a deeper hold on him? Was it the influence of the "village atheist" side of early Midwestern culture? and was he, in this respect, more dominated by the father he did not love than by the mother whom he did? Or was he simply, in the last analysis, for some unfathomed reason, incapable of that "leap into the dark" which, at one point or another, every faith demands?

III

In spite of his religious skepticism, Mark Twain was by no means free of superstition. The voodoo magic of the Negroes hovered about his childhood, and he never altogether threw off its spell. He was personally acquainted with an old, bedridden, whiteheaded slave woman who was believed to be more than a thousand years old. She had come out of Egypt with Moses, and there was a bald spot on the top of her head which had been caused by fright at seeing Pharaoh's army drowned. "Whenever witches were around she tied up the remnant of her wool in little tufts, with white thread, and thus promptly made the witches impotent." The Negroes told marvelous ghost stories, and to hear them told and thrill to them afterwards was probably the intensest form of emotional stimulation that young Sam Clemens received.

All this was fortunate from the standpoint of the artist he was to be: Negro folklore is no small element in the charm of his books. But the man was affected as well as the artist. To get out of bed on the wrong side was a bad omen for the day; he would not speak or write of an improvement in his wife's health without adding "Unberufen"; in leaving Quarry Farm, at the end of a happy summer, he must leave something behind him to insure his safe return. Thrice in his life, he saw a lunar rainbow, which he took as a sign of good fortune, and since he had come into the world with Halley's Comet in 1835, he was sure he would go out with it in 1910—which he did. His cousin, J. R. Clemens, tells an interesting story of what happened one night when he went with Mark to see William Gillette in *Secret Service*. When a black cat walked across the stage in the second act, Mark was greatly agitated: he was sure Gillette was in for some misfortune. And, sure enough, when they went back stage to see him afterwards, they found the actor binding up a finger he had cut badly on the telegraph key.

Mark Twain believed in luck. When the business crash came upon him, he was bewildered:

> There's one thing which makes it difficult for me to soberly realize that my ten year dream is actually dissolved; and that is, that it reverses my horoscope. The proverb says, "Born lucky, *always* lucky," and I am very superstitious. . . . I am so superstitious that I have always been afraid to have business dealings with certain relatives and friends of mine because they were unlucky people. All my life I have stumbled upon lucky chances of large size, and whenever they were wasted it was because of my own stupidity and carelessness. And so I have felt entirely certain that that machine would turn up trumps eventually. It disappointed me lots of times, but I couldn't shake off the confidence of a life-time in my luck.

It is an interesting statement. One cannot help wondering whether Mark Twain was, at this time, permanently disillusioned about his luck, and whether or not this had any influence on the development of his pessimism.

Just where the line is to be drawn between superstition and sensitiveness to psychic influences is a very difficult thing to determine in the present state of human knowledge. But there is no doubt that psychic phenomena always greatly interested Mark Twain.

To begin with, there is his interest in dreams. He was always dreaming, and recurrent dreams came to him through the years. No doubt "My Platonic Sweetheart" has been, in a measure, fictionized, but the long account of his dreams which he confided to his notebook in 1897 is almost as suggestive.[6] "My Platonic Sweetheart" is perhaps the most beautiful thing he ever wrote; certainly he never created a lovelier heroine. "In our dreams—I know it!—we do make the journeys we seem to make; we do see the things we seem to see; the people, the horses, the cats, the dogs, the birds, the whales, are real, not chimeras; they are living spirits, not shadows; and they are immortal and indestructible."

In a sense, then, Mark Twain's dream life was the best part of his life, for it was without guilt. This is not true of the dream life of many men; that it should have been true of him may well tell us more about his character than has yet been realized. Coleman O. Parsons has commented on the difference between his conception of dreams and that of William Dean Howells. "To Howells the mind was without pity or remorse in dreams; to Clemens it was reinstated in its kingdom of sinlessness, for it was the supernal heckling of the soul that made waking life seem intolerable to him." Like all true dreamers, like all lovers of children and animals, Mark Twain was innocent at heart. If there had been a "suppressed" evil side of him to express itself in dreams, his dream life could not have served him for a refuge as it did.

He had interesting experiences too—though he often ridicules fortune-tellers—with palmistry. Like many of the prominent artists and writers of his time, he consulted Cheiro and talked to him at some length about the possibility of our histories being written in our hands. In 1895, when he was wallowing in bankruptcy, Cheiro told him that in his sixty-eighth year he would become rich. Two years later, the prediction was repeated. On October 22, 1903, when there was little time to spare, Mark Twain signed the contract which placed all his books in the hands of Harper and Brothers and guaranteed him a handsome income.

He was much more interested in what he called "mental telegraphy" and what we call extra-sensory perception or ESP. If he were alive today, he would certainly be greatly interested in the work that has been done along this line by Dr. J. B. Rhine, Mrs. Eileen J. Garrett, and other investigators. His views are set forth in the two essays he wrote on the subject, and he speaks of

[6] *Mark Twain's Notebook*, 348–52.

it incidentally elsewhere. Some of his evidence is impressive, but his zeal weakens his argument through overemphasis. Dr. Still in a Kansas village in 1874 began the same series of experiments that Dr. Kellgren had been working on for five years in Germany. "Dr. Still seems to be an honest man; therefore I am persuaded that Kellgren moved him to his experiments by Mental Telegraphy across six hours of longitude, without need of a wire." Credulity could hardly go further. "I imagine we get most of our thoughts out of somebody else's head, by mental telegraphy—and not always out of heads of acquaintances, but, in the majority of cases, out of the heads of strangers; strangers far removed—Chinamen, Hindus, and all manner of remote foreigners whose language we should not be able to understand, but whose thoughts we can read without difficulty." Some day, he was sure, this great power would be brought under control, and we should be able at all times to call up whomever we wanted in any part of the earth and talk with him freely.

Faith healing was another interest. It would have been strange if it had not been, for when Mrs. Clemens, as a girl, was a helpless invalid, it had been a faith healer, a Dr. Newton, who had restored her to activity. Observing Oriental fakirs upon his travels, Mark Twain would sometimes commit himself to the thesis that the power of mind over the body was absolute. At one time, the nearsighted Clemenses tried applying faith-cure or mind-cure to defective sight, and all started running about without their glasses. Susy, always strongly attracted to such matters, found her eyesight improving, and Baby Jean, not to be outdone, tried faith healing on the stomachache. Mark Twain entered in his notebook the names of practitioners to whom cures had been credited. Nor did he confine himself altogether to the mind cure. Once, he was very enthusiastic about the Kellgren method, which we are told resembled osteopathy, and the family went to Sweden that Jean's epilepsy might benefit by it. At times at least, Mark Twain approved of Susy's interest in Christian Science. "I am perfectly certain that the exasperating colds and carbuncles [from which he had been suffering]," he wrote her from India, "came from a diseased mind, and that your mental science could drive them away.

. . . I have no language to say how glad and grateful I am that you are a convert to that rational and noble philosophy. Stick to it; dont let anybody talk you out of it. Of all earthly fortune it is the best, and most enriches the possessor."

This may seem surprising in view of Mark Twain's book on Christian Science, but he never opposed Christian Science as a religion, either because of its stress on spiritual healing or on account of its philosophical idealism. (He had plenty of philosophical idealism of his own in *The Mysterious Stranger*.) What he objected to in Christian Science was what seemed to him Mrs. Eddy's personal duplicity—that and the fact that he saw her building up a powerful machine which he naïvely believed would control America by the year 1940. "It was out of powers approaching Mrs. Eddy's—though not equaling them—that the Inquisition and the devastations of the Interdict grew. She will transmit hers. The man born two centuries from now will think he has arrived in hell; and all in good time he will think he knows it."

The book on Christian Science itself recognizes the reality of spiritual healing. Mrs. Eddy did not invent it or discover it; it has appeared among all peoples and in every period. What, then, is Mrs. Eddy's achievement? Simply that she has organized this force and made it available. In this aspect, "she is the benefactor of the age." Suppose she is able to help nobody except fools? "The fools, the idiots, the pudd'nheads" make up the bulk of the race anyway; her title still stands. But her services are not confined to these classes. Four-fifths of the ills from which mankind suffers are kept alive in the imagination; Christian Science can banish that four-fifths. It can destroy all fretting and anxiety, and this is a boon that "outvalues any price that can be put upon it."

Mark Twain, however, goes further than this; indeed, I cannot imagine how any Christian Scientist could ask for a higher tribute to his religion than Mark Twain pays it:

> The Christian Scientist believes that the Spirit of God (life and love) pervades the universe like an atmosphere; that whoso will study *Science and Health* can get from it the secret of how to inhale that transforming air; that to breathe it is to be made new; that

from the new man all sorrow, all care, all miseries of the mind vanish away, for that only peace, contentment, and measureless joy can live in that divine fluid; that it purifies the body from disease, which is a vicious creation of the gross human mind, and cannot continue to exist in the presence of the Immortal Mind, the renewing Spirit of God.

The Scientist finds this reasonable, natural, and not harder to believe than that the disease-germ, a creature of darkness, perishes when exposed to the light of the great sun—a new revelation of profane science which no one doubts. He reminds us that the actinic ray, shining upon lupus, cures it—a horrible disease, which was incurable fifteen years ago, and had been incurable ten million years before; that this wonder, unbelievable by the physicians at first, is believed by them now; and so he is tranquilly confident that the time is coming when the world will be educated up to a point where it will comprehend and grant that the light of the Spirit of God, shining unobstructed upon the soul, is an actinic ray which can purge both mind and body from disease and set them free and make them whole.

It is hard to believe that the writer of these lines did not understand Christian Science. It is harder to believe that he did not understand the spirit of true religion.

Mark Twain had his contacts with other fringe scientific and religious movements. In Hannibal days, he proved a wonderful subject for a visiting mesmerist; he says he faked. He seems a little hurt that palmists and phrenologists could find no evidence that he possessed a sense of humor! He read at least one Swedenborgian book at Howells' suggestion, but found that "it flies too high for me." With spiritualism his adventures were more interesting. He finds it difficult to believe that people in modern times have believed in ghosts, and in *The American Claimant* he uses Colonel Sellers' interest in "materialization" as a very ineffective element in his comedy. Yet his investigations of San Francisco mediums,[7] though sometimes disrespectfully expressed, seem to me remarkably open-minded. He cannot explain the phenomena and never expects to be able to do so, and is not really irreverent. "There was

[7] See *The Washoe Giant in San Francisco*, section V.

186

something so awful . . . about talking with living, sinful lips to the ghostly dead." Not even the fact that people have gone crazy over the new "wildcat" religions seems to him conclusive evidence against them, for he knows that the respectable, established faiths have produced their lunatics too.

As a matter of fact, psychic phenomena pursued Sam Clemens all his life. When he was four years old, his sister Margaret died: the village shoemaker claimed that weeks before, while the little girl was still strong and well, he had seen the funeral procession pass his door in a vision, exactly as it afterwards appeared. Mark Twain himself once dreamed the death of a girl he had known in school, and in 1858 he had a much more elaborate dream about his brother Henry. He saw his brother, dead, lying in a metallic casket, supported by two chairs. On his breast was a bouquet of white flowers with a single crimson bloom in the center. The dream was so vivid that he woke up the next morning believing his brother to be dead, and it was not until after he had dressed and got out into the street that he realized the truth. In June, Henry was blown up with the *Pennsylvania*. After the body had been prepared for burial, Sam found his brother in a leaden casket, exactly like the one he had seen in his dream, and whilst he stood rapt in the wonder of it, an elderly lady entered the room, bringing a floral offering. The flowers were pure white, and there was a single red rose in the center.

Many years later, in one of his skeptical moods, Mark Twain denied the reality of all psychic manifestations. When Paine reminded him of this experience, he replied, "I ask nobody to believe that it ever happened. To me it is true; but it has no logical right to be true, and I do not expect belief in it." Logic abdicates in such an answer. It was as if he knew that the "philosophy" he had developed was not big enough to satisfy all the needs of his nature, to cover all the experiences of his life.

This was not the only strange experience he had in the psychic world. I will not spoil by a paraphrase Paine's finely-told story of the billiard balls—a phenomenon to be explained on the hypothesis of dematerialization or else simply left unexplained.[8]

[8] *Mark Twain: A Biography*, III, 1407-1409 (chapter CCLX).

Once a distracted husband came to Mark Twain, fearing that his wife had met with a disaster. Mark led him straight to the ascending elevator of the hotel, confident that when the car stopped, the wife would step out of it, as she did. To Paine himself this power was once curiously exemplified when Mark Twain sent him the message, "Tell Paine I am sorry he fell and skinned his shin at five o'clock yesterday afternoon." And Paine replied, "I did fall and skin my shin at five o'clock yesterday afternoon, but how did you find it out?"

One day in Montreal, at an afternoon reception, he glimpsed across the room an old friend, a lady whom he had not seen for twenty years. He wondered why she did not come forward to speak to him, but she kept her distance, and at last he lost sight of her altogether. That night she turned up at his lecture, dressed exactly as he had seen her some hours before. "I knew you," he said to her, "I knew you the moment you appeared at the reception this afternoon." And to his utter astonishment she replied, "But I was not at the reception. I have just arrived from Quebec, and have not been in town an hour."

Somewhat different in character was the bathroom experience, just after the death of Jean. This may best be told in his own words to Paine:

> For one who does not believe in spirits I have had a most peculiar experience. I went into the bathroom just now and closed the door. You know how warm it always is in there, and there are no draughts. All at once I felt a cold current of air about me. I thought the door must be open; but it was closed. I said, "Jean is this you trying to let me know you have found the others?" Then the cold air was gone.

He did not formulate his opinions on these subjects, or, rather, he formulated them only to depart immediately from the formulation. When he came to tell the story of Joan of Arc, the psychic element puzzled him considerably, but he solved his aesthetic problem by postulating a certain naïveté on the part of the assumed narrator. He was interested in the work of the Society for

Psychical Research, and when Mrs. Clemens became interested in spiritualism, he accompanied her to séances. "I have never had an experience which moved me to believe the living can communicate with the dead," he wrote a correspondent in 1901, "but my wife and I have experimented in the matter when opportunity offered and shall continue to do so." He was willing to consider the testimony of persons he considered truthful, and Mrs. Samossoud prints a late note to her mother "because it is interesting to see that he never shut up his mind so tight that it would not unfold to the possible mysteries of an invisible world." He wrote:

> Livy, darling: Here is Rev. Dr. X furnishing some spiritualism of a most unaccountable and interesting character. This is the kind of episode that puzzles a body entirely. It isn't telepathy and it isn't clairvoyance; they can explain many, if not most of the spiritualistic wonders, but they are out of court this time. This is an altogether startling and marvelous case. Love.

It is clear, for he tells us specifically, that his interest in metempsychosis was one of the things that made Adolf Wilbrandt's play, *The Master of Palmyra,* so fascinating to him. Miss Annella Smith has also shown that several features of *Captain Stormfield* are quite in harmony with occult teaching, though I find no evidence to support her conclusion that Mark Twain was himself well versed in occult lore.

IV

What, now, did Mark Twain believe?

Early in his married life, he tried to state, in a paper that Mrs. Clemens would not let him print, the differences, as he saw them, between the God of the Bible and the God of modern thought:

> The difference in importance, between the God of the Bible and the God of the present day, cannot be described, it can only be vaguely and inadequately figured to my mind. . . .
> . . . His sole solicitude was about a handful of truculent nomads. He worried and fretted over them in a peculiarly and distractingly human way. One day he coaxed and petted them beyond their

189

deserts. He sulked, he cursed, he raged, he grieved, according to the mood and the circumstances, but all to no purpose; his efforts were all vain, he could not govern them. When the fury was on him he was blind to all reason—he not only slaughtered the offender, but even his harmless little children and dumb cattle.

To trust the God of the Bible is to trust an irascible, vindictive, fierce and ever fickle and changeful master; to trust the true God is to trust a Being who has uttered no promises, but whose beneficent, exact, and changeless ordering of the machinery of his colossal universe is proof that he is at least steadfast to his purposes; whose unwritten laws, so far as they affect man, being equal and impartial, show that he is just and fair; these things, taken together, suggest that if he shall ordain us to live hereafter, he will still be steadfast, just, and fair toward us. We shall not need to require anything more.[9]

This was a vast conception, much more rational, to Mark Twain's way of thinking, than the one he had been brought up on, but less satisfying emotionally. "For that Supreme One is not a God of pity or mercy—not as we recognize these qualities." Mark Twain accepted always the argument from design—this was one of the things that kept him from being an atheist—and so he had to account somehow for the typhus germ, the tsetse fly, and the rattlesnake. "Two things," therefore, "are quite certain: one is that God has no special consideration for man's welfare or comfort, or He wouldn't have created those things to disturb and destroy him. The human conception of pity and morality must be entirely unknown to that Infinite God, as much unknown as the conceptions of a microbe to man, or at least as little regarded."[10] It was the old, old problem of evil, always the great obstacle in the way of religious faith from the Book of Job to *The Bridge of San Luis Rey*—and beyond.

[9] See, also, the long notebook entry of May 27, 1898, in *Mark Twain's Notebook*, 36–63, and the creed quoted by Paine, *Mark Twain: A Biography*, III, 1583–84 (chapter CCXCV).

[10] See, also, however, a letter of 1889, to Livy, in which Mark Twain argues, not in harmony with the views expressed here, and much in the manner of Browning's "Saul," that, however infinitely God may surpass man, He cannot conceivably fall below him in the possession of any good quality. See *The Love Letters of Mark Twain*, 253–54.

Such speculations led him at last to a kind of vast, materialistic pantheism, suggestive, here and there, of Robert Fludd. There occurred to him "the possibility, and substantially the certainty, that man is himself a microbe, and his globe a blood corpuscle drifting with its shining brethren of the Milky Way down a vein of the Master and Maker of all things, whose body, mayhap— glimpsed part-wise from the earth by night, and receding and lost to view in the measureless remoteness of space—is what men name the Universe." Or, more elaborately:

> The suns and planets that form the constellations of a billion billion solar systems and go pouring, a tossing flood of shining globes, through the viewless arteries of space are the blood-corpuscles in the veins of God; and the nations are the microbes that swarm and wriggle and brag in each, and think God can tell them apart at that distance and has nothing better to do than try. *This*— the entertainment of an eternity. Who so poor in his ambitions as to consent to be God on those terms? Blasphemy? No, it is not blasphemy. If God is as vast as that, He is above blasphemy; if He is as little as that, He is beneath it.

What, now, of Christ? "All that is great and good in our civilization," Mark Twain wrote in 1871, "came straight from the hand of Jesus Christ." When he went to Palestine in the sixties, he gazed upon the site of the Crucifixion "with a far more absorbing interest than I had ever felt in anything earthly before." He was already trying to differentiate between traditions which are worthy of credence by their own inherent reasonableness and those other absurd traditions which are plainly the pious fictions of monks and impostures of churchmen. But this did not keep him from being impressed by the idea that he was traversing ground which had once been pressed by the feet of God.

Such a view would have seemed absurd to him in later years, yet when Orion sent him a manuscript in 1878, he objected to what he considered the irreverent attitude toward Christ expressed in it. Though taking pains to explain that "neither Howells nor I believe in . . . the divinity of the Savior," he insists that nevertheless "the Savior is . . . a sacred Personage, and a man should have no desire or disposition to refer to him lightly, profanely, or otherwise than with the profoundest reverence." One late conversation with Paine would seem to imply doubt of the historicity of Jesus, and the same point of view seems to appear in a 1908 statement to an unknown correspondent, that between A.D. 350 and A.D. 1850 Jesus and Satan "exercised a vaster influence over a fifth part of the human race than was exercised over that fraction of the race by all other influences combined." But Mark Twain was so inconsistent a thinker and speaker that one could not argue a settled disbelief in the historicity of Jesus upon such utterances as these.

Having seen Palestine, Mark Twain was sure that having been there once, Christ would not wish to come again; once he wrote Howells that he hoped He would not come again, since He had made trouble enough the first time. In his annotations in Lecky there are a number of comments more seriously disrespectful, though more toward Christianity than toward Christ; he believed that Lecky had shown both that Christianity was "the very invention of hell itself" and that it was "the most precious and elevating and ennobling boon ever vouchsafed to the world."[11] In general, however, his attitude toward Christ himself is reverential, sometimes nobly so. In one notebook passage, he calls the God of the Old Testament and the New "the Jekyl and Hyde of sacred romance." In his youth, he was shocked, in Italy, to find Christ subordinated to "some twelve or fifteen canonized Popes and martyrs"; in his old age, he was equally shocked by what he regarded as the disposition of some of his contemporaries to put Mrs. Eddy on a level with Him. He himself wrote one book that he feared might be taken as irreverent, and he kept it by him unpublished for many years. Yet this very book contains one of the most beautiful tributes ever paid to Christ in modern literature. When Captain Stormfield arrives in a section of heaven where the denizens of our particular earth are unknown, it finally occurs to him that there is one infallible way of identifying himself:

[11] See "Mark Twain's Religious Beliefs, as Indicated by Notations in His Books," *Twainian*, Fourteenth Year, May–June, pp. 1–4; July–August, pp. 1–4; Sept.–Oct., pp. 1–4; Nov.–Dec., pp. 3–4.

"Well, sir," I says, pretty humble, "I don't seem to make out which world it is I'm from. But you may know it from this—it's the one the Saviour saved."

He bent his head at the Name. Then he says, gently—

"The worlds He has saved are like to the gates of heaven in number—none can count them."

Many of Mark Twain's contemporaries believed in the existence of Satan as a spiritual being. That Mark Twain himself actually shared this belief, I greatly doubt, but, as an idea at least, Satan greatly interested him. His interest began as a boy—he was disappointed when he found that his Sunday School teacher did not care to encourage it—and it grew apace with the years. Satan seems to have appealed to him more as the principle of rebellion than as the principle of evil.[12] The classical passage, one of the prime examples of his humor, is in the essay "Concerning the Jews":

I have no special regard for Satan; but I can at least claim that I have no prejudice against him. It may even be that I lean a little his way, on account of his not having a fair show. All religions issue bibles against him, but we never hear *his* side. . . . A person who has for untold centuries maintained the imposing position of spiritual head of four-fifths of the human race, and political head of the whole of it, must be granted the possession of executive abilities of the loftiest order. . . . I would like to see him. I would rather see him and shake him by the tail than any other member of the European Concert.

Mark Twain early came to distinguish between the conventional set prayer—which was of little value in his eyes—and the prayer which is the sincere, spontaneous overflow of powerful feelings. As early as 1865 he ventures a suggestion: "How would it answer to adopt the simplicity and the beauty and the brevity and the comprehensiveness of the Lord's Prayer as a model? But

12 See two articles by Coleman O. Parsons, "The Devil and Samuel Clemens," *Virginia Quarterly Review*, Vol. XXIII (1947), 582–606, and "The Background of *The Mysterious Stranger*," *American Literature*, Vol. XXXII (1960–61), 55–74, especially pp. 60–61.

perhaps I am wandering out of my jurisdiction." Later, he was shocked by prayers for rain and other petitions which seemed to demand that the Deity upset the established order of His Creation to please the individual petitioner, and I shall have something to say later of his views concerning the appalling blasphemy of prayers for success in war. Huckleberry Finn is, as ever, the skeptic, making a determined effort to be fair and consider all sides of the question, and it comes to Huck finally that possibly "there's something in it when a body like the widow or the parson prays, but it don't work for me, and I reckon it don't work for only just the right kind." Perhaps Mark Twain came to accept Huck's opinion. It is difficult to think of him as employing systematic, private prayer, but when, shortly before his death, he was told that a convent of nuns were praying for him, he was vastly pleased: "I am grateful for the prayers of those good nuns . . . ; they have already answered themselves in giving me deep pleasure."

On one occasion, Mark Twain plays, thoughtfully enough, the role of Biblical critic. This is when he dismisses Herod's slaughter of the innocents, as reported in the Gospel According to Saint Matthew. "Tacitus makes no mention of it," he says, "and he would hardly have overlooked a sweeping order like that, issued by a petty ruler like Herod. Just consider a little king of a corner of the Roman Empire ordering the slaughter of the first-born of a lot of Roman subjects. Why, the Emperor would have reached out that long arm of his and dismissed Herod." In the creed printed in Paine's last volume, Mark Twain takes up the position that the Bible was written wholly by man, and that the world's moral laws are wholly the result of the world's experience, not the outcome of special revelations.

There was probably no phase of religious aspiration that interested Mark Twain more than the thought of life after death. Leaving Egypt as a *Quaker City* pilgrim, he says, "We were glad to have seen that land which had an enlightened religion with future eternal rewards and punishment in it, while even Israel's religion contained no promise of a hereafter." Not that he cared much for the punishment part of it; he would not roast his own enemies all through eternity, and he could not believe that God would either. Heaven, too, if there were any, was going to be something radically different from what the average Christian expected. Harps and halos might be there, but nobody was going to have much use for them, for there would be plenty of work and pain and growth and progress. Only, like all men who have loved deeply, he could not endure the thought that death was the end. Like T. T. Munger, he knew that love cannot tolerate the thought of its own end. "It has but one word—forever. Its language is 'there is no death.'" Only once in his writings do I recall its being even transiently suggested that a life lived here on this planet alone, without thought or hope of anything afterwards, might be the nobler ideal.

Since Mark Twain was not, in the theological sense at least, a Christian, immortality was not a dogma with him, but it was a hope. For, as the sorrows of life piled thick and fast upon him, he believed more and more, despite all his skepticism, that there is no sense to the universe if death ends all, and the thought of what lay beyond was often upon his mind. To be sure, there is a passage in his autobiography, recently printed by Mr. Neider, in which he declares categorically that he has lost both his faith and his interest in immortality. Nor does this stand alone. He once made a vigorous statement of his disbelief to Mrs. Thomas K. Beecher, and they drew up a contract, providing that whoever turned out to be wrong a million years hence must confess his error. But among the verses Mark Twain scribbled on the subject were these:

> If I prove right, by God His grace
> Full sorry I shall be. . . .

That is the note. "As to a hereafter," he told Paine, towards the end of his life, "we have not the slightest evidence that there is any—*no* evidence that appeals to logic and reason. I have never seen what to me seemed an atom of proof that there is a future life." And then, after waiting a long time, he added: "And yet— I am strongly inclined to expect one."

As those he loved slipped away from him, immortality became less of an intellectual and more of an emotional matter. "Let us believe it!" he writes his wife, after the death of Susy. "I will believe in it with you. It has been the belief of the wise and thoughtful of many countries for three thousand years; let us accept their verdict; we cannot frame one that is more reasonable or probable. I will try never to doubt it again." In 1903 he added that he did not object to being immortal but did not know "how to accommodate the thought." But if immortality were to be, then accommodation must come with it. "It at least cannot appal me, for I will not allow myself to believe that there is disaster connected with it. In fact, no one, at bottom, believes that; not even the priests that preach it." When Jean died, Katy Leary was sure he said to her, "Oh, Katy! She's in heaven with her mother." Mrs. Samossoud writes, "Father has often said he hoped he might die by a stroke of lightning without any warning of change from this life to the other. Sometimes he believed that death ended everything, but most of the time he felt sure of a life beyond."

So, making due allowance for buffoonery, annoyance, and exaggeration, there is less positive irreverence in Mark Twain than many persons believe. He recognizes the power of religion, and consistently maintains that he does not wish to interfere with another man's faith. There might be nothing in it, but if it served to comfort him who held it, it had still justified itself.

From one point of view, he understands true reverence better than many orthodox Christians do: he recognizes and respects *all* religious belief, not merely that which he shares, recognizes and respects it even when it manifests itself in forms quite alien or repugnant to him. No doubt this was made easier for him by the very fact that he did not regard Christianity as a unique revelation. In fact, it sometimes seemed to him that the "heathen" were in some aspects ahead of the Christians. "When he looked at the hosts of men and women kneeling in worship before the sun, by the shores of the Holy river of Ganges, in the town of Benares," writes his daughter, "he exclaimed: 'They spend hours like this while we in America are robbing and murdering.'" But in any case, the principle he lays down is perfectly sound: "True irreverence is disrespect for another man's god." For the European who treads rudely on the Arab's praying carpets, he has only contempt.

196

The same point of view comes out in Mark Twain's comments on Roman Catholic matters. As we have already seen, he was brought up to dislike Catholicism, and there are passages in *The Innocents Abroad* which make unpleasant reading for Roman Catholic readers. Yet the very frankness with which Mark Twain avows his prejudice shows that he was not wholly enslaved to it. Even that bigoted Protestant, the Connecticut Yankee, admits that "the great majority" of the parish priests were "sincere and right-hearted, and devoted to the alleviation of human troubles and sufferings." The good priest who taught Tom Canty comes in for nothing but praise in *The Prince and the Pauper*. The Roman Catholic critic, Seymour L. Gross, finds all Mark Twain's criticisms of the Church honest and sincere except when he says that Catholics believe they can "buy salvation with Masses."[13] When, in his old age, Mark Twain was asked to contribute to a Catholic magazine, he replied, "I wish I were not so hard driven; then nothing could give me more contentment than to try to write something in . . . 'Christ's Poor'; indeed you pay me a compliment which I highly value when you invite me to do so, as holding me not unworthy to appear in its pages." More interesting still is this letter to Livy: "I am very, very glad Jean is in a convent. . . . And away deep down in my heart I feel that if they make a good strong unshakable Catholic of her I shan't be the least bit sorry. It is doubtless the most peace-giving and restful of all the religions. If I had it I would not trade it for anything in the earth." Perhaps he had learned something of this from his love for Joan of Arc. Up to a point, Joan of Arc was to Mark Twain what the Blessed Virgin was to Henry Adams. But she was not the Blessed Virgin; if she had been, she might have helped him to solve his religious problem. It had always been easier for him to accept the authority of women than that of men.

Finally, of course, it has always been recognized that though Mark Twain may have rejected the theology of Christianity, he was always the child of the Christian ethic. All Americans, he

13 "Mark Twain and Catholicism," *Critic*, Vol. XVII, April–May, 1959, p. 9, 12, 88–91. This fine article says virtually everything that needs to be said on the subject.

says, whatever their religious beliefs, have the moral constitution of Christians, surely an utterance that must forever silence all accusations of pessimism! Bad conduct on the part of Americans seems actually to have shocked Mark Twain more than bad conduct on the part of other people. In 1880, petitioning Congress to enact a copyright law, he declares that he acts in the conviction that "the infusing of the spirit of God into our laws will be something better than the empty honor of putting His name in the Constitution." He is in favor of protecting foreign authors in America, even on a unilateral basis, "there being nothing in the Christian code of morals which justifies a man in requiring that another man shall promise to stop stealing from him before he will consent to stop stealing from said other man."

— V —

This chapter began with the consideration of Mark Twain's relationship to Calvinism; it must end on the same note. Intellectually, as we have seen, he was able to throw off the stamp of his early environment, but it was not only as an artist that in his inner abiding-place he was always there. He thinks—he even jokes —in terms of Calvinism; no other illustrations come so readily to his mind as those involving the old Calvinistic ideas. Even the "jackass rabbit" sits quietly "thinking about his sins." Mark Twain cannot watch Queen Victoria's Diamond Jubilee procession without being reminded of the Last Judgment—"and some of us who live to see that day will probably recall this one—if we are not too much disturbed in mind at the time." How fierce is his rebellion against a rule-of-thumb morality at the end of his touching story, "Was It Heaven? or Hell?" and how much of its power has this narrative lost by the fact that we can no longer conceive the possibility of any sane person wishing to debate the subject against him. Shortly before his death, Mark Twain wrote a series of directions designed to assist Paine in learning how to conduct himself in the life to come. "You will be wanting to slip down at night, and smuggle water to those poor little chaps [the infant damned], but don't you try it. You would be caught, and nobody in heaven would respect you after that." Humorous? Yes. But without Calvinism, without a vividly remembered Calvinism, without a Calvinism that had sunk into the marrow of his bones, such a passage could never have been written.

There are other utterances, too, which are not humorous. "God does not willingly punish us," a correspondent writes him. And he comments, "Well, why does He do it then? We don't invite it. Why does He give Himself the trouble?" (More directly, he cries, pitifully but naïvely, to Howells, after Susy's death, "Why am I robbed, and who is benefited?") The missionaries in the Congo labor to stamp out a hideous and loathsome disease. "Evidently those missionaries are pitying, compassionate, kind. How it would improve God to take a lesson from them! He invented and distributed the germ of that awful disease among those helpless, poor savages, and now He sits with His elbows on the balusters and looks down and enjoys this wanton crime. Confidentially, and between you and me—well, never mind, I might get struck by lightning if I said it." When Lecky describes the sufferings of the martyrs, who might have saved themselves with a word, Mark Twain writes in the margin, "and God did not speak it." Not even Porphyria's Lover is more shockingly anthropomorphic. Certainly, too, Twichell was well within his rights when he reproached Mark Twain for being too orthodox on the subject of total human depravity.

There is an interesting footnote in the Brashear-Rodney anthology, *The Art, Humor, and Humanity of Mark Twain,* in which the point is made that Mark Twain would have found much to interest him in Kierkegaard and in the more recent writings of such theologians as Paul Tillich and Reinhold Niebuhr. So he might well have done. But he might have found even more practical value in "Personalism," as expounded by Borden Parker Bowne and Edgar Sheffield Brightman. What he really needed was a philosophy which permitted him to see the rattlesnake and the tsetse fly as waste products in the evolutionary process, and to believe in a God of Heal, not Hurt, who did not make cancer and yellow fever, but who operated to conquer them, through human brains if necessary, a God forever impregnating the frequently intractable stuff of Creation with Himself.

Mark Twain would not, I think, have dissented from what I have written here about his Calvinism, for he was fully aware that early impressions are not lightly eradicated. "The religious folly you are born in you will *die* in," he wrote, "no matter what apparently reasonabler religious folly may seem to have taken its place meanwhile, and abolished and obliterated it." His own "apparently reasonabler religious folly" was his "Gospel" of determinism, and he himself was just on the edge of recognizing this—and its implications—when Twichell gave him a volume of Jonathan Edwards to take home and read. He "wallowed and reeked" in it until midnight; he went on "a three days' tear with a drunken lunatic." Then he wrote:

> Jonathan seems to hold (as against the Arminian position) that the Man (or his Soul or his Will) never creates an impulse itself, but is moved to action by an impulse back of it. That's sound!
>
> Also, that of two or more things offered it, it infallibly chooses the one which for the moment is most pleasing to ITSELF. *Perfectly* correct! An immense admission for a man not otherwise sane.
>
> Up to that point he could have written chapters III and IV of my suppressed "Gospel." But there we seem to separate. He seems to concede the indisputable and unshakable dominion of Motive and Necessity (call them what he may, these are *exterior* forces and not under the man's authority, guidance or even suggestion)—then he suddenly flies the logic track and (to all seeming) makes the *man* and not these exterior forces responsible to God for the man's thoughts, words, and acts. It is frank insanity.

So much for his philosophy. On his pessimism, too, Calvinism may well have exercised an influence. The thought that God has chosen a large share of the race to roast in everlasting torment, for no reason connected with their individual conduct, but simply that He has willed it so, cannot be called particularly cheerful, but Mark Twain was introduced to this idea at an early age. It is not wonderful that he rebelled, that he expressed himself wildly and "irreverently," that he sprang at the loathsome image like Shaw's Black Girl with her knobkerrie.

We know that he considered this aspect of the problem, for

he once declared that to beget a child in such a world as this, to thrust the uninvited burden of life upon a helpless creature, was a crime, as if one should insist upon building a village on the slope of a volcano, directly in the path of the lava flow. "Formerly," he observed significantly, "it was much worse than now, for before the ministers abolished hell a man knew, when he was begetting a child, that he was begetting a soul that had only one chance in a hundred of escaping the eternal fires of damnation. He knew that in all probability that child would be brought to damnation—one of the ninety-nine black sheep."

Here is an interesting phase of the psychology of our ancestors, and it may well deserve more careful consideration than it has received. "What is humanity made of," asks Gamaliel Bradford in another connection, "that it can support such pangs as these and survive?" How could men and women who were not insane go on bringing children into such a world, a world which, as they believed, was ruled by the Monster-God of *The Mysterious Stranger*? Or did they only believe such things with their minds, and did the vital Life Force in them—the True God—insist on going on in spite of their barbarous creeds? And, after all, were they much crazier than the men and women of today? It may be, as Mark Twain says, that the ministers have abolished hell, but they have certainly not abolished sin, and it is sin that creates hell, by any definition. And far worse than the threat of a lava flow is the threat of atomic destruction which we could now manage with such wonderful efficiency, yet we go on, in all nations, leaving ourselves and our children unprotected by any sane nuclear policy.

This horror, Mark Twain was fortunately spared, though he caught glimpses of it from afar off. As Professor Gross says, "Nothing is simple in Mark Twain, especially in matters of the spirit: everything is ambivalent, ambiguous, shot through with counter-impulses." The application of this is not exclusively social and religious. But it applies with special force in both these areas.

CHAPTER TEN: *Hymn to Death*

I

MARK TWAIN'S OFFICIAL BIOGRAPHER was rather inclined to minimize his pessimism. "Mark Twain," he writes, "was not a pessimist in his heart, but only by premeditation. It was his observation and his logic that led him to write those things that, even in their bitterness, somehow conveyed the spirit of human sympathy which is so closely linked to hope." Some later writers have taken it more seriously, even finding in it the key to his whole life. Perhaps it is time for a fresh evaluation of the evidence.

No man could travel farther into the Waste Land than Mark Twain goes in many considered utterances of his later years.

A myriad of men are born; they labor and sweat and struggle for bread; they squabble and scold and fight; they scramble for little mean advantages over each other; age creeps upon them; infirmities follow; shames and humiliations bring down their prides and their vanities; those they love are taken from them and the joy of life is turned to aching grief. The burden of pain, care, misery grows heavier year by year; at length ambition is dead; pride is dead; vanity is dead; longing for release is in their place. It comes at last—the only unpoisoned gift earth ever had for them—and they vanish from a world where they were of no consequence, where they have achieved nothing, where they were a mistake and a failure and a foolishness; where they have left no sign that they have existed—a world which will lament them a day and forget them forever.

Here despair is wrought into literary beauty. He can make it snap the whip of an epigram too. "Each person is born to one possession which outvalues all his others—his last breath." "Whoever has lived long enough to find out what life is, knows how deep a debt of gratitude we owe to Adam, the first great benefactor of our race. He brought death into the world." "All people have had ill luck, but Jairus's daughter and Lazarus had the worst." Like the mad priest in *John Bull's Other Island*, he thinks that this world is hell—"the true one, not the lying invention of the superstitious; and we have come to it from elsewhere to expiate our sins." It would be somewhat difficult to find bitterer words than these in which to sum up your impression of the human adventure: "Anybody that knows anything knows that there was not a single life that was ever lived that was worth living. Not a single child was ever begotten that the begetting of it was not a crime."[1]

So much for generalization. He takes the same tone as he faces the individual, the unspeakably direct fact of death. Irving goes. "It is a little reminder. My section of the procession has but a little way to go. I could not be very sorry if I tried." Hale goes. "I am as grieved to hear of his death as I can ever be to hear of the death of any friend, though my grief is always tempered with the satisfaction of knowing that for the one that goes, the hard, bitter struggle of life is ended." Gilder goes. He attends the funeral, and as he enters the church, he is heard to whisper, "I wish that I were that man lying in there."

[1] As early as 1891, Mark Twain planned a story in which Huck and Tom were to be robbed of the joy he had previously created for them. See *Mark Twain–Howells Letters*, II, 748, the passage beginning "Huck comes back, 60 years old, from nobody knows where—& crazy."

Death strikes closer home. His brother, his daughters, his beloved wife. Life crumbles in his hands, but he does not falter. He lives on himself—unfortunately. Why didn't they let him drown when he went swimming in his boyhood? Why did they have to pull him out of water, not once but several times? They "interfered with the intentions of a Providence wiser than themselves," and it is difficult for him to forgive them. "He was good," he writes his sister-in-law, when Orion is taken—"all good and sound; there was nothing bad in him, nothing base, nor any unkindness. It was unjust that such a man . . . should have been sentenced to live 72 years. It was beautiful, the patience with which he bore it." As Jean's body lies before him, that last lonely Christmas of his life, he sums it all up:

> Would I bring her back to life if I could do it? I would not. If a word would do it, I would beg for strength to withhold the word. . . . In her loss I am almost bankrupt, and my life a bitterness, but I am content: for she has been enriched with the most precious of all gifts—that gift which makes all other gifts mean and poor— death. I have never wanted any released friend of mine restored to life since I reached manhood. I felt in this way when Susy passed away; and later my wife, and later Mr. Rogers. When Clara met me at the station in New York and told me that Mr. Rogers had died suddenly that morning, my thought was, Oh, favorite of fortune—fortunate all his long and lovely life—fortunate to his latest moment! The reporters said there were tears of sorrow in my eyes. True—but they were for *me*, not for him. He had suffered no loss. All the fortunes he had ever made were poverty compared with this one.

II

But now let us turn to the other side.

It will be noted that all these expressions of extreme despair date from the last years of Mark Twain's life. What of the earlier years?

Mark Twain was not a cheerful idiot at any time. The sorrows and horrors of life saddened him from the beginning. There is some pessimism in *The Gilded Age*, and Professor Blair has re-

cently challenged the view that "the period 1876–1879 can be
called the happiest in Clemens' life."[2] But surely the Hartford
years were not predominantly unhappy. After Susy died he wrote
Livy that he had hated life from the age of eighteen, but that was
nonsense, reading back from present despair, blowing out the gas
to see how dark it is. In 1873 he sent the New York *Graphic* a list
of headlines from the morning paper—thirty-seven of them, all
relating calamities and outrages, ranging from "An Eight Year Old
Murderer" to "Two to Three Hundred Men Roasted Alive." But
he can still make a jest of such things. Life has become so dull in
America, he says, that he must go abroad for excitement. In 1880
he wrote a schoolboy correspondent both that he himself was a
happy, cheerful, fortunate man, with no complaints for how life
had treated him, and that he would not be willing to live the boy-
part of his life over again. "Indeed I *am* thankful for the wife and
the child," he writes in 1874—"and if there is one individual creature on this footstool who is more thoroughly and uniformly and
unceasingly *happy* than I am I defy the world to produce him and
prove him. In my opinion, he doesn't exist." As late as 1888, he
adds a postscript to a perfectly furious letter to Orion: "Don't
imagine . . . that I am uncomfortable or unhappy—for I *never am*.
I don't know what it is to be unhappy or uneasy; and I am not
going to learn how, at this late day." When we compare such
words as these with the late utterances already quoted, it would
seem that Mark Twain had illustrated his own aphorism: "When
a man is a pessimist before forty-eight, he knows too much; if he
is an optimist after, he knows too little."

Actually, the contrast was not as clear-cut as that, for Mark
Twain knew a good deal of happiness even in his last period. The
Old Man in *What Is Man?*—admittedly the author's *alter ego*—
claims a happy temperament, and those who knew Mark Twain
well at the end of his life make it clear that he did not go about
like a professional mourner. "I am old," he writes in 1906; "I recognize it but I don't realize it. I wonder if a person ever really ceases
to feel young—I mean, for a whole day at a time." In his paper on

2 *Mark Twain and "Huck Finn,"* chapter XI: "Mistakes and Misfortunes,
1876–1879."

the death of Jean he says he knows his temperament too well to suppose that he will be depressed permanently by even such a calamity as that, and Elizabeth Wallace has written engagingly of his gaiety in Bermuda: "Often, when the long corridor of the second floor of the hotel presented a temptingly empty avenue, he hopped, skipped, and ran, and then gave a delicious suggestion of a cakewalk. As soon as a door opened, however, he stopped and assumed a supernaturally grave aspect." Even on January 26, 1910, a month after the death of Jean, he writes, "I am happy—few are so happy."

This does not mean that he was insincere when he uttered grave counsels of despair, nor does it at all imply that he did not suffer deeply. It does mean that he was mercurial; he did not long inhabit the heights, nor did he wallow for any considerable period in the Slough of Despond. Readers of *Tom Sawyer* will remember that it is their hero's habit, every now and then, to go off by himself to meditate and wish he were dead, but they will remember, too, that a very slight change of stimulus is all that is needed to banish this mood altogether. In this respect, as in many others, we may be sure that Tom Sawyer is the true image of young Sam Clemens, and the boy Sam Clemens was the father of the man Mark Twain. "I can suck melancholy out of a song," says Jaques, "as a weasel sucks eggs." In the last analysis, there are probably no complete pessimists except those who fill our suicides' graves. Or, as Mark Twain himself puts it, "Pessimists are born not made; optimists are born not made; but no man is born either pessimist wholly or optimist wholly, perhaps; he is pessimistic along certain lines and optimistic along certain others. That is my case."

Mark Twain's own references to suicide are less numerous than might be expected of a man who so often speaks in praise of death. He tells us that in the unsettled days following his return from Hawaii, he was so depressed one morning that he placed a loaded pistol against his head but found that he lacked courage to pull the trigger; and toward the end of his life, he told Paine, one day, that he had made up his mind that, if he lived two years longer, he must put an end to himself. After Mrs. Clemens's death in Italy, he, one day, by the merest chance, saved himself from a fall through a window which would probably have killed him. He seems glad that he escaped it; he would not have the world think he had taken his own life. "You see the lightning refuses to strike me," he once remarked—"there is where the defect is. We have to do our own striking. But nobody ever gets the courage until he goes crazy." In his marginal notes on Lecky, he remarks that it always gave him pain to read of a frustrated suicide and gratitude to read of a successful one. Yet in the very year when, as he afterwards reported, he nearly shot himself in San Francisco, he produced an all-out "inspiration" letter to Will Bowen: "I am very, very sorry you cannot get well—but don't despond—it is *poison*, rank *poison* to knuckle down to care & hardships. They must come to us all, albeit in different shapes—& we may not escape them—it is not possible—but we may swindle them out of half their puissance with a stiff upper lip."[3] Much later, he wrote Howells (not about a personal problem) that he saw an argument against suicide in "the grief of the worshipers left behind, the awful famine in their hearts, these are too costly terms for the release." All in all, I cannot think of him as a promising subject for suicide. He never went crazy, and he had a great deal of endurance. He could play with the idea—as he did in that rather histrionic moment in San Francisco—for he could play with anything that was human. But suicides do not kill themselves two years hence; they do it now. He waited through all calamities for the natural end.

Albert Bigelow Paine understood Mark Twain's pessimism better than any of his critics. If he minimizes it, it is not because he is trying to make a case for Mark Twain; it is because he knows that some of Mark's utterances, quoted out of their context, are misleading. Paine lived with Mark Twain, and he knew that within ten days of his death, he wanted to buy some stocks against an inevitable coming rise in the market. Mark Twain's all-pervasive humor must often have acted as a modifying influence, though Miss Bellamy has acutely suggested that it may also have influ-

---

[3] In this connection, it is amusing to note that, alongside the savage epigrams already quoted, Mark Twain has others which are quite as cheerful as Ella Wheeler Wilcox: "The best way to cheer yourself is to try to cheer somebody else up." "Wrinkles should merely show where the smiles have been."

enced him in the opposite direction.[4] Norman Hapgood found
Mark Twain always cheerful in his old age, and quotes him, rather
amazingly, as saying, "I was happy in the early part of my life. I
am happy now, but there was a stretch of years in the middle of
my life when I was not happy—and that middle period was the
only part that was worth anything." Mark also told William Lyon
Phelps that he looked back upon his career "with considerable
satisfaction." Philosophically, he believed in "The Great Law"—
the balance of human misery and human happiness, and Coleman O. Parsons remarks that he liked to have two final words—
one hopeless and one hopeful. Thus "My Platonic Sweetheart"
stands over against *The Mysterious Stranger*. But Kenneth Lynn
adds that the power of the imagination is permitted to add an
element of hope, even at the end of *The Mysterious Stranger*.

III

When all exaggerations have been allowed for, however, Mark
Twain's pessimism still remains a sufficiently marked feature of
his thought during his later years so that one ought, if possible, to
try to sum up its genesis and growth. I will say nothing here of
purely literary influences: Schönemann, for example, suggests that
The Citizen of the World may have been important. I will pass
by, too, any suggestions which may have been made by the Scot
Macfarlane (the first name is unknown) whom young Sam Clemens met in Cincinnati: "Macfarlane considered that the animal
life in the world was developed in the course of aeons of time
from a few microscopic seed germs . . . and that this development
was progressive upon an ascending scale toward ultimate perfection until *man* was reached; and that then the progressive scheme

---

[4] *Mark Twain as a Literary Artist*, 136: "He was a humorist by virtue of his
quizzical slant on life. But the easy facility in seizing on disharmonies, the quick
perception of the fundamental incongruities in human existence which he cultivated
as part of his humorist's technique, may have contributed to his failure to achieve
harmony and unity in some of his more serious writings. Perhaps this facility and
this perception made it difficult for him to effect the reconciliation necessary for a
complete view and a true perspective of life itself—life with its innate dignities, its
myriad possibilities so sadly jumbled with obvious stupidities and injustices." See,
further, Guy A. Cardwell, "Mark Twain's Failures in Comedy, and *The Enemy
Conquered*," *Georgia Review*, Vol. XIII (1959), 424-36.

broke pitifully down and went to wrack and ruin!" Many seeds
are planted in a man's mind; only a few of them can sprout. The
problem, then, is to determine what it was in Mark Twain's temperament or experience of life that encouraged the development
of a pessimistic outlook.

First, and most obviously,[5] his personal griefs and misfortunes.
His financial failure was a terrible blow, for though he ultimately
recovered from it—though, indeed, in the end, it probably wid-
ened and deepened his consciousness of humanity's good will, in
general and toward him in particular—it was, for many years, a
great strain; he could not but be dashed by the thought that the
thing to which he had devoted so much of his energies had turned
out to be a chase after wind. But a much stronger influence was
the long series of crushing personal losses.[6] As he himself expressed
it in 1906: "Life was a fairy-tale, then, it is a tragedy now. When
I was 43 and John Hay was 41, he said that life was a tragedy after
40, and I disputed it. Three years ago he asked me to testify again:
I counted my graves, and there was nothing for me to say."

Earliest in point of time was the death of Henry Clemens in
the frightful steamboat accident of 1858. Mark Twain held himself responsible for Henry's presence on the fated steamer, and
life was never the same again. With more or less reason, as the
case may be, he also blamed himself, as we have seen, for the death
of his son Langdon. Of course, such things did not, and could not
in themselves have made Mark Twain a pessimist. But they may
have spoiled the taste of life in his mouth and inclined his mind
toward counsels of despair. After all, as Gertrude points out, Hamlet had always known that fathers die; he had always known—she
might have added—that women are false. But since he had never

[5] I am not a Freudian biographer, and I do not know everything. Therefore I
do not pretend to be able to explain Mark Twain's pessimism completely. It does
seem to me, however, that all the elements which I shall hereinafter enumerate deserve to be taken into account in *seeking* to understand it. I assert neither that they
all deserve to be weighted equally nor that other factors of equal importance may
not have entered in.

[6] If Bernard DeVoto was right in his feeling that Mark Twain's sorrows im-
paired not only his health and faith and hope but also his creativity, then the picture gains another dimension. In any event, "The Symbols of Despair" (*Mark
Twain at Work*) is the most moving account of these matters and certainly one of
the most brilliant essays that will ever be written about Mark Twain.

before personally experienced either of these things, he had only a theoretical kind of knowledge which did not prevent his entering with full zeal into the battle of life. Now he knows; his eyes are open; he will never be the old Hamlet any more. And, having the imaginative temperament, he will not stop with his own sorrows, crushing as they are. Instead, he will use them as a key to unlock the heart of humanity; through his own sympathetic imagination, he enters into the woes of all mankind, and it actually comes to seem to him as if the full weight of the griefs of all the world were resting upon his shoulders.

It is so with all men of imagination; it was so with Tennyson after the death of Hallam, as he specifically tells us in one of the many passages in *In Memoriam* that so closely echo *Hamlet*; it was so, too, with Mark Twain. "Once Twichell heard me cussing the human race, and he said, 'Why, Mark, you are the last person in the world to do that—one selected and set apart as you are.' I said, 'Joe, you don't know what you are talking about. I am not cussing altogether about my own little troubles. Any one can stand his own misfortunes; but when I read in the papers all about the rascalities and outrages going on I realize what a creature the human animal is. Don't you care more about the wretchedness of others than anything that happens to you?' Joe said he did, and shut up."

Mark Twain had not lived long before he discovered that life is a terrible thing. Indeed, he did not even have a chance to grow out of childhood first, which is a privilege the world owes to all her children but pays to few. Here is just one paragraph on the subject from the *Autobiography*:

> All within the space of a couple of years we had two or three other tragedies, and I had the ill luck to be near by, on each occasion. There was the slave man who was struck down with a chunk of slag for some small offense; I saw him die. And the young Californian emigrant who was stabbed with a bowie knife by a drunken comrade; I saw the red life gush from his breast. And the case of the rowdy young brothers and their harmless old uncle: one of them held the old man down with his knees on his breast while the

other one tried repeatedly to kill him with an Allen revolver which wouldn't go off. I happened along just then, of course.

In addition to all these unfortunates, there was the tramp confined to the village jail, to whom, in the kindness of his heart, young Sam Clemens smuggled some matches, only to see the fool burn himself to death. And—since he was apparently one of those people who do not know enough to leave horrors alone when horrors leave them alone, he also watched an autopsy on his father's body through a keyhole!

Then he grew up and went to the River—the River and the Far West. In the mining camps, he saw how the human animal behaves when the greed for gold takes possession of him and drives all other thoughts and emotions out. On the River, he met a wide variety of human types, and they did not all tend to raise his opinion of the merits of his kind. He stood up under the shock, however, for he was young and ambitious, and he had his way to make in the world. The time came later when he had made it, when his vitality did not surge so high, when his sensitiveness had grown with the years. Then he could no longer bear the thought of such things. "I have been reading the morning paper. I do it every morning—well knowing that I shall find in it the usual depravities and basenesses and hypocrisies and cruelties that make up civilization, and cause me to put in the rest of the day pleading for the damnation of the human race. I cannot seem to get my prayers answered, yet I do not despair." Paine suggested that he disregard the papers, but that was no solution. His horizon was wider now. He found the same damnable cruelties in books, and the fact that the rascals were all dead and done with did not make their rascalities hurt him less. Moreover, he knew something of science, and science had taught him that every quiet meadow is a hideous battlefield. How could he help feeling that there was something rotten at the heart of life?

Let us make no mistake about it: it was the man's tenderness that impelled him toward despair—his tenderness and his idealism and the great dreams that he had dreamed. His pessimism was not the best way to meet the problem; neither was it the worst.

And it was because he was good, not because he was bad, that he took that unhappy turning. Listen to the terrible cry of the young prince in *The Prince and the Pauper*, when he sees a girl burned at the stake: "That which I have seen, in that one little moment, will never go out from my memory, but will abide there; and I shall see it all the days, and dream of it all the nights, till I die. Would God I had been blind!"

The body of Jonathan Swift lies in Dublin Cathedral under this inscription, written by himself: "Here lies the body of Jonathan Swift, D.D., dean of this cathedral, where burning indignation can no longer tear his heart. Go, traveler, and imitate if you can a man who was an undaunted champion of liberty." The great idealists ask too much of mankind, too much of themselves; their vision of what life might be is so high that the thought of what it is becomes unendurable. Sometimes they take refuge in cynicism; they wear indifference like a piece of armor over their hearts; they tell themselves and others that they do not care. Mark Twain never got very far along that road. He had been born with his feet on the edge of utopia; no thoughtful reader of *A Connecticut Yankee* can doubt the earnestness of the sincerity of his faith in the democratic experiment. And he saw—well, he saw what all men saw in America, in the seventies and the eighties and the nineties. Or, rather, he saw what many men did not see—though it was there to be seen before their eyes. He did not always comprehend the full significance of it. He never knew just what it was that the robber barons were doing to America—some of them he counted among his personal friends—but he did know that something had gone terribly wrong. The hopes of the Enlightenment had faded. The world into which he had been born was dead, and he was roaming about in a strange new world, a world that he did not understand and could not love. You must not be discouraged, they told him. The Kingdom of God marches on; it progresses steadily, from age to age. " 'From age to age,' " he cried—"yes, it describes that giddy gait. I (and the rocks) will not live to see it arrive, but that is all right—it will arrive, it surely will."

The griefs and sorrows of Mark Twain's personal life passed over, then, by a natural transition, into his sympathy for humanity, impelling him powerfully in the direction of pessimism as he contemplates the wrongs that humanity must bear. But since men are oppressed by men, we soon run into a third cause, which I find in Mark Twain's own natural tendency to rage, violence, and exaggeration. His temper had never been of the best, and though he might have helped himself along this line, this would have required a more heroic self-discipline than he was ever disposed to impose upon himself. This was, indeed, his Achilles-heel, the place where the lime leaf clung to Siegfried, and it was through this tragic flaw that life struck at him in the end. Add the artist's natural love of strong stimuli and sensation, and we have a situation in which the rage and impatience which often appear in Mark Twain's middle period could not well have avoided passing over, by a natural development, into the pessimism of his final phase.

The connection between Mark Twain's deterministic philosophy[7] and his pessimism is now perhaps somewhat more speculative than it once appeared to be. In *Mark Twain at Work*, DeVoto saw both Mark's determinism (*What Is Man?*) and his vision of life as dream (*The Mysterious Stranger*) as phases of his attempt to free man from personal responsibility for the evils which beset him, and, more urgently, to save Mark Twain from the numerous charges which his "trained Presbyterian conscience" entered against him. More recently, Professor Alexander E. Jones has attempted to differentiate between the "serenity beyond despair" of *The Mysterious Stranger* and the "sweet (indeed almost "jaunty") reasonableness" of *What Is Man?* though he admits that the deleted concluding chapter on "The Moral Sense," in which Mark argued that man used his unique ability to distinguish between right and wrong in order that he might choose to do wrong, is "characterized by a mood of pessimism that sometimes approaches misanthropy." Nobody has ever supposed that Mark Twain was ever in practice a consistent determinist; he himself admitted that he went on to the end making moral judgments which, according to the terms of his philosophy, he had no right to make, and Professor Jones is quite right in stressing the point

[7] Which will be discussed more fully in the final chapter.

that by emphasizing the idea that though conscience is a machine, it can still be trained "to desire things which are socially desirable," Mark Twain preserved something of the Christian ethic and achieved a less pessimistic outlook than Calvinistic predestination would have made possible.[8] For all that, we have Clemens writing Howells in 1899 that "since I wrote my Bible, (last year) which Mrs. Clemens loathes, & shudders over, & will not listen to the last half nor allow me to print any part of it, Man is not to me the respect-worthy person he was before; & so I have lost my pride in him & can't write gaily nor praisefully about him any more. And I don't intend to try. I mean to go on writing, for that is my best amusement, but I shan't print much. (For I don't wish to be scalped, any more than another.)"

This is a very interesting statement, and it is noteworthy that Mark Twain here acknowledges the effect of his determinism not only upon his attitude toward men (and presumably his personal happiness) but also upon his art. And I think one may well question the idea that it is only his fear of being scalped that acts as a restraining influence upon the artist. For art—the art of the novel, in any case—deals with human beings, and if one denies human beings dignity and responsibility, how can anything one has to say about them, or anything one causes them to do in a work of art, have any importance? Persons who dislike Mark Twain's final philosophy are forever harking back to "the practical manliness and generosity of Tom and Huck" at an earlier period. It is interesting, and it may be significant, that Mark Twain himself did this. He tried to revive Huck and Tom more than once in the midnight of his despair. Once, as we have seen, he even tried to degrade them. But, do what he might, he could not make them live for him again.

Mrs. Clemens kept her husband from publishing *What Is Man?*, but she could not keep him from writing it or thinking it. If she had been able to do so, she would have served him well as writer and as man. Mark Twain was human, and he could not altogether escape the human tendency to define orthodoxy as "my

[8] See Alexander E. Jones, "Mark Twain and the Determinism of *What Is Man?*," *American Literature*, Vol. XXX (1957–58), 1–17.

doxy" and heterodoxy as "the other fellow's doxy." He himself admits this. I have found the Truth, he says, and "the rest of my days will be spent in patching and painting and puttying and caulking my priceless possession and in looking the other way when an imploring argument or a damning fact approaches." The very frankness of his admission is the best possible testimony we could have as to his fundamental sincerity, and there were many ways in which he remained astonishingly open-minded to the end. Nevertheless, once he had written *What Is Man?*, once he had talked it to his friends and defended it against their onslaughts, he had a vested interest in it, and it is difficult to believe that its influence upon him was a happy one.

IV

Mark Twain died in the first full flush of the Pollyanna optimism of our Western world. Mechanical civilization had triumphed; democracy was successful and unassailed; war was definitely a thing of the past. To be sure, there was a great deal that was wrong just now, but there was little or nothing that might not be made right once we had made up our minds to it.

To Mark Twain all this seemed a bit unconvincing. Things were happening all about him that did not quite square with the assumption that this was the best of all possible worlds. There were even times when he feared that civilization was taking the trail of the Gadarene swine down to the sea.

In such a world happiness is impossible without faith, and the faith must be inspired by something considerably larger than the "Gospel" of *What Is Man?*. In a sense, Albert Schweitzer is no more of an optimist than Samuel Clemens. "I am pessimistic," he writes, "in that I experience in its full weight what we conceive to be the absence of purpose in the course of world-happenings. Only at quite rare moments have I felt really glad to be alive. I could not but feel with a sympathy full of regret all the pain that I saw around me, not only that of men but that of the whole creation. From this community of suffering I have never tried to withdraw myself. It seemed to me a matter of course that we should all take our share of the burden of pain which lies upon the world." But

215

Schweitzer does not stop there. From the wreck of all things human, he goes on to lay hold upon that which is divine; from the natural he passes to the supernatural. Thus, in almost the same breath as that in which he has spoken of the failure of life, he can speak of himself as among those "who have won their way through to the peace which passeth all understanding," and here is the source of the strength which sustains him, and which has carried him through the herculean task he has set for himself. As Chaucer expresses it,

> Men moste axe at seyntes if it is
> Aught fair in hevene; why? for they conne telle;
> And axen fendes, is it foul in helle.

Mark Twain's soul never quite found its way into harbor, but it did not die, but went on seeking always. There are millions of men among those who never find the answer to the riddle of human life who yet see life's evils almost as clearly as Samuel Clemens saw them. They do not all become pessimists. What, then, do they do?

One of two things, I believe. Either they accept the situation, embrace the sin, make themselves a part of the bitter struggle—"Every man for himself and the devil take the hindmost"—or else they shrug their shoulders, repudiate personal responsibility for social evil, forget or try to forget, and go off

> To sport with Amaryllis in the shade,
> Or with the tangles of Neaera's hair.

Mark Twain chose neither alternative, but what he did was more uncomfortable and more noble. He could not find the supernatural solution of life's problem. He tried his best to solve it on the secular level and failed, for the simple reason that there is no secular solution. But because he was a great man, he could not rest content with that. He went about brooding over the question of human days, and he was profoundly unhappy because he could not find the answer.

216

CHAPTER ELEVEN: *Testament*

I

MARK TWAIN WAS A BORN REFORMER; nothing could be farther
from the truth than to imagine that he was a humorist pure and
simple in his early days and became interested in more serious
matters only toward the end, when personal sorrows had hurt him
and bitter reflection imposed the feeling that all was wrong with
the world. "I have always preached," he writes. "That is the reason that I have lasted thirty years. If the humor came of its own
accord and uninvited, I have allowed it a place in my sermon, but
I was not writing the sermon for the sake of the humor." Gamaliel
Bradford complains that "much of the jesting of Mark's early days
is so trivial that it distinctly implies the absence of steady thinking
on any subject." Mark had time for trivia as long as he lived, but
sometimes there was more thinking behind them than appeared
clearly. And, as Bradford himself pointed out, there was never a
time when he was indifferent to corruption and cruelty, or when
he was not ready to smite the serpent wherever it should lift its
ugly head. In Hannibal days he felt no aversion to slavery as an

institution, but he was already reacting strongly to individual cases of ill treatment.

In Nevada, we find him, for the only time in his career, wielding political influence, directly through his pen, and indirectly as the brother of Orion Clemens, secretary of the Territory. He attacked the telegraph monopoly, extortionate undertakers, journalistic indifference to local evils, and much besides. Even the piece about the Empire City Massacre was intended to expose the habit of "cooking dividends." It is difficult, writes Miss Bellamy with simple justice, "to see how anyone could have expressed himself more directly regarding the life about him." His fight against municipal, and particularly police, corruption in San Francisco, is well known, and since the *Call* lacked the courage or the decency to print what he wrote about these things, he sent it back to Joe Goodman in Virginia City, and Joe printed it. Soon they were calling him "The Moralist of the Main," and I have no doubt political corruptionists were also calling him other names less complimentary and less printable.

He brought the habits he had formed on the Comstock with him to the East Coast. He had caricatures of the Erie Railroad Ring running through his *Burlesque Biography* (1870), and though he did not initiate the fight against Tammany, nobody contributed to it more spectacularly. When the big boss was finished, one New York paper quipped,

> *Who killed Croker?*
> *I, said Mark Twain,*
> *I killed Croker,*
> *I, the Jolly Joker.*

In a dream he once saw a procession of all the persons killed and injured in American railroad accidents during the year. He attacked the mounting expenses of government, fraudulent income tax returns, and the abuse of the insanity plea in capital cases.[1]

[1] There is a horrible description of an execution witnessed by Mark Twain in *Republican Letters*, 43–46. He went because he thought he "ought to have a lesson" and characteristically chose one of the worst of assassins. He does not take a definite stand on capital punishment as such. In Australia, he thought that many

The reform tendency runs all through Mark Twain's career. The shortcomings of the jury system are attacked in *Roughing It*; *Life on the Mississippi* contains a strong plea for cremation; the feud as an institution gets a rough going-over in *Huckleberry Finn*;[2] and the monstrous wickedness of war is excoriated in *The Mysterious Stranger*. Examination of the letters and speeches indefinitely lengthens the list of "causes" in which Mark Twain was interested. He spoke out on what displeased him in Hartford as well as elsewhere, and he would not have been himself if his protest had not sometimes taken fantastic forms. "In 1888, the city, at the instigation of a prominent citizen and 'skunk,' moved a street light from Mark's gates to the corner of Forest Street, and Mark spitefully contracted for his own light and police protection and planned to refuse taxes except on his house and land."[3] When sufficiently roused, he was capable of uncomfortable personal exertion in the public welfare, as when he prosecuted the cabman who had overcharged Katy Leary.

The two great satires are, however, *The Gilded Age* and *A Connecticut Yankee*. Whatever may be said of the former from a strictly literary standpoint, it is so significant a social document that it has given its name to a period. "Alone among the novelists of his time," DeVoto writes of Mark Twain, "he concerns himself with the national muck. In him only exist the boom towns, the railroad builders, the Dilworthies, the lobbyists, the gallicized Irish, society swelling to a gimcrack pretension with the manure of empire under its finger nails, the monster fungus of the gilded age." The *Yankee* is, however, a much greater book, and that criti-

of the convicts who had been sent out there ought to have been hanged, transportation being too cruel and unfair a punishment; he also wanted imprisonment for life for the man who killed the Empress of Austria, as the severer punishment of the two and not conferring celebrity. In the McFarland-Richardson case in Buffalo *Express* days, he said that McFarland ought to be tried not for killing Richardson but for mistreating his wife. Henry Ward Beecher married Mrs. McFarland to Richardson on his death-bed; as Abby Sage Richardson she later dramatized *The Prince and the Pauper*. See Martin B. Fried, "Mark Twain in Buffalo," *Niagara Frontier*, Vol. V (1959), 89–110.

[2] At one time, Mark Twain considered treating dueling and lynching in *Huckleberry Finn*, as well as feuding.

[3] Kenneth R. Andrews, *Nook Farm*, 125, which see, for further criticism of Hartford.

cism is particularly obtuse which sees Mark Twain, in the *Yankee*, deserting the problems of his own time to blow off steam on the perfectly safe subject of the iniquities of sixth-century England.[4] When Mark Twain made a romance out of his parable, he proved not that he was a coward but rather that he was an artist, and not simply a pamphleteer.

The artist has an advantage over the pamphleteer, too, in the matter of securing a hearing, and the humorist has an advantage over the avowedly serious artist. Men will often tolerate in jest what they cannot bear to have said in earnest, and there is always at least a chance that somebody may be intelligent enough to discover the virtue of the jest. Paine glances at this circumstance when he tells us that in the campaign of 1884, Mark Twain made speeches for Cleveland "which invited the laughter of both parties, and were universally quoted and printed without regard to the paper's convictions."

There was a strong note of chivalry running through Mark Twain's record as a reformer; temperamentally he was always on the side of the underdog. He might or he might not believe in the cause, he might or he might not admire the people involved, let him be convinced that an injustice was being practiced, and he would immediately constitute himself counsel for the defense. Thus he opposed the Bell Bill, which proposed to outlaw osteopathy in the state of New York, and though he had no love for Mormons, and no sympathy with their peculiar tenets, he denounced the persecution under which they had suffered.

He admits only one racial prejudice—against the French. "I am quite sure that (bar one) I have no race prejudices, and I think I have no color prejudices nor caste prejudices nor creed prejudices. Indeed, I know it. I can stand any society. All that I care to know is that a man is a human being—that is enough for me; he can't be any worse."[5] His record is not quite that clear. At one

4 See John B. Hoben, "Mark Twain's *Connecticut Yankee*: A Genetic Study," *American Literature*, Vol. XVIII (1946–47), 197–218.

5 The anti-French feeling was due to Mark Twain's abhorrence of Latin attitudes toward sex. "France has neither winter nor summer nor morals—apart from these drawbacks it is a fine country." Even in *Captain Stormfield* there is a fling about liking to look at a Frenchman, "if I ever have the luck to catch him engaged

time, in his youth, he shared mildly in the Know-Nothing sus-
picion of "foreigners," but this did not go very deep. Not much
can be claimed for his sensitiveness to Indian abuses,[6] but he did
better by the Chinese. "I am not fond of Chinamen, but I am still
less fond of seeing them wronged and abused." His speaking out
for them against police brutality in San Francisco was one of
the noblest actions of his life. He supported the Burlingame
Treaty of 1868; at one time, he saw no objection to Chinese becoming American citizens.

Apparently there was only one family of Jews in school in
Hannibal. "It took me a good while to get over the awe of it. To
my fancy they were clothed invisibly in the damp and cobwebby
mold of antiquity. They carried me back to Egypt, and in imagination I moved among the Pharaohs and all the shadowy celebrities of that remote age." In Palestine he was less romantic
about Jews. "How they ever came to be the chosen people of the
Lord," he declared in a passage in the *Alta California* letters not
reprinted in *The Innocents Abroad*, "is a mystery which will stag-
ger me from this day forth till I perish." As a mature man, he
was considered a great friend and admirer of the Jews, though it
is true that even the essay "Concerning the Jews" perpetuates
some anti-Semitic stereotypes. This, however, was ignorance on
Mark Twain's part, not malice, as he showed promptly when the
matter was brought to his attention.[7] He also perpetuates myths
friendly to the Jews, as when he commits himself to the popular
notion that Jewish brains are superior to Gentile brains.

Since Mark Twain was born in a slaveholding state, his attitude toward Negroes is more interesting. Though he was never an
abolitionist, he always loved the black face. "I have seen but few
niggers," says Captain Stormfield, "that hadn't their hearts in the
right place." Mark Twain had a hump to get over before he could
accept citizenship for Negroes, but he made it—"Pap" Finn is

in anything that ain't indelicate." It is ironical that the human being Mark Twain
admired most should have been not only French but the national heroine of France.

[6] See Fred W. Lorch, "Mark Twain's Early Views on Western Indians,"
Twainian, Vol. IV, April, 1945, pp. 1–2.

[7] All the important data concerning Mark Twain's attitude toward Jews are
assembled and interpreted by Philip S. Foner, in *Mark Twain, Social Critic*, 222–36.

never more hateful than in his loathing for the Negro who was a professor in a college and who could vote—and once, with his weakness for prophecies, he even foresaw Negro supremacy in America by 1985. He admired Frederick Douglass, and had a picture of Prudence Crandall, one of the early desegregationists in American education, in his billiard room. He was so much more tolerant of human shortcomings in Negroes than in members of his own race that Mrs. Clemens finally suggested that he might save himself a good deal of wear-and-tear if he made it a rule to consider every man colored until he was proved white. Mark Twain gave at least one reading for a Negro church in Hartford; he also put a Negro student through Yale, as a part of the "reparation due from every white to every black man." Whatever wrong thing a Negro may do, he believed, white men are responsible for nine-tenths of the guilt accruing, and "The United States of Lyncherdom" and other utterances on the same nauseating subject were brave, passionate, and high-minded. Did any white man ever deal more justly and more understandingly with the Negro race than Mark Twain did in *Pudd'nhead Wilson*, where all its faults are so mercilessly revealed, and all its wrongs and courage set forth, so utterly without any sense of racial superiority?[8] When Negroes object to Jim in *Huckleberry Finn*, one can only regret that they are behaving as stupidly as white folks often do, for surely Jim is one of the noblest characters in American literature.[9] Yet there is another touch in the same novel which cuts even deeper in its implications for race relations, and this comes when Huck tells Aunt Sally about the steamboat accident:

"Good gracious! [she exclaims] anybody hurt?"

[8] See Anne P. Wigger, "The Composition of Mark Twain's *Pudd'nhead Wilson and Those Extraordinary Twins*: Chronology and Development," *Modern Philology*, Vol. XXXV (1957-58), 93–102: "Tom ponders which is 'base or high' in him, his white or his Negro blood, and Twain states that either is high if not debased by slavery. Tom is base because of the effects of slaveowning. He is brutal because of slaveowning heredity, and his inherent brutality is reinforced by his training as a white master; he is cowardly because the Negro blood in him has had to submit to generations of slaves and slaveowners, and is the corrupting force in Tom's nature."

[9] See Frances V. Brownell, "The Role of Jim in *Huckleberry Finn*," *Boston University Studies in English*, Vol. I (1955-56), 74–83.

"No'm. Killed a nigger."

"Well, it's lucky; because sometimes people do get hurt."

Mark Twain was also friendly to organized labor, "the sole present help of the weak against the strong." His most advanced statement in behalf of the laboring man was made before the Monday Evening Club, in Hartford, in 1886, in a paper called "The New Dynasty."[10] Through organization and the use of the ballot, he saw labor achieving many of the privileges it has since won, and his heart was with the cause. Howells's Socialistic ideas did not greatly tempt him, however, and he criticized what seemed to him unethical union practices. "How will he [the working man] use his power? *To oppress*—at first. For he is not better than the masters that went before; nor pretends to be. The only difference is, he will oppress the few, they oppressed the many; he will oppress the thousands, they oppressed the millions; but he will imprison nobody, he will massacre, burn, flay, torture, exile nobody, nor work any subject eighteen hours a day, nor starve his family."

II

In Mark Twain's own view in later years, the most important aspect of his Testament was the idea of mechanistic determinism that he called his "Gospel." As he expressed it to Paine in 1906, "When the first living atom found itself afloat on the great Laurentian sea, the first act of that first atom led to the *second* act of that first atom, and so on down through the succeeding ages of all life, until, if the steps could be traced, it would be shown that the first act of the first atom had led inevitably to the act of my standing here in my dressing-gown at this instant talking to you."

Obviously they could not be traced, and the theory, therefore, remained theory. But Mark Twain assumed its truth.

From this presupposition it follows inevitably that man is a machine, an impersonal engine. "Whatsoever the man is, is due

[10] See Paul J. Carter, Jr., "Mark Twain and the American Labor Movement," *New England Quarterly*, Vol. XXX (1957), 383–88. Cf. Foner, *Mark Twain, Social Critic*, 176–79.

to his *make,* and to the *influences* brought to bear upon it by his heredities, his habitat, his associations. He is moved, directed, COMMANDED by *exterior* influences—*solely.* He originates nothing, not even a thought."

Logically, this point of view would seem to destroy all personal responsibility for conduct. No merit attaches to the good man, no blame to the bad. "There are gold men, and tin men, and copper men, and steel men, and so on—and each has the limitations of his nature, his heredities, his training, and his environment." Unselfish action is impossible. *"From his cradle to his grave a man never does a single thing which has any* FIRST AND FOREMOST *object but one—to secure peace of mind, spiritual comfort, for* HIMSELF.*"* This does not mean that all men are forever exploiting their fellows. In the development of life from the primordial seed it has fortunately come about that some men find satisfaction through doing good, through sacrificing themselves instead of exploiting themselves. "A man performs but *one* duty —the duty of contenting his spirit, the duty of making himself agreeable to himself. If he can most satisfactorily perform this sole and only duty by *helping* his neighbor, he will do it; if he can most satisfactorily perform it by *swindling* his neighbor, he will do that."

As we have already seen, if Mark Twain is anything he is a moralist, yet there seems no room for morality in this philosophy of life. He tries hard to bring about a *rapprochement* between his mind and his moral judgments. There is a noble passage in A *Connecticut Yankee,* where, anticipating his later, full-grown determinism, he writes:

All that is original in us, and therefore fairly creditable or discreditable to us, can be covered up and hidden by the point of a cambric needle, all the rest being atoms contributed by, and inherited from, a procession of ancestors that stretches back a billion years to the Adam-clan or grasshopper or monkey from whom our race has been so tediously and ostentatiously and unprofitably developed. And as for me, all that I think about in this plodding sad pilgrimage, this pathetic drift between the eternities, is to look out and humbly live a pure and high and blameless life, and save that one microscopic atom in me that is truly *me*; the rest may land in Sheol and welcome for all I care.

And in *What Is Man?* itself we read: "Diligently train your ideals *upward* and *still upward* toward a summit where you will find your chiefest pleasure in conduct which, while contenting you, will be sure to confer benefits upon your neighbor and the community."

Obviously there are logical difficulties here. As Paine, who himself accepted Mark Twain's philosophy, remarked, "Once admit the postulate that existence is merely a sequence of cause and effect beginning with the primal atom, and we have a theory that must stand or fall as a whole. We cannot say that man is a creature of circumstance and then leave him to select his circumstance, even in the minutest fractional degree." But it is clear that simply because he saw man as the product of his heredity and his environment, Mark Twain was also convinced that almost anything could be done through training. "Training is everything," he says. "The peach was once a bitter almond; cauliflower is nothing but cabbage with a college education." Almost two-thirds of *What Is Man?*, as Frank C. Flowers has pointed out, is devoted to "training the machine." A man is not free to do what he likes; he must content his inner master, but the inner master can be trained to desire noble and socially desirable things. "In other words, the human mechanism can be trained in virtue but deserves no personal credit for righteous behavior. [Mark] Twain's obvious satisfaction in his 'gospel' was due in no small part to this triumph over Pride, traditionally the oldest and deadliest of mortal sins."[11] So here again we see Mark Twain robbing Peter to pay Paul, throwing away the traditional Christian sanctions for righteous conduct, yet in his own somewhat eccentric way determined to save righteousness.

Once, with bitter irony, Mark Twain employed the deterministic philosophy to flay a wrongdoer far more thoroughly and

[11] Alexander E. Jones, "Mark Twain and the Determinism of *What Is Man?*," *American Literature*, Vol. XXX (1957–58), 1–17. My discussion of Mark Twain's determinism is considerably indebted to the article.

mercilessly than he could have achieved it upon any other basis. He wrote, it will be recalled, "A Defence of General Funston" for his treacherous capture of Aguinaldo, during the Spanish-American War in the Philippines. Funston, urged Mark Twain, was not to blame for what he did: he was only following the natural bent of his nature, even as Washington did. "In each case, the basis or moral skeleton of the man was inborn disposition—a thing which is as permanent as rock, and never undergoes any actual or genuine change between cradle and grave." Funston's "It took as naturally to moral slag as Washington's took to moral gold, but only It was to blame, not Funston." It would be as unfair to blame him for this "as it would be to blame him because his conscience leaked out through one of his pores when he was little—a thing which he could not help, and he couldn't have raised it, anyway."

Mark Twain's determinism has been attributed to the influence of various writers upon him—Lecky, Hobbes, Mandeville, Locke, Hume, Newton, and others. In 1898, having read a book by Sir John Adams, he wrote that savant to thank him for having revealed the "exterior sources" of some of his ideas to him. "I have never read Locke nor any other of the many philosophers quoted by you," he declared. "So, all these months I have been thinking the thoughts of illustrious philosophers, and didn't know it. I merely knew that they were not *my* thoughts; that they all came from the outside; that neither I nor those philosophers nor any other person has ever had a thought which was his own; a thought born on the premises; a thought not brought in from the outside." And he goes on to find it "a little pathetic to reflect that man's proudest possession—his mind—is a mere machine; an automatic machine; a machine which is so wholly independent of him that it will not even take a *suggestion* from him, let alone a command, unless it suits its humour."[12] Where the idea of Mark Twain's determinism came from originally may admit of wide conjecture, but his acceptance of it seems more closely connected with his own personal and emotional needs than he here suggests. That it actu-

[12] The letter has been printed by Lawrence C. Powell, "An Unpublished Mark Twain Letter," *American Literature*, Vol. XIII (1941–42), 405–407. Cf. Sir John Adams, "Mark Twain, Psychologist," *Dalhousie Review*, Vol. XIII (1933–34), 417–26.

ally satisfied those needs is, as has already been indicated, something worse than doubtful, but it does seem clearly to represent an attempt to do so. If there were contradictory elements in Mark Twain's philosophy, there were contradictory elements in his personality also, and he had to live with all of them. It is not at all unusual to wish to eat one's cake and keep it too.

III

Mark Twain was not a "joiner." It was not his habit to delegate his right to make decisions to others; despite his philosophy, he found "spiritual comfort" and "peace of mind" only in standing firmly on his own feet and being responsible to nobody. So it was very natural that he should have no interest in political parties as such, and should pass at will from one party to another, giving his vote to the best man available, regardless of party affiliations. "It is not *parties* that make or save countries or that build them to greatness—it is clean men, clean ordinary citizens, rank & file, the masses." At one time, he proposed to organize a "casting vote party," which should consist of a body of independent voters, nominating no candidate of their own, but throwing their support to the best man nominated by the established parties. Such an organization, he believed, must hold the balance of power in any election, thus compelling all regular parties to put their best candidates forward.

His political inheritance was Whig. In 1860 he supported Bell and Everett; thereafter he voted Republican when he voted at all, except when his conviction that Blaine was dishonest caused him to turn "Mugwump" and support Cleveland.[13] Even in 1908, the last Presidential election of his life, he voted for Taft, despite his conviction that, as Theodore Roosevelt's candidate, he represented the establishment of a dynasty.

The earliest campaign in which Mark Twain took a keen interest was that of 1876, when Hayes's commitment to civil service and decent government won his passionate allegiance, and he was

13 The famous story in *Mark Twain's Autobiography*, II, 13–26, about Twichell's nearly losing his church because he voted for Cleveland is an example of Mark's remembering what did not happen. Twichell opposed Blaine and voted the Prohibition ticket. There is nothing to indicate that his congregation objected.

confident that the country would go to hell if Tilden won. (Later he decided that Hayes's election had been a "steal.") He was, of course, an almost ecstatic admirer of Grant[14]—"The presidency can't add anything to Grant—he will shine on, without it. It is ephemeral, he is eternal"—and, when the time came, almost as enthusiastic about Garfield, for whom he made a campaign speech in Hartford. When Garfield lay dying of an assassin's wound in 1881, Mark canceled a humorous lecture, because he could not bear the thought of giving it at such a time, or of having it reported along with the President's death. The Howellses had close personal ties with Garfield, but Mark, sternly honorable as always, would not use his avenue to the President to get an appointment even for Charley Fairbanks, not thinking him qualified for the post he sought.[15] In view of Mark Twain's general economic ignorance, as shown, for example, in his comments on free silver[16]— in 1900 he refused to vote, McKinley being disqualified as an imperialist and Bryan by his economic heresy—his opposition to a high tariff, during his later years, is surprising. It may be remembered that Theodore Roosevelt, himself, by profession at least, an innocent in the realms of high finance, regarded the tariff as "only a question of expediency."

Mark Twain's comparative indifference to party politics does not mean, of course, that he was not interested in the democratic experiment. His political democracy rested on the soundest possible foundation, the one foundation without which political democracy can never be notably successful—I mean his social democracy. "There are no common people," he declares, "except in the highest spheres of society"—which is, perhaps, only an inverted form of social snobbery, and he generously acknowledged that in the last analysis civilization must rest upon the hewers of wood and the drawers of water.

Such a man was not likely to have much sympathy with kings. "There never was a throne which did not represent a crime." It sounds a little hysterical today, now that kings are no longer dan-

[14] See letter to Howells, Nov. 17, 1879, *Mark Twain–Howells Letters*, I, 278–80.
[15] *Mark Twain to Mrs. Fairbanks*, 240–43.
[16] Cf. Foner, *Mark Twain, Social Critic*, 98, 263.

228

gerous and, even from the extreme republican point of view, have been succeeded by so much more menacing evils. "Another throne has gone down, and I swim in oceans of satisfaction. I wish I might live fifty years longer; I believe I should see the thrones of Europe selling at auction for old iron." He goes to Bayreuth, and the town is so full of royalty that he has difficulty in getting accommodations. "The damned Royalty gets ahead of me every time! They get ahead of everything!" Yet it is this man who must be singled out for special attention on the part of royalty, who sooner or later meets most of the royalty of his time, and who, for all his boasted democracy, finds himself pleased by the attention of these criminals, and as grateful for their favors as any good monarchist could be!

But alas! democracy calls for much more than merely getting rid of kings, and if Mark Twain did not know this at the outset, he came to realize it bitterly long before the end. As early as Muscatine *Journal* days, he was thrilled by American historic buildings, and convinced of the necessity to preserve them—a much less common point of view in those days than it is now. As long as he lived, he felt an upsurge of patriotism whenever he returned to America. In 1888, incensed by Matthew Arnold's criticism of American newspapers, he went so far as to argue that the first function of a newspaper was not to give the news—this was secondary—but to keep the people "in love with their country and its institutions, and shielded from the allurements of alien and inimical systems." For all that, he was to live to realize the importance of teaching *dis*loyalty and to perceive that "My country, right or wrong!" was no less servile or immoral than "The King can do no wrong!" The Yankee declares that brutal laws are impossible in a democracy, but Mark Twain was not always sure of this. He hits the stupidity of Congress as early as the *Innocents*, and there has never been a much more appalling picture of governmental corruption than is presented in *The Gilded Age*. Colonel Sellers is genuinely hurt when Washington suggests that he ought to be in Congress: "I don't think there has ever been anything in my conduct that should make you feel justified in saying a thing like that." When Stormfield was broken into, Clemens warned the burglars that if they persisted in their evil ways, they might sooner or later expect to wind up in the Senate. His final devastating judgment is summed up in one of the *Equator* aphorisms: "It could probably be shown by facts and figures that there is no distinctly native American criminal class except Congress."

Of course there is exaggeration here for humorous effect, but it is not all exaggeration. And the problem of democratic government in America involved more than the criminal impulses of congressmen. The plain truth of the matter was that the hopes of the fathers had not been fulfilled. America had escaped the exploitation of royal houses, only to fall into the hands of other exploiters instead. Even universal suffrage, that foolproof safety valve, had turned out far from infallible in practice. In all too many cases, it meant government by the ignorant, by the incompetent, by those whose votes could be bought or unfairly controlled. He made various suggestions toward solving this problem —limiting the suffrage, or giving extra votes for property and learning, as in "The Curious Republic of Gondour." As early as 1875, he told the Hartford Monday Evening Club that it was absurd to weigh the vote of a fool or a scoundrel as heavily as that of "a president, a bishop, a college professor, a merchant prince." Always fascinated by the English landscape, Clemens went through almost every variety of admiration and detestation of English political arrangements, but there were times when he thought America might take a lesson even from that monarchical land. (Disraeli had advocated plural voting, as Mark did in "Gondour.") But in his heart he knew that no political gadget would solve a problem which, in the last analysis, was rooted in the fundamental stuff of a weak and defective human nature. "There is one thing that always puzzles me: as inheritors of the mentality of our reptile ancestors we have improved the inheritance by a thousand grades; but in the matter of the morals which they left us we have gone backward in many grades." And so, in his old age, he saw America becoming, as he called it, a monarchy. We call it a dictatorship. The battle had been fought on this side of the Atlantic, and here too it had been lost.

IV

Of all the problems of government, the one about which Mark Twain appears to have felt most deeply is the problem of war and peace. This may best be approached in connection with the national emergencies which he was called upon to face in the course of his life.

The Mexican War (which was hardly a national emergency) was relatively unimportant. He was too young to be greatly affected by it; neither did he develop a critical attitude. He was pleased by the rhythm of marching feet, and wished he were old enough to march away himself, but that was impossible. According to his own account in *Life on the Mississippi*, he was, during his St. Louis days, once a member of a body of young men under military command, who had been organized for the purpose of quelling a mob, but the account has so plainly been "doctored" for burlesque purposes that it is difficult to make any definite assertion about it.

Similar difficulties arise when we try to interpret his Civil War experiences. If, as has been conjectured, he had something to do with military matters in New Orleans, before participating in the adventures of the loosely organized Missouri group of which he wrote in "The Private History of a Campaign That Failed," we know nothing about it, except that the Quintus Curtius Snodgrass letters leave us with the impression that he did not enjoy it. The "Private History" itself was obviously designed not as history but as literature; Paine himself pointed out that the killing of the soldier is fiction, while Goodpasture complains that Paine himself sees the episode in terms of a Tom Sawyer lark, impossible for an ex-Mississippi pilot, nearly twenty-six years of age. DeVoto at one time accepted Absalom Grimes's account of the campaign at face value, but M. M. Quaife, who edited Grimes's book, was later more than doubtful about it. Super-patriots have called Mark Twain a deserter—which, under the conditions which existed in 1861 Missouri, is idiocy—and pacifists are tempted to interpret his French leave as an act of principle, reading back into the Civil War period his later well-known detestation of war.

The thing that really needs explaining is not why Mark Twain left when he did but how he ever got mixed up in such a loosely organized military adventure to begin with, and this probably cannot be understood without more knowledge than we possess of the state of the Border mind in 1861. Clemens, as we have seen, had registered his wish to avoid the secession crisis by voting for Bell and Everett. Both in the state and in the Clemens family, sympathies between North and South were clearly divided.[17] It seems clear that Sam had no desire to be pressed into dangerous service as a Mississippi pilot under military direction, and until the opportunity came to go west with Orion, he may well have been at a loose end. Even today, when military service, like everything else, is as highly organized as it was unorganized in Mark Twain's Missouri, the army itself finds many men psychologically unqualified for military life. Mark Twain would not have required many such experiences as he has recorded in the "Private History" to discover that he was one of them—if he had had the brains he was born with, he would have known it from the beginning—and when we remember that he was a man of imagination, even the killing of the soldier is not wholly deprived of its hypothetical impact upon his mind by the fact that it never happened. Genius anticipates experience, as the Brontës and a thousand others prove, and Mark Twain had surely gone far enough in his "military" life to realize that sooner or later he would be called upon to do something like this.

It has been suggested that, especially in view of his later admiration for Lincoln, Grant, and other Civil War heroes, and the implied commitment to the Union cause, he may, in later years, have been somewhat uneasy about his Civil War record. Susy's biography of her father omits the Civil War altogether, taking him directly from the river to Nevada Territory; Goodpasture therefore conjectured that "evidently Mark had never talked about his army life in her presence." Professor Gerber, too, points out that an anonymous account of Mark's war experiences had been published in Keokuk, Iowa, just before he wrote the "Private History," and adduces various other evidence to support the view that if he

[17] See Samuel C. Webster, *Mark Twain, Business Man*, chapter VII: "Border State Confusion."

were ever to feel the need of justifying his record, it would most likely be at this time.

On the other hand, the "Private History" is not, in any sense, a justification; instead it brought that period of his life before the attention of a great many people who would otherwise never have thought of it. There is not in the "Private History" or in other utterances of Mark Twain any suggestion that he was ashamed of what he did in 1861, and with a man of his capacity for self-reproach, this seems difficult to reconcile with the hypothesis of guilt. Certainly his slur at Samuel J. Tilden's Civil War record, when Tilden was a candidate for President, would seem to violate the rule that people who live in glass houses ought to be careful about throwing stones, and indeed it would have been bad taste under any circumstances. Introducing Henry Watterson, at a Lincoln's Birthday celebration in Carnegie Hall, in 1901, Mark Twain declared, "I was born and reared in a slave state, my father was a slave owner; and in the Civil War I was a second lieutenant in the Confederate service." As a euphemistic way of putting the matter, this surely takes high rank. It does not seem really apologetic, however, and the only statement I find anywhere which would seem to indicate that Mark was troubled by any conflict between his own Civil War record and his admiration for Grant on the one hand, or the conviction he was developing on the subject of war and peace on the other, comes when he says that he admired Grant not so much for winning the war as for ending it. In another connection, he says the same thing about Joan of Arc.[18]

All in all, though I cannot but regard any suggestion of moral turpitude in connection with Mark Twain's Civil War record as ridiculous, I must also say that his whole contemporary Civil War

[18] The three most important articles on Mark Twain's Civil War experiences are A. V. Goodpasture, "Mark Twain, Southerner," *Tennessee Historical Magazine*, Series II, Vol. I (1931), 253–60; Fred W. Lorch, "Mark Twain and the 'Campaign That Failed'," *American Literature*, Vol. XII (1940–41), 254–70; John C. Gerber, "Mark Twain's 'Private Campaign'," *Civil War History*, Vol. I (1955), 37–60. Absalom Grimes's account of "Campaigning with Mark Twain" is chapter I in M. M. Quaife, ed., *Absalom Grimes, Confederate Mail Runner* (Yale University Press, 1926); for Quaife's doubts, see "Mark Twain's Military Career," *Twainian*, N.S. Vol. III, June, 1944, pp. 4–7. See, further, the account of Mark Twain's Civil War experience in the New York *Times*, Oct. 7, 1877, reprinted in *The Twainian*, Thirteenth Year, March–April, 1954, pp. 1–2.

attitude shows little political intelligence. In Virginia City he associated with Union men and "secesh" men with fine impartiality, and it must have been difficult for anyone to find out where his sympathies lay.[19] As late as 1864 he stipulates that he must not be required to write editorials on politics or Eastern news generally, as he takes no interest in such matters. In one letter he even declares, "If the war will let us alone, we can get rich." Only one letter, published recently in *American Heritage*,[20] shows a keener and more intelligent interest in the issues of the conflict than is elsewhere to be postulated.

The Spanish-American War was a very different matter. At the beginning, indeed, he was taken in by it. His chivalry, his sentimentalism, his hatred of monarchy betrayed him. "I have never enjoyed a war—even in written history—as I am enjoying this one. For this is the worthiest one that was ever fought, so far as my knowledge goes. It is a worthy thing to fight for one's freedom; it is another sight finer to fight for another man's. And I think this is the first time it has been done." He was writing from Vienna, and all the factors in the situation were not yet clear to him. His letter to Pond is jocose, but it leaves no doubt where he stands. "Old as I am, I want to go to the war myself. And I should do it, too, if it were not for the danger."

Then certain things happened. The theater of conflict shifted to the Pacific Ocean. Funston captured Aguinaldo "by methods which would disgrace the lowest blatherskite that is doing time in any penitentiary." An Iowa newspaper printed a letter written by an American soldier to his mother. "We never left one alive," wrote this noble specimen of unselfish American idealism. "If any one was wounded, we would run our bayonets through him." Despite the idealistic motives we had professed, we seized the Philippines. To Clemens, as to William Vaughn Moody, Carl Schurz, William and Henry James, Finley Peter Dunne, and so many others, this seemed a base betrayal of American idealism, and the jester grew overnight into the stature of a major prophet. He called

[19] See Smith and Anderson, *Mark Twain of the "Enterprise,"* 17–19.
[20] "Two Civil War Letters," *American Heritage*, Vol. VIII, No. 6 (Oct., 1957), 62–63.

the war "a land-stealing and liberty-crucifying crusade." "I am opposed," he wrote, "to having the eagle put its talons on any other land." McKinley had "polluted" the flag; perhaps it might now represent us more accurately if we were to have "the white stripes painted black and the stars replaced by the skull and crossbones."

He rewrote "The Battle Hymn of the Republic" to express twentieth-century ideals. The last stanza reads:

In a sordid slime harmonious, Greed was born in yonder ditch;
With a longing in his bosom—for other's goods an itch;
Christ died to make men holy, let men die to make us rich;
Our god is marching on.

In the terrible scenario he blocked out for a pageant known as "The Stupendous Procession," The Twentieth Century appeared as "a fair young creature, drunk and disorderly, borne in the arms of Satan," while Christendom was "a majestic matron in flowing robes drenched with blood." On her head was "a golden crown of thorns, impaled on its spine the bleeding heads of patriots who died for their country—Boers, Boxers, Filipinos; in one hand a slingshot in the other a Bible, open at the text—'Do unto others,' etc."

Other events of the period continued his political education. His visit to South Africa had prepared him for the Boer War, and in 1897, when he wrote his "Letters to Satan," he had informed that plenipotentiary that it was quite unnecessary "to grease Mr. Cecil Rhodes's palm any further, for I think he would serve you just for the love of it." Introducing Winston Churchill at a dinner in New York in 1900, he held forth on the kinship between England and America, concluding with the observation that since the two nations were now "kin in sin," the bond ought to be closer than ever. Continuing the argument in private, Churchill fell back on the bromide, "My country, right or wrong." "Ah," said Mark Twain, "when the poor country is fighting for its life, I agree. But this was not your case." And in the book he gave Churchill, he inscribed bitingly, "To do good is noble; to teach others to do good is nobler; and no trouble."

He had had no need, this time, to wait for the course of the hostilities themselves to open his eyes. At the moment the British ultimatum expired, he wrote in his journal, "Without a doubt the first shot in the war is being fired to-day in South Africa *at this moment. Some* man had to be the first to fall; he has fallen. Whose heart is broken by this murder? For be he Boer or be he Briton, it is murder, & England committed it by the hand of Chamberlain & his Cabinet, the lackeys of Cecil Rhodes & his Forty Thieves, the South Africa Company." He wrote a pro-Boer article, then decided not to publish it. "For England must not fall; it would mean an inundation of Russian and German political degradations which would envelop the globe and steep it in a sort of Middle-Age night and slavery which would last till Christ comes again. Even wrong—and she is wrong—England must be upheld. He is an enemy of the human race who shall speak against her now."

It was an amazing *non sequitur,* and we ought not to be surprised if we find that the principles Mark Twain deduced from his war experiences were not altogether consistent. As late as 1901, in the Henry Watterson speech which has already been referred to, he espouses patriotism. "We of the South were not ashamed, for, like the men of the North, we were fighting for flags we loved; and when men fight for these things, and under these convictions, with nothing sordid to tarnish their cause, that cause is holy, the blood spilt for it is sacred, the life that is laid down for it is consecrated." When he is writing of foreigners, the tone is the same, as in the extraordinary passage from *Following the Equator:* "Patriotism is Patriotism. Calling it Fanaticism cannot degrade it; nothing can degrade it. Even though it be a political mistake, and a thousand times a political mistake, that does not affect it; it is honorable—always honorable, always noble—and privileged to hold its head up and look the nations in the face." And China: "I am with the Boxers every time. The Boxer is a patriot. He loves his country better than he does the countries of other people. I wish him success."

He can go even further than this. He had a childish sort of admiration for West Point, and West Point is one of the institutions with which the Connecticut Yankee blesses Arthurian England. As an "Innocent," he seems to approve Spain's "big-stick" policy against the Moors, and his defense of the Jews apparently assumes that if a man is to be a good citizen, he must be prepared, in time of war, to fight for his country, though, to be sure, he elsewhere declares that he would not fight for a cause of which his conscience did not approve, for he always believed that true loyalty is "loyalty to one's country, not to its institutions or its officeholders." Once he speaks fearfully of the "Yellow Peril." And even in his most disillusioned nonfiction work, *Following the Equator*, he goes out of his way to plead for a great merchant marine, which shall make it possible for the United States "to assert and maintain her rightful place as one of the Great Maritime Powers of the Planet."

There are times, however, when he disclaims patriotism altogether. Macfarlane's influence may have survived here, for the Scot laid heavy stress on the idea that man is "the sole animal in whom was fully developed the base instinct called *patriotism*." At one time, Mrs. Fields gathered the impression that Mark was not a patriot: "He is so unhappy and discontented with our government that he says he is not conscious of the least emotion of patriotism in himself. He is overwhelmed with shame and confusion and wishes he were not an American." He himself feared that patriotism, as commonly taught to children, would make a worse, not a better, country for us in the end: "We teach the boys to atrophy their independence. We teach them to take their patriotism at second-hand; to shout with the largest crowd without examining into the right or wrong of the matter—exactly as boys under monarchies are taught and have always been taught."

Mark Twain's instinctive, personal reaction to war was always one of intense aversion. Huck Finn turns physically sick at the sight of the feud, disgusted by the slaughter and killing practiced by the damned human race. When Clemens heard that the notorious General Blucher had received an honorary degree from Oxford, he was shocked, and the luster of his own honor was dimmed in his eyes. "Blucher a doctor like myself! And people like that, who delight in murder and rapine, receive honorary degrees!" He was shocked by the piling up of armaments, and he took no stock in the notion that the way to prevent war is to be ready for it. "Tolstoy was right," he cries, "in calling army life 'a school for murder.'" Elsewhere he speaks of "that enslaver of nations, the standing army." Nobody spoke out more boldly and effectively than Mark Twain against the Belgian atrocities in the Congo, and nobody was more horrified that the United States should have been the first power officially to accept Leopold's overlordship there. His "Thanksgiving Sentiment" of 1904 (unpublished) offered thanks for the circumstance of our having recognized the "pirate flag" and "become responsible through silence for the prodigious depredations & multitudinous murders committed under it upon the helpless natives," ending with the "blessed hope" that when, "in the Last Great Day," Leopold should be "confronted with his unoffending millions upon millions of robbed, mutilated & massacred men, women & children, & required to explain, he will be as politely silent about us as we have been about him."

It was under the influence of his hatred of imperialism that Mark Twain came, then, to write the caustic commentaries which make it possible for us to claim him, today, at his best, as a prophet of the modern peace movement. "All Christendom is a soldier camp," he cried. "The poor have been taxed in some nations to the starvation point to support the giant armaments which Christian governments have built up, each to protect itself from the rest of the Christian brotherhood, and incidentally to snatch any scrap of real estate left exposed by a wealthy owner." With such ideas in mind, he wrote his powerful story, "The War Prayer,"[21] and prepared his magnificent

Greeting From the Nineteenth to the Twentieth Century

I bring you the stately matron named Christendom, returning, bedraggled, besmirched, and dishonored, from pirate raids in Kiao-Chou, Manchuria, South Africa, and the Philippines, with her soul full of meanness, her pocket full of boodle, and her mouth full of

[21] In *Europe and Elsewhere.*

238

pious hypocrisies. Give her soap and a towel, but hide the looking-glass.

Is it any wonder that Ceylon's Prime Minister Bandaranaike asked, after his election in April, 1956, "How could I be hostile to a country that produced Mark Twain?"

Yet Mark Twain was not a consistent pacifist. He was so thoroughly committed to the cause of political democracy that it was difficult for him not to feel that violence was righteous if it resulted in overthrowing an unjust or tyrannical government. This point of view he seems to have developed under the influence of his enthusiasm for the French Revolution, of which he derived his impressions largely from Carlyle and Dickens, though his enthusiasm surpasses that of either one. "When I finished Carlyle's French Revolution in 1871," he wrote Howells in 1887, "I was a Girondin; every time I have read it since, I have read it differently —being influenced and changed, little by little, by life and environment (and Taine and St. Simon): and now I lay the book down once more, and recognize that I am a Sansculotte!—And not a pale, characterless Sansculotte, but a Marat. Carlyle teaches no such gospel: so the change is in me—in my vision of the evidences." Two years later, he speaks of the Revolution as, "next to the 4th of July and its results . . . the noblest and holiest thing and the most precious that ever happened on this earth."

Some persons could reason thus concerning the French Revolution—way off, so safe, a hundred years past—and still shrink from applying the same kind of reasoning to the problems of their own time. Not so Mark Twain, not with the toiling, sweating, suffering millions of Russia groaning and dying before his metaphorical eyes. "What is the Czar of Russia but a house afire in the midst of a city of eighty millions of inhabitants?" If redress cannot come in any other way, he is even ready to sanction a private revolution. "Of course I know that the properest way to demolish the Russian throne would be by revolution. But it is not possible to get up a revolution there; so the only thing left to do, apparently, is to keep the throne vacant by dynamite until a day when candidates shall decline with thanks." In "The Czar's Soliloquy," published in 1905, in *The North American Review*, and not yet included in Mark Twain's collected works, the question is considered in some detail, and the Czar is made to say that the moralists protect his family from the just reward of their crimes by teaching that assassination is a crime, while the plain truth of the matter is that the Romanoffs, having made themselves independent of the law, must be regarded as outlaws, and "outlaws are a proper mark for anyone's bullet." And there is a story about Mark Twain rising in his place after having heard George Kennan describe the Siberian mines, in a Lowell Lecture at Boston, and exclaiming in "a voice choked with tears": "If such a government cannot be overthrown otherwise than by dynamite, then thank God for dynamite!" When Theodore Roosevelt brought about the end of the Russo-Japanese War, Mark Twain's love of peace came into conflict with his desire to see a real revolution in Russia, and the latter proved stronger. Had the war been allowed to continue, Japan must, he believed, have thoroughly trounced Russia, and the chains of Russian political enslavement would have been cut then and there. This time he did not speak out, but privately he could find nothing too harsh to say of those who were so obtuse as to prevent this consummation, and, as he believed, postpone indefinitely the day of Russian freedom.

This seems unequivocal enough. "All gentle cant and philosophizing to the contrary notwithstanding," says the Yankee, "no people in the world ever did achieve their freedom by goody-goody talk and moral suasion; it being immutable law that all revolutions that will succeed, must *begin* in blood, whatever may answer afterward." In *propria persona*, Mark Twain adds, "Do these liberation-parties think that they can succeed in a project which has been attempted a million times in the history of the world and has never in one single instance been successful—the 'modification' of a despotism by other means than bloodshed?"

But if this was the wave of the future, it was not the kind of future Mark Twain would have been glad to see. There were times when, in spite of himself, Mark Twain glimpsed that future, and recoiled from it with something of the shocked humanity of the young heroine of *Berkeley Square*. Like his younger contemporary,

240

H. G. Wells, he had long realized the increasing futility and hopelessness of the armament race. He had observed, too, the fact that armaments were changing, that if war was to survive as an institution, its character must be radically changed. Paine says that he foretold World War I as early as 1909, and DeVoto has shown how, in "Sold to Satan" and a number of unpublished sketches, he rather astonishingly anticipated certain aspects of our recent scientific "progress" and the problems it poses for the future of mankind. These anticipations lack the ponderousness of Henry Adams's kindred speculations, but in their own darting, volatile way, they are not necessarily less penetrating.[22]

Mark Twain's aging eyes were clouded as he peered into the future, clouded by anxiety and fear. There was science. He had always believed in it. It was lifting the curse of backbreaking labor from mankind, making it possible for men to devote their energies to the business of developing an abundant material and spiritual life. It was demolishing ancient superstitions too, so that a man's soul, as well as his body, might stand upright at last, and really feel at home in this world in which he must live. But now it seemed as though science had prostituted itself. Man's moral and spiritual development had not kept pace with his technological development. It was Caliban, not Prospero, that ruled the island, and the very thing that had been counted upon to redeem humanity might, in the end, turn out to be the thing that would destroy it altogether. He had had his doubts and fears for a long time. At the end of *A Connecticut Yankee* he had even described how it might come. His readers had taken it for burlesque, but he knew that it might some day be enacted in bitter earnest. Not even the torpedo, filled "with Greek fire and poisonous and deadly missiles," by whose aid Colonel Sellers hoped to be able to take St. Louis, was quite so absurd as it had been taken to be. The Colonel never completed his torpedo, because he was never able to get hold of his Greek fire. Some day men would get it; what must happen then? One day the Kaiser was reported as having spoken about sending his U-boats to invade England, and Mark's imagination set to work and developed a Wellsian kind of defense. But it was always

22 See "The Easy Chair," *Harper's Magazine*, Vol. CXCII (1946), 309–12.

easier to destroy than it was to build, and the defenses did not seem to keep pace somehow.

In *The Mysterious Stranger* he passed the ages in review. What did progress amount to except building ever deadlier and deadlier weapons? And what had Christianity, for all its boasted lip service of peace, ever done to arrest this development. Young Satan himself was shocked as he contemplated it:

> In five or six thousand years five or six high civilizations have risen, flourished, commanded the wonder of the world, then faded out and disappeared; and not one of them except the latest ever invented any sweeping and adequate way to kill people. They all did their best—to kill being the chiefest ambition of the human race and the earliest incident in its history—but only the Christian civilization has scored a triumph to be proud of. Two or three centuries from now it will be recognized that all the competent killers are Christians; then the pagan world will go to school to the Christian—not to acquire his religion, but his guns. The Turk and the Chinaman will buy those to kill missionaries and converts with.

Sometimes it even seemed to Mark Twain, in his despair, that there was no use grieving over these things; a race capable of such stupidity and cruelty deserved nothing better than to be destroyed.

Mark Twain was not insensitive to the considerations which led men like Rudyard Kipling and Theodore Roosevelt to support imperialism. Sometimes, briefly, he was even moved by them. In the early days, he believed, for a little while, that we should annex Hawaii, and for commercial reasons at that. Much later he wrote:

> The signs of the times show plainly enough what is going to happen. All the savage lands in the world are going to be brought under the subjugation of the Christian governments of Europe. I am not sorry but glad. . . . The sooner the seizure is consummated the better for the savages. The dreary and dragging ages of bloodshed and disorder and oppression will give place to peace and order and the reign of law.

In the light of what has happened in the world since Mark Twain's time, this point of view is not absurd. If Kipling's brand of imperialism could have been made to work permanently, the world would undoubtedly be a more peaceful place to live in than it is today. So would it be also if Germany had won World War I. But when Mark Twain was at his best, he was too sensitive to be able to bring himself to do evil that good might come. He was too much of a rebel for that, not enough of a "yes-sayer" to life; he did not, in this sense, "accept the universe." In this aspect, Huck Finn, accepting hell rather than betraying Nigger Jim, represents his creator well. Perhaps this may even have something to do with Mark Twain's never really having become a believer. But it may well be that God more loves that kind of rebellion—and that it holds more promise for the Kingdom of God on earth—than many men's acceptance. Theodore Roosevelt was not an insensitive man, but Lord Bryce, who knew him well, once remarked that he "wouldn't always look at a thing." Mark Twain looked at things until they nearly struck him blind, and when, at times, he failed to do this, he went most dangerously astray. We have had our Russian revolution, for example, blood and all, but it would be difficult to show that it has achieved the results which Mark Twain desired.

V

I find little evidence to support the once-popular view that Mark Twain was a social critic who hid his light under a bushel. It is true that he withheld some of his later utterances from publication. And in at least one instance—the Russo-Japanese War—his private conviction and his public utterance were diametrically opposed to each other.[23] Since, however, this was a matter in which there was a conflict within Mark Twain himself, it was a special case. Undoubtedly there were times when prudential considerations prevailed with Mark Twain, but this does not cancel out the fact that he did speak out—often violently—on a larger number of vital issues than any other writer of his time. On many occasions he went far enough to alienate many important contemporaries and be called very unpleasant names. I would add that, though I have no proof that Mark Twain himself was actu-

[23] Foner, *Mark Twain, Social Critic*, 120–21.

ated by this consideration, many of his utterances were so violent that, from the standpoint of policy alone, he was well advised to suppress some of them. He was a more, not a less, effective social critic because he did this. If you hammer people's sensibilities incessantly, they come to expect it from you as a matter of course, and are consequently unaffected by it. Theoretically it is possible to reply that Mark Twain should have spoken more calmly. Being Mark Twain, he could not have done this. And every man—artist, reformer, statesman—must be allowed to function as himself, in accordance with the demands of his own temperament. If he cannot do this, he will not be able to function at all.

On the other hand, if Mark Twain was no coward as a social critic, he was (as he was in every other aspect), quicksilverish, temperamental, and unpredictable. When those who found themselves allied with him in the various reforms he sponsored, expected him to take out a union card, and play the game according to the rules, they were generally disappointed. "My instincts and interests are merely literary," he wrote on one occasion, "they rise no higher; & I scatter from one interest to another, lingering nowhere. I am not a bee, I am a lightning-bug." When he wrote *King Leopold's Soliloquy*, he warned his friends that he was going to stop there, not becoming involved in the organized Congo Reform movement in any way. This time he was better than his word, for he became vice president of the association and participated directly in their efforts to bring pressure to bear in Washington and in London. When, however, they attempted to arrange a lecture tour for him, he rebelled. "I shall not make a second step in the Congo matter, because that would compel a third . . . & a fourth & a fifth, & so on. I mean a *deliberate* second step; what I may do upon sudden *impulse* is another matter—*they* are out of my control." Exactly. But a man of letters does not become a coward simply because, having spoken out, he declines to stop being a man of letters in order to become a full-time or professional propagandist.

At the close of *The Education of Henry Adams*, the author speculates on the possibility that "perhaps some day—say 1938, their centenary—" he and his two closest friends might be permitted to return to this earth for a holiday, "to see the mistakes of their own lives made clear in the light of the mistakes of their successors; and perhaps then," he continues, "for the first time since man began his education among the carnivores, they would find a world that sensitive and timid natures could regard without a shudder." For his sake, one may hope that Henry Adams did *not* return in 1938, nor in any year since 1938, and the same may be said of Mark Twain. His admirers have often commented on what he escaped by not being obliged to live through two world wars and their aftermath, nor, in many aspects, would what now passes for peace in America have pleased him much better. Though it is always dangerous to speculate concerning what great men of the past would believe about controversial issues of the present, we cannot avoid attempting to do this if our heroes are to continue to have any vital meaning for us. I believe that William Dean Howells, who could speak without a shudder of "the destiny of the future state, which will at once employ and support all its citizens," might well approve of the peaceful revolution which has taken place during recent years, both in Britain and in the United States, but I feel quite sure that Mark Twain would decidedly disapprove of it. According to his own statement, Franklin D. Roosevelt took the phrase "New Deal" from *A Connecticut Yankee*. Mark Twain might have been seduced by the New Deal in some of its humanitarian aspects, but he would certainly have been antagonized by its bureaucracy and standardization, its centralization, its militarism, and its emphasis upon security at the expense of individualism. His attitude toward Franklin Roosevelt's methods of intervening in World War II would, I believe, have been quite those of Charles A. Beard. And words fail me when we come to the greatest atrocity in all recorded history, the dropping of the atomic bombs on Hiroshima and Nagasaki, by the direction of an American President. I even think that, for once, they might have failed him.

It is a sobering thought that the President who dropped those bombs comes from Mark Twain's own state of Missouri, and admires the great writer very much. Mark Twain would seem to have become a permanent part of the American legend, and there has never been a time when his reputation stood higher than it stands today. Nevertheless, such an anomaly cannot but cause one to wonder how long his spirit and what seems to be the spirit of modern America may be able to meet, or whether, if he survives, his image may not be as distorted as organized Christianity has often distorted Christ's. Nor is it only the tremendous moral problems involved in high matters of national policy that give one pause here. Can the Man in the Gray Flannel Suit really meet "the Lincoln of our literature"? Can the great rebel make a vital contact with us, under all our sleek conformities?

Mark Twain himself once remarked that in this country we have three inestimable blessings—freedom of thought, freedom of expression, and the prudence never to indulge either of them. If this was true in his day, it is ten times truer now. Naturally this does not lessen his greatness or his importance. There are currents and counter-currents in every age, and those who determine dominant policies and set current standards do not speak for all of us. Moreover, as C. S. Lewis has reminded us, when poisons become fashionable, they do not cease to kill. It has happened before that a whole generation has missed the truth of life; it can happen again. In such times the memory of a great humanist and individualist is the shadow of a great rock in a weary land, but it may also be more than that—an inspiration and a genuine creative and regenerative force.

Bibliography

THE FIRST EDITION OF THIS BOOK contained a very full Mark Twain bibliography up to 1935. If I were to reprint this bibliography in its entirety, adding the plethora of materials that have appeared since, the result might, I fear, be somewhat overwhelming. Moreover, extensive listings, not available in 1935, have since appeared, notably in Robert E. Spiller, *et al.*, eds., *Literary History of the United States*, III, and its *Bibliography Supplement*, ed. Richard M. Ludwig (M, 1948, 1959); E. Hudson Long, *Mark Twain Handbook*; Lewis Leary, *Articles on American Literature, 1900–1950* (Duke University Press, 1954); and my own *Cavalcade of the American Novel* (Holt, 1952).

I have given a rather full listing for Mark Twain's own writings, plus all the books and pamphlets about him which I think worth listing for any reason. I have listed all the articles which seem to me of biographical significance and a selection of articles which have only critical significance. But I have not reprinted from my first edition the names of any of the books primarily devoted to other subjects which contain incidental references to Mark Twain.

The following abbreviations have been employed:

ABC	American Book Company	MT	Mark Twain
AL	*American Literature*	NAR	*North American Review*
AM	*American Monthly*	NEQ	*New England Quarterly*
AQ	*American Quarterly*	Okla	University of Oklahoma
AS	*American Speech*		Press
BCC	Book Club of California	OM	*Overland Monthly*
Bkm	*Bookman* (New York)	OSAHQ	*Ohio State Archaeological*
Ce	*Century Magazine*		*and Historical Quarterly*
CE	*College English*	PBSA	*Papers of the Bibliographi-*
Col	*Colophon*		*cal Society of America*
DR	*Dalhousie Review*	PHR	*Pacific Historical Review*
GR	*Georgia Review*	PMLA	*Publications of the Modern*
H	Harper & Brothers		*Language Association*
HaM	*Harper's Magazine*	PQ	*Philological Quarterly*
HaW	*Harper's Weekly*	PS	*Pacific Spectator*
HL	Huntington Library	S	Charles Scribner's Sons
HLQ	*Huntington Library*	SAQ	*South Atlantic Quarterly*
	Quarterly	SEP	*Saturday Evening Post*
HM	Houghton Mifflin Co.	SMUP	Southern Methodist Uni-
HUP	Harvard University Press		versity Press
IJHP	*Iowa Journal of History*	SUP	Stanford University Press
	and Politics	UCP	University of California
IMH	*Indiana Magazine of*		Press
	History	UKCR	*University of Kansas City*
IMTS	International Mark Twain		*Review*
	Society	UNCP	University of North Caro-
LB	Little, Brown and Company		lina Press
M	The Macmillan Company	UTSE	*University of Texas Studies*
MHR	*Missouri Historical Review*		*in English*
MLN	*Modern Language Notes*	VQR	*Virginia Quarterly Review*
MLQ	*Modern Language Quarterly*	WHR	*Western Humanities*
MP	*Modern Philology*		*Review*
MSUP	Michigan State University		
	Press		

The standard bibliography is Merle Johnson, A *Bibliography of the Works of MT*, etc., Revised Edition (H, 1935). See, also, Floyd Stovall, ed., *Eight American Authors: A Review of Research and Criticism* (Modern Language Association, 1956); Roger Asselineau, *The Literary Reputation of MT from 1910 to 1950* (Paris, Librairie Marcel Didier, 1954); Edgar M. Branch, "A Chronological Bibliography of the Writings of Samuel L. Clemens," AL, Vol. XVIII (1946–47), 109–59.

The "Definitive Edition" of MT's Works (37 vols., Gabriel Wells, 1923–25), is generally considered the most desirable. Harpers "Storm-field Edition" was printed from the same plates. I have, however, used the old Harpers "Uniform [trade] Edition," which comprises the following titles: *The Adventures of Huckleberry Finn; The Adventures of*

Tom Sawyer; The American Claimant and Other Stories and Sketches; Christian Science; A Connecticut Yankee in King Arthur's Court; Europe and Elsewhere; Following the Equator; The Gilded Age (with Charles Dudley Warner); *In Defense of Harriet Shelley and Other Essays; The Innocents Abroad; Life on the Mississippi; The Man That Corrupted Hadleyburg and Other Stories and Essays; The Mysterious Stranger and Other Stories; Personal Recollections of Joan of Arc; The Prince and the Pauper; Pudd'nhead Wilson and Those Extraordinary Twins; Roughing It; Sketches New and Old; The $30,000 Bequest and Other Stories; Tom Sawyer Abroad, Tom Sawyer, Detective, and Other Stories; A Tramp Abroad; What Is Man? and Other Essays.*

Additional MT material will be found in the following books: *Adventures of Thomas Jefferson Snodgrass*, ed. Charles Honce (Covici Fried, 1928); *The Autobiography of Mark Twain*, ed. Charles Neider (H, 1959);[1] *A Champagne Cocktail and A Catastrophe: Two Acting Charades* (privately printed by Robin and Marian McVicars, 1930); *Concerning Cats: Two Tales*, with an introduction by Frederick Anderson (BCC, 1959); *The Curious Republic of Gondour, and Other Whimsical Sketches* (Boni & Liveright, 1919); *Edmund Burke on Croker and Tammany* (New York, Order of Acorns, 1901); *Letters from Honolulu*, ed. John W. Nickerson (Honolulu, Thomas Nickerson, 1939); *Letters from the Sandwich Islands*, ed. G. Ezra Dane (SUP, 1938); *Jim Smiley and His Jumping Frog* (Chicago: Pocahontas Press, 1940); *The Letters of Quintus Curtius Snodgrass*, ed. Ernest E. Leisy (SMUP, 1946); *MT and Hawaii*, ed. Walter Francis Frear (privately printed at the Lakeside Press, 1947);[2] *MT in Eruption*, ed. Bernard De Voto (H, 1940),[3] *MT of the "Enterprise,"* etc., ed. Henry Nash Smith and Frederick Anderson (UCP, 1957); *MT: San Francisco Correspondent*, etc., ed. H. N. Smith and F. Anderson (BCC, 1957); *MT's Autobiography*, ed. Albert Bigelow Paine (2 vols., H, 1924);[4] *MT's [Date, 1601.] Conversation As it was by the Social Fire-*

[1] This is the latest volume of selections from Mark Twain's autobiography, arranged chronologically, and with some material not included in earlier editions.

[2] This volume also contains a 246-page study by Judge Frear of Mark Twain's connections with Hawaii.

[3] Selected material from the autobiography, with a heavy emphasis upon social criticism.

[4] The earliest collection of material from the autobiography to be published in book form. A good many selections, however, were published in *The North American Review* during Mark Twain's lifetime, and Paine did not reprint all of these. See DeLancey Ferguson, "The Uncollected Portions of Mark Twain's Autobiography," AL, Vol. VIII (1936–37), 37–46.

side in the Time of the Tudors, ed. Franklin J. Meine (privately printed for the MT Society of Chicago, 1939);[5] *MT's Letters in the Muscatine "Journal,"* ed. Edgar M. Branch (MT Association of America, 1942); Coley B. Taylor, *MT's Margins on Thackeray's "Swift"* (Gotham House, 1935); *MT's Speeches* (H, 1910); *MT's Travels with Mr. Brown,* etc., ed. Franklin Walker and G. Ezra Dane (Knopf, 1940); *The £1,000,000 Bank Note* (H, 1917); *The Pains of Lowly Life* (London, Anti-Vivisection Society, 1900); *The "Quaker City" Holy Land Excursion: An Unfinished Play* (privately printed, 1927); *Queen Victoria's Jubilee: The Great Procession of June 22, 1897,* etc. (n.p., n.d.); *Republican Letters,* ed. Cyril Clemens (IMTS, 1941);[6] *Report from Paradise* (H, 1952); *Sketches of the Sixties,* etc. by Bret Harte and MT (San Francisco, John Howell, 1926); *Slovenly Peter* (*Der Struwwelpeter*), translated from the German of Heinrich Hoffmann by MT (H, 1935); *Traveling with the Innocents Abroad,* etc., ed. Daniel Morley McKeithan (Okla, 1958);[7] *Washington in 1868,* ed. Cyril Clemens (IMTS, 1943).[8] See, also, the edition of *Life on the Mississippi,* illustrated by Thomas Hart Benton, and published by The Limited Editions Club, 1944, with an introduction by Edward Wagenknecht "and a number of previously suppressed passages, now printed for the first time, and edited with a note by Willis Wager." For additional items, consult Merle Johnson, *Bibliography.*

Further writing by MT will be found in the following serials: Paul Bander, "MT and the Byron Scandal," *AL*, Vol. XXX (1958–59), 467–85; Bradford A. Booth, "MT's Comments on Holmes's *Autocrat*," *AL*, Vol. XXI (1949–50), 256–63, and "MT's Comments on Bret Harte's Stories," *AL*, Vol. XXV (1953–54), 492–95; Minnie M. Brashear, "MT Juvenilia," *AL*, Vol. II (1930), 25–53; "A Capable Humorist," *HaW*, Vol. LIII, Feb. 20, 1909, p. 13; "Carl Schurz, Pilot," *HaW*, Vol. L (1906), 727; "The Carnegie Spelling Reform," *HaW*, Vol. L (1906), 488; Edwin H. Carpenter, Jr., "Mining Methods in Catgut Cañon," *PHR*, Vol. XVIII (1949), 109–11; Paul J. Carter, "MT Describes a San Francisco Earthquake," *PMLA*, Vol. LXXII (1957), 997–1004,

---

[5] This is the best of a considerable number of more or less privately circulated printings of Mark Twain's bawdy classic.

[6] In connection with this work, see the discussion in *AL*, Vol. XIII (1942), 439–40; Vol. XIV (1943), 430–31; Vol. XVI (1944), 32–34.

[7] The *Innocents Abroad* material, in its original, newspaper-correspondence form.

[8] See note 6 above.

"MT and the American Labor Movement," *NEQ*, Vol. XXX (1957), 382–88, and "MT Materials in the New York Weekly Review," *PBSA*, Vol. LII (1958), 56–62; "Concerning Copyright," NAR, Vol. CLXXX (1905), 1–18; "The Czar's Soliloquy," NAR, Vol. CLXXX (1905), 321–26; "A Defence of General Funston," NAR, Vol. CLXXIV (1902), 613–24; "Fenimore Cooper's Further Literary Offenses," *NEQ*, Vol. XIX (1946), 291–301; DeLancey Ferguson, "MT's Lost Curtain Speeches," *SAQ*, Vol. XLII (1943), 262–69; "Forty-three Days in an Open Boat," *HaM*, Vol. XXIV (1866), 104–13; "Ghost Lore on the Mississippi," *PS*, Vol. II (1948), 485–90; "A Gift from India," *Critic*, Vol. XXVIII (1896), 285–86; "The Gorki Incident," *Slavonic and East European Review*, Vol. XXII (1944), 37–38; "How I Secured a Berth," *Galaxy*, Vol. XI (1871), 285–86; "James Hammond Trumbull," *Ce*, Vol. LV (1897), 154–55; "John Hay and the Ballads," *HaW*, Vol. XLIX (1905), 1530; Fred W. Lorch, "MT's Orphanage Lecture," *AL*, Vol. VII (1935-36), 453–55, "MT's Sandwich Islands Lecture at St. Louis," *AL*, Vol. XVIII (1946-47), 299–307, "MT's Lecture from *Roughing It*," *AL*, Vol. XXII (1950-51), 290–307, "Mark Twain's 'Artemus Ward' Lecture on the Tour of 1871-72," *NEQ*, Vol. XXV (1952), 327–43, and "MT's 'Morals' Lecture During the American Phase of His World Tour in 1895-1896," *AL*, Vol. XXVI (1954-55), 52–66; Robert J. Lowenherz, "MT on Usage," *AS*, Vol. XXXIII (1958), 70–72; "MT's Introductory Remarks at the Time of Churchill's First American Lecture," *American Notes and Queries*, Vol. V (1946), 147–48; "Memoranda," *Galaxy*, Vol. IX (1870), 717–26, 858–67; Vol. X (1870), 133–41, 286–87, 424–32, 567–76, 726–35, 876–85; Vol. XI (1871), 150–59, 312–21; William C. Miller, "MT at the Sanitary Ball—and Elsewhere," *California Historical Society Quarterly*, Vol. XXXVI (1957), 35–40; W. B. Moffett, "MT's Lansing Lecture on *Roughing It*," *Michigan History*, Vol. XXXIV (1950), 144–70; E. F. Peabody, "MT's Ghost Story," *Minnesota History*, Vol. XVIII (1937), 28–35; Horace Reynolds, "MT's Queer Newspaper," *Christian Science Monitor*, July 29, 1952, p. 9; "Simplified Spelling," *Putnam's Magazine*, Vol. I (1906), 219–20; "An Unbiased Art Criticism," *Californian*, March 18, 1865; Arthur L. Vogelback, "MT: Newspaper Contributor," *AL*, Vol. XX (1948-49), 111–28, "MT and the Fight for Control of the *Tribune*," *AL*, Vol. XXVI (1954-55), 374–75, and "MT and the Tammany Ring," *PMLA*, Vol. LXX (1955), 69–77; "Wanted—A Universal Tinker," *Ce*, N.S. Vol. IX (1885), 318 (signed "X.Y.Z."); Carolyn Wells, "An Item of Interest," New York *American*, Sept. 19, 1933; "Why Not Abolish It?," *HaW*, Vol. XLVII (1903), 732.

The most important collections of MT's letters are in Albert Bigelow Paine, ed., *MT's Letters* (2 vols., H, 1917); Samuel C. Webster, *MT, Business Man* (Little, Brown, 1946); Dixon Wecter, ed., *The Love Letters of MT* (H, 1949), and *MT to Mrs. Fairbanks* (HL, 1949); Henry Nash Smith, William M. Gibson, and Frederick Anderson, eds., *MT-Howells Letters* (2 vols., HUP, 1960). See, also, *MT's Letter to the California Pioneer* (Oakland, DeWitt and Snelling, 1911); *MT and Fairhaven* (Fairhaven, Mass., The Millicent Library, 1913); Cyril Clemens, ed., *MT the Letter Writer* (Meador, 1932); Benjamin De Casseres, ed., *When Huck Finn Went Highbrow* (New York, Thomas F. Madigan, 1934); Letter to Chatto and Windus, in *The Letters of Western Authors* (BCC, 1935); Theodore Hornberger, ed., *MT's Letters to Will Bowen* (University of Texas, 1941); Dixon Wecter, ed., *MT in Three Moods* (Friends of Huntington Library, 1948); Thomas H. English, ed., *MT to Uncle Remus, 1881-1885* (Emory University Library, 1953); Arlin Turner, ed., *MT and George W. Cable: The Record of a Literary Friendship* (MSUP, 1960).

The following serials also contain MT letters: C. J. Armstrong, "John L. RoBards—A Boyhood Friend of MT," *MHR*, Vol. XXV (1931), 493-98; Bradford A. Booth, "MT's Friendship with Emeline Beach," *AL*, Vol. XX (1947-48), 219-30; M. M. Brashear, "An Early MT Letter," *MLN*, Vol. XLIV (1929-30), 256-59; William B. Gates, "MT to his English Publishers," *AL*, Vol. XI (1939-40), 78-80; Seymour L. Gross, "MT on the Serenity of Unbelief: An Unpublished Letter to Charles Warren Stoddard," *HLQ*, Vol. XXII (1958-59), 260-62; Benjamin Lease, "MT and the Publication of *Life on the Mississippi*," *AL*, Vol. XXVI (1954-55), 248-50; Letter to Samuel Hopkins Adams, *Collier's*, Vol. XXXVII, Sept. 22, 1906, pp. 16-17; Letter about the Japanese Schoolboy, *Collier's*, Vol. XLI, Aug. 8, 1908, p. 22; Letter to George Harvey, *HaW*, Vol. L, March 27, 1909, p. 6; Letter to the Editor of *The Spectator*, *Bkm*, Vol. XXXIII (1911), 114-15; "Letters Young MT Wrote in 1856," *Kansas City Star Magazine*, March 21, 1926; Fred W. Lorch, "A MT Letter," *IJHP*, Vol. XXVIII (1930), 268-76, "MT's Trip to Humboldt in 1861," *AL*, Vol. X (1938-39), 343-49, and "MT's Early Nevada Letters," pp. 468-88; "MT for Jerome," *HaW*, Vol. LXIX (1905), 1238; D. M. McKeithan,

"A Letter from MT to Francis Henry Skrine in London," *MLN*, Vol. LXIII (1948), 134–35; James C. Olson, "MT and the Department of Agriculture," *AL*, Vol. XIII (1941–42), 408–10; Lawrence C. Powell, "An Unpublished MT Letter," *AL*, Vol. XIII (1942), 405–407; Dorothy Quick, "My Author's League with MT," *NAR*, Vol. CCXLV (1938), 315–29; C. E. Schorer, "MT's Criticism of *The Story of a Country Town*," *AL*, Vol. XXVII (1955–56), 109–12; John R. Schultz, "New Letters of MT," *AL*, Vol. VIII (1936), 47–51; "Some Unpublished Letters by MT," *Overland Monthly*, Vol. LXXXVII (1929), 115 ff.; L. C. Wimberly, "MT and the Tichenor Bonanza," *AM*, Vol. CLXXII, Nov. 1943, p. 117, 119; Robert Wuliger, "MT on *King Leopold's Soliloquy*," *AL*, Vol. XXV (1953–54), 234–37.

The following books and pamphlets have been published about MT: George Ade, *One Afternoon with MT* (MT Society of Chicago, 1939); Jerry Allen, *The Adventures of MT* (LB, 1954); Kenneth R. Andrews, *Nook Farm: MT's Hartford Circle* (HUP, 1950); Gladys Carmen Bellamy, *MT as a Literary Artist* (Okla, 1950); Ivan Benson, *MT's Western Years* (SUP, 1938); Walter Blair, *MT and "Huck Finn"* (UCP, 1960); Edgar M. Branch, *The Literary Apprenticeship of MT* (University of Illinois Press, 1950); Minnie M. Brashear, *MT, Son of Missouri* (UNCP, 1934); Van Wyck Brooks, *The Ordeal of MT* (Dutton, 1920); Henry Seidel Canby, *Turn West, Turn East, MT and Henry James* (HM, 1951); Guy A. Cardwell, *Twins of Genius* (MSUP, 1953); Edwin H. Carpenter, Jr., *MT: An Exhibition*, etc. (HL, 1947); Clara Clemens, *My Father MT* (H, 1931);[9] Cyril Clemens, *MT and Mussolini* (IMTS, 1934), *My Cousin MT* (Emmaus, Pa., Rodale Press, 1939), and *Young Sam Clemens* (Portland, Maine, Leon Tebbetts Editions, 1942); Will M. Clemens, *MT, His Life and Work* (San Francisco, The Clemens Publishing Co., 1892); Bernard DeVoto, *MT's America* (LB, 1932),[10] and *MT at Work* (HUP, 1942); DeLancey Ferguson, *MT, Man and Legend* (Bobbs-Merrill, 1943); Henry W. Fisher, *Abroad with MT and Eugene Field*, etc. (New York, Nicholas L. Brown, 1922); Philip S. Foner, *MT, Social Critic* (New York, International Publishers, 1958); William R. Gillis, *Gold*

[9] Further commentary by Clara Clemens on her father will be found in her other two books: *My Husband Gabrilowitsch* (H, 1938) and *Awake to a Perfect Day* (Citadel, 1957), and in her introduction to *Slovenly Peter*.

[10] Now published by HM. See, also, two essays by DeVoto—"MT: The Ink of History" and "MT and the Limits of Criticism"—in his *Forays and Rebuttals* (LB, 1936).

Rush Days with MT (A. and C. Boni, 1930); Caroline Thomas Harnsberger, MT, *Family Man* (Citadel, 1960); Edgar T. Hemminghaus, *MT in Germany* (Columbia, 1939); Archibald Henderson, *MT* (Stokes, 1910); W. D. Howells, *My* MT (H, 1911); John T. Krumpelmann, MT *and the German Language* (Louisiana State University Press, 1953); Jervis Langdon, *Samuel Langhorne Clemens: Some Reminiscences and Some Excerpts from Letters and Unpublished Manuscripts* (n.p., n.d.); Mary Lawton, *A Lifetime with* MT: *The Memories of Katy Leary*, etc. (Harcourt, Brace, 1925); Stephen Leacock, MT (Appleton, 1933); Lewis Leary, MT (University of Minnesota Press, 1960); Oscar Lewis, *The Origin of the Celebrated Jumping Frog of Calaveras County* (BCC, 1931); S. B. Liljegren, *The Revolt against Romanticism in American Literature as Evidenced in the Works of S. L. Clemens* (Upsala, A-B Lundequistska Bokhandeln, 1945); Kenneth S. Lynn, MT *and Southwestern Humor* (LB, 1960); Effie M. Mack, MT *in Nevada* (S, 1947); MT *in Hartford* (MT Library and Memorial Commission, 1958); Alma B. Martin, *A Vocabulary Study of "The Gilded Age"* (IMTS, 1930); Edgar Lee Masters, MT: *A Portrait* (S., 1938); D. M. McKeithan, *Court Trials in* MT *and Other Essays* (The Hague, Martinus Mijhoff, 1950); Charles Neider, MT *and the Russians: An Exchange of Views* (Hill and Wang, 1960); Albert Bigelow Paine, MT: *A Biography* (3 vols., H, 1912), *The Boys' Life of* MT (H, 1916), and *A Short Life of* MT (H, 1920); William S. C. Pellowe, MT, *Pilgrim from Hannibal* (Hobson Book Press, 1946); Opie Read, MT *and I* (Reilly & Lee, 1940); Arlin Turner, *Mark Twain and George W. Cable: The Record of a Literary Friendship* (MSUP, 1960); Elizabeth Wallace, MT *and the Happy Island* (McClurg, 1913); Dixon Wecter, *Sam Clemens of Hannibal* (HM, 1952).

Two valuable anthologies of MT's writings have been published: Bernard DeVoto, ed., *The Portable* MT (Viking Press, 1946) and M. M. Brashear and Robert M. Rodney, eds., *The Art, Humor, and Humanity of* MT (Okla, 1959). Fred Lewis Pattee, ed., MT: *Representative Selections* (ABC, 1935) is much inferior but contains an excellent bibliography. Svend Petersen, ed., MT *and the Government* (Caxton Printers, 1960) is simply a collection of MT's utterances on the subject of government. Hal Holbrook, MT *Tonight!* (Ives Washburn, 1959) gives an account of his adventures impersonating MT on the stage, with the text of the selections read. Arthur L. Scott, ed., MT: *Selected Criticism* (SMUP, 1955) is a very good collection. E. Hudson Long, MT *Handbook* (Hendricks House, 1957) provides wise guidance for the reader of MT. Caroline T. Harnsberger, *MT at Your Fingertips* (Beechhurst Press, 1948) is a topical index; it also contains some material not printed elsewhere.

Important critical essays on MT in larger works devoted to American literature include C. Hartley Grattan's, in John Macy, ed., *American Writers on American Literature* (Liveright, 1931); Walter Fuller Taylor's, in *The Economic Novel in America* (UNCP, 1942); Alexander Cowie's, in *The Rise of the American Novel* (ABC, 1948); Dixon Wecter's, in Robert E. Spiller *et al.*, eds., *Literary History of the United States* (M, 1948); Edward Wagenknecht's, in *Cavalcade of the American Novel* (Holt, 1952).

Henry A. Pochmann, "The Mind of MT," thesis (M.A.), University of Texas, 1924, was an important pioneering study of MT's reading. Katharine Seymour Day, "MT's First Years in Hartford, and Personal Memories of the Clemens Family," thesis (M.A.), Trinity College, 1936, has some material not elsewhere available.

For works on MT in foreign languages, see Long, *MT Handbook*, 431–34. Probably the most important are Friedrich Schönemann, *MT als literarische Persönlichkeit* (Jena, Verlag des Frommanschen Buchhandlung—Walter Biedermann, 1925) and Leon Lemonnier, *MT: l'homme et son oeuvre* (Paris, Librairie Arthème Fayard, 1946). The current Soviet line on MT is represented by M. Mendelson, *MT* (Moscow, Fskblksm Molodaya Gvardiya, 1939).

As this book is prepared for the press in September, 1960, the following books have been announced for publication. None, however, were available to be drawn upon for the volume in hand: MT, *Contributions to the Galaxy* (Scholars Reprints and Facsimiles); Paul Fatout, *MT on the Lecture Circuit* (Indiana); Milton Meltzer, *MT Himself* (Crowell); Charles Neider, *The Travels of MT* (Coward-McCann); Franklin R. Rogers, *MT's Burlesque Patterns* (SMUP).

The remainder of this bibliography is devoted to a list of articles about MT, mostly in periodicals.

Sir John Adams, "MT, Psychologist," *DR*, Vol. XIII (1933–34), 417–26; Richard P. Adams, "The Unity and Coherence of *Huckleberry Finn*," *Tulane Studies in English*, Vol. VI (1956), 87–103; Chester A. Allen, "MT and Conscience," *Literature and Psychology*, Vol. VII (1957), 17–21; Jerry Allen, "Tom Sawyer's Town," *National Geographic Magazine*, Vol. CX (1956), 121–40; Richard D. Altick, "MT's Despair: An Explanation in Terms of His Humanity," *SAQ*, Vol.

XXXIV (1935), 359–67; C. J. Armstrong, "MT's Early Writings Discovered," *MHR*, Vol. XXIV (1930), 485–501.

Paul Baender, "MT and the Byron Scandal," *AL*, Vol. XXX (1958–59), 467–85; Howard Baetzhold, "MT's 'First Date' with Olivia Langdon," *Missouri Historical Society Bulletin*, Vol. XI (1955), 155–57, and "MT: England's Advocate," *AL*, Vol. XXVIII (1956–57), 328–46; J. Christian Bay, "*Tom Sawyer, Detective:* The Origin of the Plot," in *Essays Offered to Herbert Putnam*, etc. (YUP, 1929); Dan Beard, "MT as a Neighbor," *American Review of Reviews*, Vol. XLI (1910), 705–709; Warren Beck, "Huck Finn at Phelps Farm," *Archives des Lettres Modernes*, Vol. III, Nos. 13–15 (1958); Gladys C. Bellamy, "MT's Indebtedness to John Phoenix," *AL*, Vol. XIII (1941), 29–43; Adolph B. Benson, "MT's Contacts with Scandinavia," *Scandinavian Studies*, Vol. XIV (1937), 159–67; George I. Bidewell, "MT's Florida Years," *MHR*, Vol. XL (1946), 159–73; Robert W. Bingham, "Buffalo's MT," *Museum Notes, Buffalo Historical Society*, Vol. II, Nos. 4–6 (1935); Walter Blair, "On the Structure of Tom Sawyer," *MP*, Vol. XXXVII (1939–40), 75–88, and "The French Revolution and Huckleberry Finn," *MP*, Vol. LV (1957–58), 21–35; Harold Blodgett, "A Note on MT's Library of Humor," *AL*, Vol. X (1938–39), 78–80; Bradford A. Booth, "MT's Comments on Holmes's *Autocrat*," *AL*, Vol. XXI (1949–50), 456–63; Gamaliel Bradford, "Mark Twain," in his *American Portraits, 1875–1900* (HM, 1922); Edgar M. Branch, "The Two Providences: Thematic Form in *Huckleberry Finn*," *CE*, Vol. XI (1950), 188–95; Frances V. Brownell, "The Role of Jim in *Huckleberry Finn*," *Boston University Studies in English*, Vol. I (1955), 74–83; Louis J. Budd, "MT Plays the Bachelor," *WHR*, Vol. XI (1957), 157–67, "Twain, Howells, and the Boston Nihilists," *NEQ*, Vol. XXXII (1959), 368–71, and "The Southward Currents under Huck Finn's Raft," *Mississippi Valley Historical Review*, Vol. XLVI (1959), 222–37; Tom Burnam, "MT and the Paige Typesetter: A Background for Despair," *WHR*, Vol. VI (1951–52), 29–36; Ruth A. Burnet, "MT in the Northwest, 1895," *Pacific Northwest Quarterly*, Vol. XLII (1951), 187–202; Katherine Buxbaum, "MT and the American Dialect," *AS*, Vol. II (1927), 232–36.

Guy A. Cardwell, "MT's Hadleyburg," *Ohio State Archaeological and Historical Quarterly*, Vol. LX (1951), 257–64, "MT's Failures in Comedy and *The Enemy Conquered*," *GR*, Vol. XIII (1959), 424–36, "The Influence of William Dean Howells upon MT's Social Satire," *University of Colorado Studies, Series in Language and Literature*, No.

4 (1953), 93-100, and "MT: 'Moralist in Disguise,'" same, No. 6 (1957), 65-78, "MT and the American Labor Movement," *NEQ*, Vol. XXX (1957), 383-88, "Olivia Clemens Edits *Following the Equator*," *AL*, Vol. XXX (1958-59), 194-209, and "The Influence of the Nevada Frontier on MT," *WHR*, Vol. XIII (1959), 61-70; John W. Chapman, "The Germ of a Book: A Footnote on MT," *AM*, Vol. CL (1932), 720-21; Cyril Clemens, "The True Character of MT's Wife," *MHR*, Vol. XXIV (1929), 40-49; J. R. Clemens, "Some Reminiscences of MT," *OM*, Vol. LXXXVII (1929), 102; Rufus A. Coleman, "MT in Montana, 1895," *Montana Magazine of History*, Vol. III, Spring, 1953, pp. 9-17, and "MT's Jumping Frog: Another Version of the Famed Story," same, 29-30, and "Trowbridge and Clemens," *MLQ*, Vol. IX (1948), 216-23; Lane Cooper, "MT's Lilacs and Laburnams," *MLN*, Vol. XLVII (1932), 85-87; William A. Corey, "Memories of MT," *OM*, Vol. LXVI (1915), 263-65; James M. Cox, "*Pudd'nhead Wilson*: The End of MT's American Dream," *SAQ*, Vol. LVIII (1959), 251-63; Alexander Cowie, "MT Controls Himself," *AL*, Vol. X (1938-39), 488-91; Leo P. Coyle, "MT and William Dean Howells," *GR*, Vol. X (1956), 302-11; Roger P. Cuff, "MT's Use of California Folklore in his Jumping Frog Story," *Journal of American Folklore*, Vol. LXV (1952), 155-58; Sherwood Cummings "MT's Social Darwinism," *HLQ*, Vol. XX (1956-57), 163-75, and "Science and MT's Theory of Fiction," *PQ*, Vol. XXXVII (1958), 26-33.

Durant da Ponte, "Some Evasions of Censorship in *Following the Equator*," *AL*, Vol. XXIX (1957-58), 92-95; Dan DeQuille, "Reporting with MT," *Californian Illustrated Magazine*, Vol. IV (1893), 170-79; Bernard DeVoto, "MT and the Genteel Tradition," *Harvard Graduates' Magazine*, Vol. XL (1931-32), 155-63; Leon T. Dickinson, "Marketing a Best Seller: MT's *Innocents Abroad*," *PBSA*, Vol. XLI (1947), 107-22, "MT's Revisions in Writing *The Innocents Abroad*," *AL*, Vol. XIX (1947-48), 139-57, and "The Sources of *The Prince and the Pauper*," *MLN*, Vol. LXIV (1949), 103-106; Stanley T. Dormer, "MT as a Reader," *Quarterly Journal of Speech*, Vol. XXXIII (1947), 308-11; Theodore Dreiser, "Mark the Double Twain," *English Journal*, Vol. XXIV (1935), 615-27; Max Eastman, "MT's Elmira," *HaM*, Vol. CLXXV (1938), 620-32, reprinted in *Heroes I Have Known* (Simon and Schuster, 1942); Frances G. Emberson, "MT's Vocabulary: A General Survey," *University of Missouri Studies*, Vol. X, No. 3 (1935); Frances G. Emberson and Robert L. Ramsay, "A MT Lexicon," same, Vol. XIII, No. 1 (1938).

Mary Mason Fairbanks, "The Cruise of the *Quaker City*," etc., *Chautauquan*, Vol. XIV (1892), 429-32; Paul Fatout, "MT Lectures in Indiana," *IMH*, Vol. XLVI (1950), 363-67, "MT's First Lecture: A Parallel," *PHR*, Vol. XXV (1956), 347-54, "The Twain-Cable Readings in Indiana," *IMH*, Vol. LIII (1957), 19-28, and "MT, Litigant," *AL*, Vol. XXXI (1959-60), 31-45; P. J. Federico, "MT as an Inventor," *Journal of the Patent Office Society*, Vol. VIII (1925), 75-79; DeLancey Ferguson, "The Uncollected Portions of MT's *Autobiography*," *AL*, Vol. VIII (1936-37), 37-46, "MT and the Cleveland *Herald*," same, 304-305, " 'The Petrified Truth,' " *Col*, N.S. Vol. II, No. 2 (1937), 189-96, "Huck Finn Aborning," *Col*, N.S. Vol. III, No. 2 (1938), 171-80, "The Case for MT's Wife," *University of Toronto Quarterly*, Vol. IX (1939-40), 9-21, and "MT's Comstock Duel: The Birth of a Legend," *AL*, Vol. XIV (1942-43), 66-70; George Feinstein, "MT's Idea of Story Structure," *AL*, Vol. XVIII (1946-47), 160-63; Leslie Fiedler, "Come Back to the Raft Ag'in, Huck Honey!," *Partisan Review*, Vol. XV (1948), 664-71; John T. Flanagan, "MT on the Upper Mississippi," *Minnesota History*, Vol. XVII (1936), 369-84; Ray W. Frantz, "The Role of Folklore in *Huckleberry Finn*," *AL*, Vol. XXVIII (1956-57), 314-27; Martin B. Fried, "MT in Buffalo," *Niagara Frontier*, Vol. V (1959), 89-110; Otto Friedrich, "MT and the Nature of Humor," *Discourse*, Vol. II (1959), 67-86; E. S. Fussell, "The Structural Problem of *The Mysterious Stranger*," *Studies in Philology*, Vol. LXIX (1952), 95-104.

John C. Gerber, "MT's 'Private Campaign,' " *Civil War History*, Vol. I (1955), 37-60, and "The Relation between Point of View and Style in the Works of MT," in Harold C. Martin, ed., *Style in Prose Fiction* (Columbia, 1959); William M. Gibson, "MT and Howells: Anti-Imperialists," *NEQ*, Vol. XX (1947), 435-70; A. V. Goodpasture, "MT, Southerner," *Tennessee Historical Magazine*, Series II, Vol. I (1931), 253-60; Edgar H. Goold, Jr., "MT on the Writing of Fiction," *AL*, Vol. XXVI (1954-55), 52-66; Seymour L. Gross, "MT and Catholicism," *Critic*, Vol. XVII (April-May, 1959), 9, 12, 88-91; Thomas A. Gullason, "The 'Fatal' Ending of *Huckleberry Finn*," *AL*, Vol. XXIX (1957-58), 86-91; Allen Guttmann, "MT's *Connecticut Yankee*: Affirmation of the Vernacular Tradition," *NEQ*, Vol. XXXIII (1960), 232-37.

Frank Harris, *Contemporary Portraits*, Fourth Series (Brentano's, 1923); Julian Hawthorne, "MT as I Knew Him," *OM*, Vol. LXXXVII (1929), 111, 128; Edgar H. Hemminghaus, "MT's German Provenience," *MLQ*, Vol. VI (1945), 459–78; Maurice Hewlett, "Mark on Sir Walter," *Sewanee Review*, Vol. XXIX (1921), 130–33; John B. Hoben, "MT's *A Connecticut Yankee*: A Genetic Study," *AL*, Vol. XVIII (1946–47), 197–218, and "MT: On the Writer's Use of Language," *AS*, Vol. XXXI (1956), 163–71; H. H. Hoeltje, "When MT Spoke in Portland," *Oregon Historical Quarterly*, Vol. LV (1954), 73–81; Daniel G. Hoffman, "Jim's Magic: Black or White?" *AL*, Vol. XXXII (1960), 47–54; John W. Hollenbach, "MT, Story-Teller, at Work," *CE*, Vol. VII (1946), 303–12; Robert M. Hughes, "A Deserter's Tale," *Virginia Magazine of History and Biography*, Vol. XXXIX (1931), 21–28; Robert Hunting, "MT's Arkansas Yahoos," *MLN*, Vol. LXXIII (1958), 264–68; Dudley R. Hutcherson, "MT as a Pilot," *AL*, Vol. XII (1940–41), 353–55.

George Wharton James, "MT and the Pacific Coast," *Pacific Monthly*, Vol. XXIV (1910), 115–34; Burges Johnson, "A Ghost for MT," *AM*, Vol. CLXXXIX, May, 1952, pp. 65–66; Alexander E. Jones, "Heterodox Thought in MT's Hannibal," *Arkansas Historical Quarterly*, Vol. X (1951), 244–57, "MT and Freemasonry," *AL*, Vol. XXVI (1954–55), 363–73, "MT and Sexuality," *PMLA*, Vol. LXXI (1956), 595–616, and "MT and the Determinism of *What Is Man?*," *AL*, Vol. XXX (1957–58), 1–17; Joseph Jones, "The Duke's Tooth-Powder Racket," *MLN*, Vol. LXI (1946), 468–69; L. Clark Keating, "MT and Paul Bourget," *French Review*, Vol. XXX (1956–57), 342–49; E. W. Kemble, "Illustrating *Huckleberry Finn*," *Col*, Part I (1930); Albert R. Kitzhaber, "MT's Use of the Pomeroy Case in The Gilded Age," *MLQ*, Vol. XV (1954), 42–56; Ada M. Klett, "Meisterschaft, or the True State of MT's German," *German Review*, Vol. VII (Dec. 1940), 10–11; Sydney J. Krause, "T's Method and Theory of Composition," *MP*, Vol. LVI (1958–59), 167–77.

Lauriat Lane, Jr., "Why *Huckleberry Finn* Is a Great World Novel," *CE*, Vol. XVII (1956–57), 1–5;[11] Stephen Leacock, "MT and Canada," *Queen's Quarterly*, Vol. XLII (1935), 68–81; Lewis Leary, "Tom and Huck: Innocence on Trial," *VQR*, Vol. XXX (1954), 417–30; F. R. Leavis, "MT's Neglected Classic: The Moral Astringency of *Pudd'nhead Wilson*," *Commentary*, Vol. XXI (1956), 128–36; Ernest

---

[11] Cf., in the same issue, William Van O'Connor, "Why *Huckleberry Finn* Is Not the Great American Novel" (pp. 6–10). See also replies by Gilbert M. Rubenstein, "The Moral Structure of *Huckleberry Finn*," *College English*, Vol. XVIII (1956–57), 72–76, and Walter Blair, "Why Huck and Jim Went Downstream," pp. 106–107, and the rejoinders by O'Connor and Lane, pp. 108–109.

E. Leisy, "MT's Part in *The Gilded Age*," AL, Vol. VIII (1936–37), 445–48, and "MT and Isaiah Sellers," AL, Vol. XIII (1941–42), 398–404; E. James Lennon, "MT Abroad," *Quarterly Journal of Speech*, Vol. XXXIX (1953), 197–200; Richard G. Lillard, "Contemporary Reaction to 'The Empire City Massacre,' " AL, Vol. XVI (1944–45), 198–203; E. Hudson Long, "Sut Lovingood and MT's *Joan of Arc*," *MLN*, Vol. LXXIV (1949), 37–39; C. Grant Loomis, "Dan DeQuille's MT," PHR, Vol. XV (1946), 336–47; Fred W. Lorch, "MT in Iowa," *IJHP*, Vol. XXVII (1929), 408–56, "Lecture Trips and Visits of MT in Iowa," same, 507–47, "The Tradition," "Molly Clemens's Note Book," "Literary Apprenticeship," "Adrift for Heresy," "The Closing Years," *Palimpsest*, Vol. X (1929), 353–86, "A Source for MT's 'The Dandy Frightening the Squatter'," AL, Vol. III (1931), 309–13, "MT's Trip to Humboldt in 1861," AL, Vol. X (1938–39), 343–49, "MT and the 'Campaign That Failed'," AL, Vol. XII (1940–41), 254–70, "A Note on Tom Blankenship," same, 351–53, "Albert Bigelow Paine's Visit to Keokuk in 1910," *IJHP*, Vol. XLII (1942), 192–97, "MT's Philadelphia Letters in the Muscatine *Journal*," AL, Vol. XVII (1945–46), 348–52, " 'Doesticks' and *Innocents Abroad*," AL, Vol. XX (1948–49), 124–25, "Cable and His Reading Tour with MT in 1884–85," AL, Vol. XXIII (1951–52), 471–86, "MT's 'Sandwich Islands' Lecture and the Failure at Jamestown, New York, in 1869," AL, Vol. XXV (1953–54), 314–25,[12] "MT's Lecture Tour of 1868–69: 'The American Vandal Abroad'," AL, Vol. XXVI (1954–55), 515–27, "Julia Newell and MT on the *Quaker City* Holy Land Excursion," *Rock County Chronicle* (Janesville, Wisconsin), Vol. II (1956), 13–25, "MT's Public Lectures in England in 1873," AL, Vol. XXIX (1957–58), 297–302, and "Hawaiian Feudalism in MT's *A Connecticut Yankee in King Arthur's Court*," AL, Vol. XXX (1958–59), 50–66.

T. O. Mabbott, "MT's Artillery: A Mark Twain Legend," MHR, Vol. XXV (1930), 23–69; Leo Marx, "Mr. Eliot, Mr. Trilling, and *Huckleberry Finn*," *American Scholar*, Vol. XXII (1952–53), 423–40; John C. McCloskey, "MT as Critic in *The Innocents Abroad*," AL, Vol. XXV (1953–54), 139–51; Dwight Macdonald, "MT: An Unsentimental Journey," *The New Yorker*, April 9, 1960, pp. 160–96; D. M. McKeithan, "More About MT's War with English Critics of America," *MLN*, Vol. LXIII (1948), 221–28, and "Madame Laszowska Meets MT," *Texas Studies in Literature and Language*, Vol. I

---

[12] Cf. the reply by Alexander E. Jones, "MT and the 'Many Citizens' Letter," AL, Vol. XXV (1954–55), 421–25, and Professor Lorch's rejoinder, pp. 426–27.

(1959), 62–65; Walter Meserve, "Colonel Sellers as a Scientist," *Modern Drama*, Vol. I (1958–59), 151–56; Harold Meyer, "MT on the Comstock," *Southwest Review*, Vol. XII (1927), 197–207; H. E. Mierow, "Cicero and MT," *Classical Journal*, Vol. XX (1924–25), 167–69; William C. Miller, "MT's Source for 'The Latest Sensation' Hoax?," *AL*, Vol. XXXII (1960), 75–78; Marion Montgomery, "The New Romantic *vs.* the Old: MT's Dilemma in *Life on the Mississippi*," *Mississippi Quarterly*, Vol. XI (1958), 79–82; Olin H. Moore, "MT and Don Quixote," *PMLA*, Vol. XXXVII (1922), 324–46; W. R. Moses, "The Pattern of Evil in *Adventures of Huckleberry Finn*," *GR*, Vol. XIII (1959), 161–66.

Russel B. Nye, "MT in Oberlin," *OSAHQ*, Vol. XLVII (1938), 69–73; James C. Olson, "MT and the Department of Agriculture," *AL*, Vol. XIII (1941–42), 408–10; G. Harrison Orians, "Walter Scott, MT, and the Civil War," *SAQ*, Vol. XL (1940), 342–59; Robert Ornstein, "The Ending of Huckleberry Finn," *MLN*, Vol. LXXIV (1959), 698–702; E. P. Pabody, "MT's Ghost Story," *Minnesota History*, Vol. XVIII (1937), 28–35; Albert Bigelow Paine, "Innocents at Home," *Collier's*, Vol. LXXV, Jan. 3, 1925, pp. 5–6, 45, "MT at Stormfield," *HaW*, Vol. CXVIII (1909), 955–58; Coleman O. Parsons, "The Devil and Samuel Clemens," *VQR*, Vol. XXIII (1947), 582–606, and "The Background of *The Mysterious Stranger*," *AL*, Vol. XXXII (1960), 47–54; Wilfred Partington, "MT—in Love, in Anger, and in Bibliography," *Bkm*, Vol. LXXVI (1933), 313–24, III–IV; Charles O. Paullin, "MT's Virginia Kin," *William and Mary College Quarterly Historical Magazine*, Vol. XV, Series 2 (1935), 294–98; H. Houston Peckham, "The Literary Status of MT, 1877–1900," *SAQ*, Vol. XIX (1920), 332–40; William Lyon Phelps, "MT," *Yale Review*, Vol. XXV (1935–36), 291–310; Michael J. Phillips, "MT's Partner," *SEP*, Vol. CXCII (Sept. 11, 1920), 22–23, 69–70, 73–74; V.R., "Walter Scott and the Southern States of America," *Notes & Queries*, Vol. CLXIX (1935), 328–30; William H. Rideing, "MT in Clubland," *Bkm*, Vol. XXXI (1910), 379–82; E. Arthur Robinson, "The Two 'Voices' in *Huckleberry Finn*," *MLN*, Vol. LXXV (1960), 204–208; Louis D. Rubin, Jr., "Tom Sawyer and the Use of Novels," *AQ*, Vol. IX (1957), 209–16.

Paul Schmidt, "MT's Satire on Republicanism," *AQ*, Vol. V (1935), 344–56; Friedrich Schönemann, "MT and Adolf Wilbrandt," *MLN*, Vol. XXXIV (1919), 372–74, "MT's Weltanschauung," *Englische Studien*, Vol. LV (1921), 53–84, "Mr. Samuel Langhorne Clemens," *Archiv*, Vol. CXLIV (1923), 184–213, and "MT's Huckleberry

Finn," *Archiv*, Vol. CXCII (1956), 273–89; Arthur L. Scott, "*The Innocents Abroad* Revaluated," *WHR*, Vol. VII (1952–53), 213–23, "MT Looks at Europe," *SAQ*, Vol. LII (1953), 399–413, "MT's Revisions of *The Innocents Abroad* for the British Edition of 1872," *AL*, Vol. XXV (1953–54), 43–61, "MT Revises *Old Times on the Mississippi*," *Journal of English and Germanic Philology*, Vol. LIV (1955), 634–38, "The *Century Magazine* Edits *Huckleberry Finn*," *AL*, Vol. XXVII (1955–56), 356–62, and "MT: Critic of Conquest," *DR*, Vol. XXXV (1955–56), 45–53; Charles E. Shain, "The Journal of the *Quaker City* Captain," *NEQ*, Vol. XXVIII (1955), 388–94; Joseph Slater, "Music at Col. Grangerford's: A Footnote to *Huckleberry Finn*," *AL*, Vol. XXI (1949–50), 108–11; Annella Smith, "MT—Occultist," *Rosicrucian Magazine*, Vol. XXVI (1934), 65–68; Henry Nash Smith, " 'That Hideous Mistake of Poor Clemens's,' " *Harvard Library Bulletin*, Vol. IX (1955), 145–80, and "MT's Images of Hannibal: From St. Petersburg to Eseldorf," *UTSE*, Vol. XXXVII (1958), 1–23; G. R. Stewart, "Bret Harte upon MT in 1866," *AL*, Vol. XIII (1941–42), 263–64; Albert E. Stone, Jr., "The Twichell Papers and MT's *A Tramp Abroad*," *Yale University Library Gazette*, Vol. XXIX (1955), 151–64, and "MT's *Joan of Arc*: The Child as Goddess," *AL*, Vol. XXXI (1959–60), 1–20; Jessie B. Strate, "MT and Geography," *Journal of Geography*, Vol. XXIII (1924), 81–92; Louis Hall Swain, "MT as a Music Critic," *Furman Bulletin*, Vol. XIX, No. 9 (April, 1937), 48–53.

Caroline Ticknor, "MT's Missing Chapter," *Bkm*, Vol. XXXIX (1914), 298–309; James N. Tidwell, "MT's Representation of Negro Speech," *AS*, Vol. XVII (1942), 174–76; Juliette A. Trainor, "Symbolism in *A Connecticut Yankee in King Arthur's Court*," Vol. LXVI (1951), 382–85; Arlin Turner, "James Lampton, MT's Model for Colonel Sellers," *MLN*, Vol. LXX (1955), 592–94, and "MT, Cable, and 'A Professional Newspaper Liar,' " *NEQ*, Vol. XXVIII (1955), 18–33; Joseph H. Twichell, "MT," *HaM*, Vol. XCII (1896), 817–27; Charles Vale, "MT as an Orator," *Forum*, Vol. XLIV (1910), 1–13; A. L. Vogelback, "The Publication and Reception of *Huckleberry Finn* in America," *AL*, Vol. XI (1939–40), 260–72, and "*The Prince and the Pauper*: A Study in Critical Standards," *AL*, Vol. XIV (1942–43), 48–54; Leo von Hibler, "MT und die deutsche Sprache," *Anglia*, Vol. LXV (1941), 206–13.

H. H. Waggoner, "Science in the Thought of MT," *AL*, Vol. VIII (1936–37), 357–70; Franklin Walker, "An Influence from San Francisco on MT's The Gilded Age," AL, Vol. VIII (1936), 63–66; H. R. Warfel, "George W. Cable Amends a MT Plot," AL, Vol. VI (1934–35), 328–31; Edward Wasiolek, "The Structure of Make-Believe: Huckleberry Finn," UKCR, Vol. XXIV (1957–58), 97–101; E. A. Weatherly, "Beau Tibbs and Colonel Sellers," MLN, LIX (1944–45), 310–13; Doris and Samuel Webster, "Whitewashing Jane Clemens," Bkm, Vol. LXI (1925), 531–35; Dixon Wecter, "MT as Translator from the German," AL, Vol. XIII (1941), 257–64, and "MT and the West," HLQ, Vol. VIII (1944–45), 359–77; Mort Weisinger, "Listen! MT Speaking," SEP, Vol. XXCCI, July 3, 1948, p. 12; Ray B. West, Jr., "MT's Idyl of Frontier America," UKCR, Vol. XV (1948), 92–104; Victor Royce West, "Folklore in the Works of MT," University of Nebraska Studies in Language, Literature, and Criticism, No. 10 (1930); Frank M. White, "MT as a Newspaper Reporter," Outlook, Vol. XCVI (1910), 961–67; B. J. Whiting, "Guyuscutus, Royal Nonesuch and Other Hoaxes," Southern Folklore Quarterly, Vol. VIII (1944), 251–75; Anne P. Wigger, "The Source of Fingerprint Material in MT's Puddn'head Wilson and Those Extraordinary Twins," AL, Vol. XXVIII (1956–57), 517–20, and "The Composition of MT's Pudd'nhead Wilson and Those Extraordinary Twins: Chronology and Development," MP, Vol. XXXV (1957–58), 93–102; Robert A. Wiggins, "MT and the Drama," AL, Vol. XXV (1953–54), 279–86; Cecil B. Williams, "MT: American Paradox," Bulletin of the Oklahoma Agricultural and Mechanical College, Vol. XLVIII, No. 25 (1951), 14–21; Mentor L. Williams, "MT's Joan of Arc," Michigan Alumnus Quarterly Review, Vol. LIV (1948), 243–50; Robert H. Wilson, "Malory in the Connecticut Yankee," UTSE, 1948, pp. 185–206; Owen Wister, "In Homage to MT," HaM, Vol. CLXXI (1935), 547–56; Homer E. Woodbridge, "MT and the Gesta Romanorum," Nation, Vol. CVIII (1919), 424–25; S. J. Woolf, "Painting the Portrait of MT," Collier's, Vol. XLV, May 14, 1910, pp. 42–44; Mary A. Wyman, "A Note on MT," CE, Vol. VII (1946), 438–43; Norris W. Yates, "The 'Counter-Conversion' of Huckleberry Finn," AL, Vol. XXXII (1960), 1–10; James Harvey Young, "Anna Dickinson, MT, and Bret Harte," Pennsylvania Magazine of History and Biography, Vol. LXXVI (1952), 39–46.

The MT Quarterly, later The MT Journal, has been published by the IMTS since 1936. The Twainian has been published since 1939, first by The MT Society of Chicago, then by The MT Research Foundation. The Bookman published a MT number in June, 1910 (Vol.

XXXI) and *The Mentor* in May, 1924 (Vol. XII). The articles in these periodicals are not listed separately in this bibliography, though some of them are referred to in footnotes.

A Commentary on Mark Twain Criticism
and Scholarship Since 1960

SINCE THE REVISED EDITION of *Mark Twain, The Man and His Work* came out in the spring of 1961, a really immense amount of Mark Twain material has been published, and now that still another printing of this book is called for, it has seemed good to both the author and the publisher to take some account of these items. Harper & Row will soon be launching their new "Manuscript Edition" of Mark Twain's works, which will be the first that has been edited by scholars, and the University of California Press plans to supplement this with twelve volumes culled mainly from the Mark Twain Papers. See Paul Baender and Frederick Anderson, "Twain[1] in Progress: Two Projects," *American Quar-*

[1] Though I find much to praise in the work of the younger MT scholars, I cannot but deplore their growing tendency to refer to their subject as "Twain." "Twain" is not a surname. "Mark twain" is a river term, indicating safe water, and is a unit. I do not see how it can be divided. It would no doubt be possible to argue that since Samuel L. Clemens took "Mark Twain" as his pseudonym, he *used* it as a name, and that "Twain" thus, in effect, *became* a surname, but I do not understand how any person possessing any linguistic sense could be impressed by such an argument. It is also true, of course, that our author has often

terly, Vol. XVI (1964), 621–23. The publication of these works will mark the end of one era in Mark Twain scholarship and the beginning of another.

What follows is not exactly a bibliographical study nor exactly critical evaluation but something which lies somewhere between the two. My revised edition of 1961, text and bibliography together, was intended not only to express my personal vision of Mark Twain but also to sum up the state of knowledge at the time it appeared. In this new section, my primary interest has been to brief my reader on the directions in which scholarship has traveled since and to indicate the sources that must be consulted to bring the record up to date. To all intents and purposes I have confined myself to materials in English. I have not tried to list everything, and my analyses and evaluations range all the way from comparative elaboration to the vanishing point.

Though my revised edition appeared in the spring of 1961, it was prepared for the press in September, 1960; its bibliography, therefore, does not embrace all 1960 items, some of which, consequently, appear here, along with a few waifs and strays that are even earlier. For the years 1960–1965 I have depended largely upon the annual bibliographies in *PMLA*. This section is being prepared in September 1966, that is before 1965 material has been indexed with any approach to completeness. I have drawn my 1966 references from many sources, but I do not flatter myself that I have caught everything. I have deliberately refrained from reading the Mark Twain section of James A. Woodress, ed., *American Literary Scholarship 1964* (Duke University Press, 1965).

The Twainian is devoted exclusively and the *Mark Twain Journal* largely to Mark Twain material. Some of the articles published in these serials but not all are itemized hereinafter; a general reference is also indicated. The same applies to the special Mark Twain numbers published by *American Book Collector*,

been affectionately called "Mark," but since Mark is a common given name, this seems to me to stand upon a somewhat different basis. Clemens sometimes signed "Mark," but he never thought or spoke of himself as "Twain." The climax of absurdity along this line has been achieved by Leslie F. Chard II, who, in AQ, Vol. XVI (1964), 596, writes of MT's mother as "Mrs. Twain"!

Vol. X, June, 1960; *American Quarterly*, Vol. XVI, Winter, 1964; and *Midcontinent American Studies Journal* (then known as *Journal of the Central Mississippi Valley American Studies Association*), Vol. I (1960).

I have, wherever possible, standardized titles, using italics for books and quotation marks for articles, etc. In addition to the abbreviations listed on page 248, the following are hereinafter employed:

ABC	*American Book Collector*
ArizQ	*Arizona Quarterly*
BSTCF	*Ball State Teachers College Forum*
BNYPL	*Bulletin of the New York Public Library*
Cr	Thomas Y. Crowell Company
D	Doubleday & Company
Ex	*Explicator*
HH	Hanover House
HR	Harper & Row
HF	*Adventures of Huckleberry Finn*
IUP	Indiana University Press
MASJ	*Midcontinent American Studies Journal*
MTJ	*Mark Twain Journal*
MQ	*Mississippi Quarterly*
NCF	*Nineteenth Century Fiction*
Tw	*Twainian*
YUP	Yale University Press

I

A good deal of fresh material by MT himself has been published during our period. The most important single item is the miscellany, *Letters from the Earth* (HR, 1962). This was prepared for publication by Bernard DeVoto as far back as 1939 but was withheld by MT's daughter, the late Clara Samossoud, because of what she considered the shocking character of such pieces as "Papers of the Adam Family," "The Damned Human Race," and "Letters from the Earth" itself. In 1940, too, Mrs. Samossoud prevented DeVoto from including in *MT in Erup-*

tion the five 1906 dictations which Charles Neider has now published as "Reflections on Religion," *Hudson Review*, Vol. XVI (1963), 329–52.[2] *Letters from the Earth* also contains, besides other, minor items, much more of the late experimental, uncompleted work, "The Great Dark," than DeVoto published in 1942 in his *MT at Work*.

Though all students of MT may be expected to agree on the importance of making these writings available, their total effect is disappointing from the point of view of literary quality; neither do they greatly modify what we already knew about MT. Because he fails to define his position, his anti-religious screeds lack real critical value. He scatters his shot and attacks from all directions simultaneously; neither does he seem to have made up his mind whether he is attacking God or merely false ideas of God. Useful correctives are at hand in Caroline Thomas Harnsberger, *MT's Views on Religion* (Evanston, Illinois, The Schori Press, 1961), which makes available the marginal notes MT entered in his copy of Rufus K. Noyes's *Views of Religion* (1906), and in MT's annotations in his copy of Lecky, as printed in *Tw*, 21st Year, November–December, 1962, pp. 1–2. "If I have understood this book aright," MT wrote of Lecky, "it proves two things beyond shadow or question: 1. That Christianity is the very invention of Hell itself; 2. & that Christianity is the most precious and elevating and ennobling boon ever vouchsafed to the world." Mrs. Harnsberger's quotations show that MT was no atheist, that he was constantly preoccupied with the thought of God, and that his rejections and acceptances were profoundly conditioned by his early midwestern environment. For that matter, the fourth dictation in the "Reflections" is itself definitely theistic, though the God postulated in it is not likely to be of much use to mortals.

A number of articles published during the period also bear on

---

[2] Mrs. Samossoud finally lifted the ban on *all* her father's unpublished writings, partly at least to refute the claim of Russian critics that MT's anti-religious, anti-imperialistic, and anti-capitalistic utterances were being suppressed in the United States. See M. O. Mendelson, "MT's Unpublished Literary Heritage," *Soviet Review*, Vol. II, September, 1961, pp. 33–53; R. D. Lakin, "MT and the Cold War," *Midwest Quarterly*, Vol. II (1961), 159–67; and the introduction to *Life As I Find It*, where Charles Neider pertinently inquires whether Russian editions of MT plan to include his remarks on international copyright!

the religious question. Thomas Andersson, "MT's Views on Politics, Religion, and Morals," *Moderna Språk*, Vol. LVII (1963), 283–89, though a useful compilation, has nothing new, either in data or in interpretation. Aurele A. Durocher has taken another look at "MT and the Roman Catholic Church," *MASJ*, Vol. I, Fall, 1960, pp. 32–43, and Louis J. Budd, "MT on Joseph the Patriarch," *AQ*, Vol. XVI (1964), 577–86, studies his attitude toward, and use of, a particular Bible character. Richard Greenleaf's "MT and the Bishop of Woolwich," *Religion in Life*, Vol. XXXV (1965–66), 122–31, is an illuminating dialogue which draws freely on both "Reflections on Religion" and *Honest to God*. Sherwood Cummings also skirts the fringes of MT's religious problem in two articles describing his ambivalent attitude toward science and technology—"MT's Acceptance of Science," *Centennial Review*, Vol. VI (1962), 245–61, and "MT and the Sirens of Progress," *MASJ*, Vol. I, Fall, 1960, pp. 17–24. Joseph O. Baylen, "MT, W. T. Stead and 'The Tell-Tale Hands,' " *AQ*, Vol. XVI (1964), 606–12, writes of palmistry, which is not a religious subject but does touch upon MT's interest in occultism.

Franklin R. Rogers has published MT's unfinished novel, *Simon Wheeler, Detective* (New York Public Library, 1963), impeccably edited and with a masterly introduction. Badly confused and absurdly complicated, the story turns out to be quite as flawed a piece of art as it was reputed to be, yet the best of it has an unmistakable charm. Essentially, *Simon Wheeler, Detective* burlesques detective stories in general and the methods of Allan Pinkerton in particular. Its use of feud materials antedates *HF* and may have contributed to it. Si Wheeler's dream ties up with "Captain Stormfield's Visit to Heaven," and the runaway horse episode shows MT making use of a Quarry Farm happening of summer 1877. On the whole, however, the work is more like *Pudd'nhead Wilson* than any other of MT's published novels.

Much less can be claimed for the Mark Twain–Bret Harte play, *Ah Sin*, recovered from an amanuensis copy, "apparently prepared for the early rehearsals of the play," now in the Barrett Library of American Literature at the University of Virginia, and printed in a really exquisite format for the members of the Book

Club of California in 1961. One cannot but wonder whether beautiful bookmaking has ever before been expended upon material less worthy of it. The editor, Frederick Anderson, remarks justly that "while *Ah Sin* is not the poorest work by either man, it is not far from it." On the stage it may have been barely passable; on the printed page, it comes close to being unreadable.

II

Next to publishing fresh MT material, the best thing is to revive and make available materials hitherto uncollected. In *MT's San Francisco* (McGraw-Hill, 1963), edited by Bernard Taper, selections from MT's journalistic writings of 1863–66, chosen to reveal the city of the time and to illustrate MT's development as a writer, have been presented in a rather luxurious format.

MT on the Art of Writing (Buffalo, The Salisbury Club, 1961) is a charming little book in which M. B. Fried rescues three interesting little articles from the files of the Buffalo *Express*. In " 'Review of Holiday Literature,' " *CE*, Vol. XXV (1963), 182–86, Arthur L. Scott reprints a "Carl Byng" item from the *Express*, December 24, 1870, and conjecturally assigns it to MT. It is a Mother Goose book that is being reviewed, but only "The Cat and the Fiddle" is discussed. A more elaborate job of excavation from *Express* files was undertaken by Henry Duskis in *The Forgotten Writings of MT* (Philosophical Library, 1963), but Mr. Duskis has not reprinted any of the selections as they appeared in the *Express* but simply weaves long quotations from them into his own summary and commentary. His book will be useful, therefore, only until somebody else has done a better job.

There is nothing at which to cavil, on the other hand, in Bruce R. McElderry's edition of MT's *Contributions to* The Galaxy, 1868–1871 (Scholars' Facsimiles and Reprints, 1961); although most of the significant material given here has been reprinted elsewhere, it is valuable to have it all in order and in facsimile, with such admirable annotation.

In 1964, Charles E. Tuttle reprinted, in Rutland, Vermont, *A Cure for the Blues*, which is one of the most important testimonials we have to MT's appetite for what he called "hogwash" in literature. The attractive little volume also contains the complete text of the novel which inspired the essay, *The Enemy Conquered; or, Love Triumphant,* by S. Watson Royston (MT called him "G. Ragsdale McClintock"), and a review of the latter from the *Yale Literary Magazine.*

In *NEQ,* Vol. XXXIV (1961), 228–39, Hamlin Hill reprinted from *The American Publisher,* September–October, 1871, "MT's 'Brace of Brief Lectures on Science,'" with comments on their implications for the author's scientific knowledge and interests. In "Samuel Clemens, Sub Rosa Correspondent," *English Language Notes,* Vol. I (1964), 270–73, Dewey Ganzel reprints two hitherto unknown *Quaker City* letters to the New York *Herald.* The letters themselves are of no interest, but Ganzel's suggestion that MT was writing for the *Herald* sub rosa while officially a *Tribune* correspondent raises interesting questions. "The New Dynasty," MT's strongest pro-labor utterance, was reprinted in *Tw,* 19th Year, September–October, 1960, pp. 2–4. Kenneth E. Carpenter, "An Unrecorded MT," *PBSA,* Vol. LV (1961), 236–39, pointed out that "The Czar's Soliloquy" was first published in book form, in Geneva, in the Russian language, by the Socialist Revolutionary party in 1905. "MT's Marginal Notes on 'The Queen's English,'" *Tw,* 25th year, No. 2, March–April, 1966, pp. 1–4, reprints what Mark had to say about G. Washington Moon's *Learned Men's English,* etc. (Routledge, 1892). To all this may be added two straight bibliographical investigations—Lawrence E. Mobley, "MT and the *Golden Era,*" *PBSA,* Vol. LVIII (1964), 8–23, and Martha A. Turner, "MT's 1601 Through Fifty Editions," *MTJ,* Vol. XII, Summer, 1965, pp. 10ff., which supplements the bibliography in Meine's edition of 1601 and may awaken in some readers the same kind of astonishment which Touchstone experienced upon first discovering that breaking of ribs could be entertainment for ladies.

MT's Letters from Hawaii, edited by A. Grove Day (Appleton-Century, 1966) does not actually enlarge the canon, but it does make available to the general reader material which previously had to be sought for through out-of-print books. In fact, all twenty-five of the pieces which Mark Twain wrote in 1866 for the Sacramento *Union* have hitherto appeared together only in Walter F. Frear's *MT in Hawaii*, which was a private, limited edition.

General Grant, by Matthew Arnold, with a Rejoinder by MT, edited by John Y. Simon (Southern Illinois University Press, 1966) reprints one of MT's speeches, never before correctly given in print since it was delivered before the Army and Navy Club of Connecticut in 1887 and reported in the Hartford *Courant*.

More important than either of these is a charming little book edited by Arthur Scott, *On the Poetry of MT: with Selections from his Verse* (University of Illinois Press, 1966), which provides a fascinating footnote on a minor aspect of a great talent. It is a pity that the Estate did not see fit to permit Mr. Scott to make a really definitive collection of MT's verses. Nevertheless we have more (sixty-five items) between these covers than we have ever had before, together with a valuable introduction which invites us to rethink the whole question of MT's relationship to verse-making.

Charles Neider's activities as an editor of MT require separate consideration. His most important publication of the period was *Life As I Find It* (HH, 1961), a very large volume, reprinting from many sources and including considerable material which had not hitherto been available in book form. One very important item in *Life As I Find It* is "Defence of General Funston," which had not previously been reprinted from *The North American Review* of May, 1902. Neider also prints an omitted chapter from *The Prince and the Pauper* and the "suppressed" chapter of *Life on the Mississippi*, which, though he neglects to mention it, had previously appeared in the edition published in 1944 by the Limited Editions Club and the Heritage Press. He also began an important pioneering work by reprinting a number of interviews with MT from the New York press. (To these should be added the Pacific Northwest items given in *Tw*, 24th Year, January–February, 1965, pp. 1–3).

Mr. Neider's favorite word is "complete," but (as he himself is sometimes driven to point out in his introductions) he seldom uses it correctly. His lines of classification frequently overlap, and he has a tendency to define literary terms to suit himself. He has now given us *The Complete Short Stories of MT* (HH, 1957); *The Complete Humorous Sketches and Tales of MT* (HH, 1961); and *The Complete Essays of MT* (D, 1963), all useful books, containing much material that it would have been much harder to get at without him. He was more original in *The Travels of MT* (Coward-McCann, 1961), where he arranged by places selections from all MT's travel books, but *The Adventures of Colonel Sellers* (D, 1965), "being MT's share of *The Gilded Age*," extracted and presented separately as a masterpiece of fiction, does not seem to me to have been one of his better ideas. An original study of MT, presumably biographical and critical, by Mr. Neider has been announced for publication in January, 1967, by Horizon Press, but this is not available for examination as this bibliography goes to press.

Finally, it is interesting to note that two writers have sought to reduce the MT canon. In "MT and the Quintus Curtius Snodgrass Letters," *Journal of the American Statistical Association,* Vol. LVIII (1963), 85–96, Charles S. Brinegar applied statistical analysis of the elements of style to show that MT did *not* write these pieces sometimes attributed to him, and in "The Quintus Curtius Snodgrass Letters: A Clarification of the MT Canon," *AL*, Vol. XXXVI (1964), 31–37, Allan Bates argued against MT's authorship on non-stylistic grounds.

Naturally only a few of the many editions of individual works by MT published since 1960 can or need be listed here. Facsimiles of the first editions of *HF* and *A Connecticut Yankee*, with introductions by Hamlin Hill, were published by Chandler Publishing Company, San Francisco, in 1962 and 1963 respectively. Sculley Bradley, R. C. Beatty, and E. H. Long brought out an edition of *HF* containing an annotated text, background and source material, and selected criticism through Norton in 1961. Walter Blair's *Selected Writings of MT*, in "Riverside Editions" (HM, 1962), is a fine collection, including, besides much shorter, and some very early material, the whole of "The Man That Corrupted Hadleyburg" and *The Mysterious Stranger*, and constituting a valuable companion to Blair's *HF* in the same series in 1958. The most beautiful editions of MT ever published are those brought out by the George Macy Companies, which embrace both the Limited Editions Club and the Heritage Press. *Tom Sawyer, HF, A Connecticut Yankee, Life on the Mississippi,* and *Slovenly Peter* all antedate our period, which saw *The Innocents Abroad* (1962), *The Prince and the Pauper* (1964), and *A Tramp Abroad* (1966), all with introductions by the present writer.

MT has also been subjected to the ordeal by "casebook," that peculiarly trying contemporary phenomenon which finds its only possible justification in the fact that teachers of composition in American colleges and universities do not trust their students to indicate sources honestly when they prepare what both they and many of their instructors idiotically persist in describing as "research papers." (To make the whole thing as ridiculous as possible, the student is now given all the materials he is supposed to use within a single pair of covers, which would, of course, make "research" impossible even if he were capable of it.) It must be admitted, however, that the material included in many of these "casebooks" makes good reading. On MT we have had *MT's Frontier,* ed. James E. Camp and X. J. Kennedy (Holt, 1963); *Huck Finn and His Critics,* ed. Richard Lettis, Robert F. McDonnell, and William E. Morris (M, 1962); and *MT's Wound,* ed. Lewis Leary (Cr, 1962). This last is a scrupulously fair account of the long controversy precipitated by Van Wyck Brooks's "suppression theory," as set forth in 1920 in *The Ordeal of MT,* followed by selections illustrating almost every conceivable point of view. The whole thing adds up to the fullest treatment of the subject ever made, though since no qualified writer now accepts the Brooks hypothesis, some may consider that it comes under the heading of beating a dead horse. Among the writers of our period, only E. Hudson Long has seen fit to devote an article to the "suppression" theory—"T's Ordeal in Retrospect," *Southwest Review,* Vol. XLVIII (1963), 338–48.

Three anthologies call for notice also. In *MT and the Damned Human Race* (Hill & Wang, 1962), Janet Smith offered selections from MT's later writings on public affairs, topically arranged with introduction and notes, and in *MT and the Government* (Caxton

Printers, 1960), Svend Peterson gave us selections, alphabetically arranged, on "such subjects as War, Taxes, and Politicians." In *MT: A Collection of Critical Essays* (1962) in Prentice-Hall's "Twentieth Century Views" series, Henry Nash Smith collected twelve essays, beginning with Brooks but mostly post–1950, with a valuable introduction on trends and tendencies in MT criticism. He earns special gratitude for including a translation of Maurice LeBreton's "MT: An Appreciation," from *Revue Anglo-Americaine*, 1934.[3]

III

The largest collection of MT letters to appear during our period was *MT's Letters to Mary*, ed. Lewis Leary (Columbia University Press, 1961). Mary Benjamin married the youngest son of MT's benefactor, the Standard Oil magnate, Henry H. Rogers. MT first wrote to her when her engagement was announced and continued to the end of his life. He predicted that she would ultimately be installed on the thirteenth floor of Heaven and hoped that he himself might be smuggled in to visit her; as long as she lived, she said of her "Uncle Mark," "I shall see him again." Previously unpublished letters to a much younger girl are included in Dorothy Quick's irresistible book, *Enchantment: A Little Girl's Friendship with MT* (Okla, 1961). Besides the reading delight which they offer, both these works illustrate MT's tenderness and capacity for both finding happiness and creating it for others during the very years when many critics have seen him as totally committed to pessimism, cynicism, and despair. For an absent-

---

[3] Smith remarks of the book in hand: "In *Mark Twain: The Man and His Work* (1935) Edward Wagenknecht attempted to free himself from the obsessive concern with biography by adopting a topical arrangement, with chapters devoted to the writer's experience, his temperament, his conceptions of technique, and so on; but the man is still more prominently displayed than his work, and there is virtually no effort to deal with specific books." It is amazing that so good a scholar should so completely misunderstand a simple book. *MT: The Man and His Work* is completely biographical in its interest, and never pretended to be anything else. I use the topical method because my book is a psychograph, not a chronological biography (Mr. Smith is apparently not familiar with psychography), and I deal with MT's writings only as they illuminate his personality, never for their own sake. It is possible, of course, that he may have been misled by an unsuitable title; see p. vii of the present volume.

minded man of his irritable temperament, the lengths to which he would go to make Dorothy comfortable when she came to stay with him are really amazing.

In "Dear Master Wattie: The MT–David Watt Bowser Letters," *Southwest Review*, Vol. XLV (1960), 105–21, Pascal Covici, Jr., printed the text, with commentary, of all the letters that have survived of those which passed between MT and a twelve-year-old Dallas boy, beginning in 1880. See, further, "MT's Letter to the Texas Schoolboy," *Tw*, 19th Year, March–April, 1960, pp. 2–3, and Tony Tanner, "MT and Wattie Bowser," *MTJ*, Vol. XII, Spring, 1963, pp. 1–6. Until now, all the child friends of MT's concerning whom we have had any knowledge have been girls. These letters show that he was also capable of being sympathetic toward little boys.

In *The Pattern for MT's* Roughing It: *Letters from Nevada by Samuel and Orion Clemens, 1861–62*, "University of California Publications, English Studies," 23 (University of California Press, 1961), Franklin R. Rogers reprints and analyzes elaborately four letters which MT wrote to the Keokuk, Iowa, *Gate City*, 1861–62. "In "Letters from MT to William Walter Phelps, 1891–93," *HLQ*, Vol. XXVII (1964), 375–81, Arthur L. Scott discusses MT's correspondence with an American minister to Berlin, but though he quotes from the letters he does not print them. For other letters, see Morton N. Cohen, "MT and the Philippines," *MASJ*, Vol. I, Fall, 1960, pp. 25–31, an important letter illustrating MT's anti-imperialism; "Edward H. House, *Prince and the Pauper* Dramatization," *Tw*, 22nd Year, March–April, 1963, pp. 1–3, May–June, pp. 2–4; Otto Hietsch, "MT und Johann Strauss," *Jahrbuch für Amerikastudien*, Vol. VIII (1963), 210–11; John J. Weishert, "Once Again: MT and German," *MTJ*, Vol. XII, Summer, 1965, p. 17; William White, "MT to the President of Indiana University," *AL*, Vol. XXXII (1961), 461–63, an important and endearing letter, reflecting MT's affection for his wife, his loneliness after her death, his response to appreciation, and his interest in ESP. Letters from various persons to Albert Bigelow Paine on business connected with the MT Estate ran through several issues of *Tw*, 24th Year (1965).

IV

The following general biographical and/or critical studies have been published during our period: Justin Kaplan's *Mr. Clemens and MT: A Biography* (Simon and Schuster, 1966); Milton Meltzer's *MT Himself: A Pictorial Biography* (Cr, 1961); Frank Baldanzas's *MT, An Introduction and Interpretation* (1961) in the Barnes & Noble "American Authors and Critics" series; Douglas Grant's *Twain* (1962), published in Edinburgh in the Oliver and Boyd "Writers and Critics" series; Karl-Heinz Schönfelder's *MT: Leben, Persönlichkeit und Werk* (Halle: VEB, Verlag Sprache und Literatur, 1961); May McNeer's *America's MT* (HM, 1962).

Of these the most important is Mr. Kaplan's book, which contains the most detailed biography of Mark Twain's mature life outside of Paine. Curiously, Mr. Kaplan begins with Mark at the age of thirty, a circumstance which leaves DeLancey Ferguson's *MT, Man and Legend* still the only critical biography which covers the whole life. Mr. Kaplan sometimes uses Freudian methods but he uses them discriminatingly, and though it is possible to quarrel with his interpretations here and there, it should be stated with emphasis that he has written an excellent book. It is only unfortunate that he should have been subjected to the indignity of the ridiculous overpraise which reviewers in general have lavished upon him. Professor Howard Mumford Jones started it all by "booming" Mr. Kaplan's book in advance of publication, whereupon nearly everybody else proceeded to climb on the bandwagon, possibly to prove that they were all as erudite as Professor Jones (which they are not), and possibly to save themselves the trouble of independent reading and evaluation.

Milton Meltzer's book contains about 600 pictures, many of which concern MT's world more than MT himself, and a text derived mainly from his own words. Baldanza, Grant, and Schönfelder are all paperbacks of the general handbook variety. May McNeer's book, which was written for children, does not always differentiate sufficiently between MT fact and legend, but almost any lover of MT will enjoy the gorgeous illustrations by the author's husband, Lynd Ward.

There have also been some Russian studies which, unfortunately, I cannot read, and upon which I therefore cannot report.

Most or the biographical studies have concerned specialized subjects. Hamlin Hill, *MT and Elisha Bliss* (University of Missouri Press, 1964) not only develops MT's relationship to the American Publishing Company in detail and gives an interesting account of "subscription" publishing, but also argues the influence of "subscription" methods in MT's art. Paul Fatout's *MT in Virginia City* (IUP, 1964) adds new material and recovers lost writings from the period indicated,[4] and his *MT on the Lecture Circuit* (IUP, 1960) builds up our knowledge of all Mark's public speaking. This should be supplemented by a number of articles about the world tour. Four of these are by Coleman O. Parsons —"MT in Australia," *Antioch Review*, Vol. XXI (1961), 455–68; "MT in New Zealand," *SAQ*, Vol. LXI (1962), 51–76; "MT: Sightseer in India," *MQ*, Vol. XVI (1963), 76–93; and "MT in Ceylon," *Tw*, 22nd Year, January–February, 1963, p. 4, and March–April, pp. 3–4. See, further, Robert D. Wallace, "MT on the Great Lakes," *Inland Seas*, Vol. XVII (1961), 181–86; George Mackaness, "MT's Visit to Australia," *ABC*, Vol. XII, May, 1962, pp. 7–10.

Paul Baender, "Alias Macfarlane: A Revision of MT Biography," *AL*, Vol. XXXVIII (1966), 187–97, suggests that "Macfarlane" was a persona for MT's later pessimistic ideas concerning man and not, as has hitherto been believed, an actual person whom he met early in life and who influenced his thinking. Ray

---

[4] I am somewhat doubtful that Mr. Fatout has correctly explained the origin of "MT's Nom de Plume," *AL*, Vol. XXXIV (1962), 1–7, which is summarized in *MT in Virginia City*. Leisy and Benson have already thoroughly demolished the Isaiah Sellers hypothesis to which Paine and MT himself adhered, but this does not necessarily mean that the one Mr. Fatout favors—which is that Sam Clemens said "Mark twain" when he wanted two drinks charged to him in Western barrooms—is necessarily the only alternative. I think there is no doubt that Sam did more drinking during his Western years than we have hitherto supposed, but I am not quite convinced that a river man would use the term indicated in the milieu and the manner indicated. It seems strained and self-conscious. Fatout suggests that MT was later ashamed of this and that he invented the Sellers yarn to cover it up. But no invention would have been necessary. It would have been quite as convincing to say that he had adopted the river term indicating safe water and let it go at that. There is no relationship between the use of Sellers' name and the hypothetical desired erasure of the barroom.

B. Browne, "MT and Captain Wakeman," *AL*, Vol. XXIII (1961), 320–29, deals with the man who served as a model for Captain Stormfield. Louis J. Budd, "Twain Could Mark the Beat," *MSAJ*, Vol. IV, Spring, 1963, explores MT's dancing. Max Eastman, "MT and Socialism," *National Review*, Vol. X (1961), 154–55, argues that MT's failure to embrace Socialism, in spite of his sympathy for the underdog, shows that he understood both human nature and the romantic, oversimplified, and intellectually naïve character of the Marxist point of view. Herbert Feinstein, "MT and the Pirates," *Harvard Law School Bulletin*, Vol. XIII, No. 5, 1962, pp. 6–18, concerns MT as opponent by legal means of literary piracy. Dewey Ganzel, "Clemens, Mrs. Fairbanks, and *Innocents Abroad*," *MP*, Vol. LXIII (1965), 128–40, argues that Mrs. Fairbanks was a great friend to Clemens and "a true and generous lady," but not an important literary influence on the *Innocents* or anything else. Another article by Ganzel concerns "MT and John Camden Holten," *Library*, Vol. XX, (1965), 230–42. Herbert E. Klingelhofer, "MT, Edited and Bowdlerized," *Manuscripts*, Vol. XI, Fall, 1959, pp. 3–12, reviews MT's disagreement with T. Douglas Murray over the piece which finally became his essay, "Saint Joan of Arc." George Monteiro, "A Note on the MT–Whitelaw Reid Relationship," *Emerson Society Quarterly*, No. 19 (1960), 20–21, relates hitherto unknown facts about the *Tribune* review of *The Prince and the Pauper* and shows that MT's mistrust of Whitelaw Reid was better grounded than he himself later came to believe. John Q. Reed, "MT, West Coast Journalist," *Midwest Quarterly*, Vol. I (1960), 141–61, concerns the development of MT, especially as a stylist, during his Western years. Jon Swan, "Innocents at Home," *American Heritage*, Vol. XVI, No. 2 (February, 1965), gives a full and interesting account of the Gorky incident. Donald H. Welsh, "Sam Clemens's Hannibal," *MASJ*, Vol. III, Spring, 1962, pp. 28–53, builds up background materials from contemporary newspapers.

The subjects of the following articles will be clear from their titles: C. Merton Babcock, "MT and Mencken: A Literary Relationship," *Menckeniana*, No. 14, (1965), 4–5; James M. Cox, "Walt Whitman, MT, and the Civil War," *Sewanee Review*, Vol.

LXIX (1961), 185–204; Vincent L. Eaton, "MT, Washington Correspondent," *Manuscripts*, Vol. XI, Fall, 1959, pp. 3–12; Chris Kanellakon, "MT and the Chinese," *MTJ*, Vol. XI, Fall, 1961, pp. 7ff.; Robert D. Lundy, "MT and Italy," *Studi Americani*, IV (1958), 135–49; Gordon Roper, "MT and His Canadian Publishers," *ABC*, Vol. X, June, 1960, pp. 13–30; Pat M. Ryan, Jr., "MT, Frontier Theater Critic," *ArizQ*, Vol. XVI (1960), 197–209; James B. Stronks, "MT's Boston Stage Debut as Seen by Hamlin Garland," *NEQ*, Vol. XXXVI (1963), 85–86; James W. Tuttleton, "Twain's Use of Theatrical Traditions in the Old Southwest," *Classical Language Association Journal*, Vol. VIII (1964), 190–97; Alfred Vagts, "MT at the Courts of the Emperors," *Jahrbuch für Amerikastudien*, Vol. IX (1964), 149–51; Carl Vitz, "J. B. Pond and Two Servants," *Bulletin Historical and Philosophical Society of Ohio*, Vol. XVII (1959), 277–84.

The biographers have also been concerning themselves with MT's family. Now that Van Wyck Brooks's charges against Olivia Langdon Clemens are no longer taken seriously, we should not expect to find very much about her, but James M. Cox, "The Muse of Samuel Clemens," *Massachusetts Review*, Vol. V (1963), 127–41, constitutes what I would call the best and most profound examination that has been made of Mrs. Clemens's relationship to her husband both as man and as writer. Effie Mona Mack, historian of Nevada and author of *MT in Nevada*, published "Orion Clemens, 1825–1897: A Biography," in *Nevada Historical Society Quarterly*, Vol. IV, Nos. 3–4 (1964), and Rachel M. Varble wrote a long book called *Jane Clemens: The Story of MT's Mother* (D, 1964). The scholarly value of this work is lessened by the fact that the author has chosen to write without documentation, in a straight narrative style, but it is still the product of long and careful research. MT weaves in and out of the narrative, but he is no more important in it than Jane's other children; it is not essentially a MT book. I should say that its primary value lies in the detailed picture it gives of how MT's ancestors —and ours—lived.

Of wider appeal is Edith Colgate Salsbury's *Susy and MT: Family Dialogues* (HR, 1965). All lovers of MT have loved Susy and hoped that she might someday have a book of her own. *Susy and MT* is somewhat less a book about her than its title might indicate. it is rather a detailed picture, woven from many sources, of the life of the Clemens household during the twenty-four years of her life. Considerable new material appears in it. Before reading it, I was inclined to be wary of the dialogue method of presentation; its use now seems to me to have been quite justified by the results obtained.

V

A number of important specialized critical studies of MT have been published: Louis J. Budd, *MT, Social Philosopher* (IUP, 1962); Pascal Covici, Jr., *MT's Humor: The Image of a World* (SMU, 1962); Franklin R. Rogers, *MT's Burlesque Patterns, as Seen in the Novels and Narratives, 1855–85* (SMU, 1960); Henry Nash Smith, *MT: The Development of a Writer* (HUP, 1962); Roger B. Salomon, *Twain and the Image of History*, and Albert E. Stone, Jr., *The Innocent Eye: Childhood in MT's Imagination* (both, YUP, 1961). The year 1966 brought also *MT and the Backwoods Angel, The Matter of Innocence in the Works of Samuel L. Clemens* (Kent State University Press) and James M. Cox, *MT: The Fate of Humor* (Princeton University Press), both of which appeared too late to be examined here.

The reader who comes to Budd's book fresh from reading the proletarian critic Philip S. Foner's *MT, Social Critic* (1958) may well wonder whether both writers are discussing the same man. Foner's emphasis was upon what Mark himself called his "Sansculotte" aspect; Budd leaves the impression of a generally "Republican" outlook. Though Foner is still useful for certain materials and emphases, Budd's is distinctly the better book— more knowledgeable, more scholarly, more disinterested. He has no axe to grind, yet objective as he is, he gives at least one reader the impression that he himself is somewhat more "liberal" than he thinks of Sam Clemens as having been. J. Harold Smith's article, "MT's Basic Political Concepts: Men, Parties, Democracy," *Missouri Historical Review*, Vol. LIX (1965), 349–54, is a good summary but has no new material.

Covici's book wanders at times from its announced subject, but it says much that is penetrating, along with much else that seems to me strained and far-fetched. Other considerations of MT's humor during the period were Gerhard Friedrich, "Erosion of Values in Twain's Humor," *CEA Critic*, Vol. XXII, September, 1960, pp. 108ff.; John Gerber, "MT's Use of the Comic Pose," *PMLA*, Vol. LXXVII (1962), 297–304; William C. Havard, "MT and the Political Ambivalence of Southwestern Humor," *MQ*, Vol. XVII (1964), 95–106.

Rogers's thesis is that MT's "distinctive structural technique" developed "from his apprenticeship in burlesque," with *HF* as the climax of the process. He has importantly reinforced the growing tendency of critics to see MT as a conscious literary artist rather than the "divine amateur" he was once considered. Smith's primary concern is with MT's style, but he assumes a relationship between style and both "questions of meaning" and "ethical ideas." Beginning with the apprentice writing, in which Mark was capable of using "all the stereotypes of conventional rhetoric" and also of suddenly deflating "the mood he has created by a comic turn," he proceeds to the writer's "nearest approach to the full embodiment of vernacular values in fiction" in *HF*. The British MT specialist, Tony Tanner, also writes about "Samuel Clemens and the Progress of a Stylistic Rebel," in *British Association for American Studies*, n.s. No. 3, December, 1961, pp. 31–42. (See also his book, *The Reign of Wonder* [Cambridge University Press, 1966]).

Yale University Press published the books by Salomon and Stone on the same day—the first time, to my knowledge, that any publisher has ever thus handled two studies of MT. Both are excellent, representing the new MT scholarship at its best, and because of its endearing subject, the Stone book has a charm all its own. It should be noted, too, that *Joan of Arc* and *The Mysterious Stranger* are importantly treated in both these works (Salomon sees the latter as one aspect of MT's escape from history), but the treatment of the *Joan of Arc* is especially important because of the critical neglect that this novel has suffered. There will never again be any excuse for viewing it as a sentimental aberration on the part of an aging writer; it was quite in the main stream of the thought as well as the literary activity of its time. With Stone, see Jim Hunter, "MT and the Boy-Book in 19th-Century America," *CE*, Vol. XXIV (1963), 430–38, and Tony Tanner, "The Literary Children of James and Clemens," *NCF*, Vol. XVI (1961), 205–18 ("James thought the gain of maturity worth the loss of innocence: Clemens did not"); with Salomon, see Clinton S. Burhans, Jr., "MT's View of History," *Papers of the Michigan Academy of Science, Arts, and Letters*, Vol. XLVI (1961), 617–27.

Among critical articles, E. H. Cady, "Howells and Twain: The World in Midwestern Eyes," *BSTCF*, Vol. III, Winter, 1962–63, pp. 3–8, traces the wisdom and realism of both writers to their midwestern heritage; Curtis Dahl's uncommonly novel and suggestive "MT and the Moving Panoramas," *AQ*, Vol. XIII (1961), 20–32, not only establishes MT's interest but suggests a hitherto unrecognized influence upon his art; Franklin L. Jensen, "MT's Comments on Books and Authors," *Emporia State Research Studies*, Vol. XII, No. 4 (June, 1964), is a useful compilation of MT's comments on many works, but the author does nothing to remedy the lack he complains of in the way of an over-all evaluation of MT as a critic; A. N. Kaul's chapter on MT in *The American Vision: Actual and Ideal Society in Nineteenth-Century Fiction* (YUP, 1963) concentrates on social criticism; Sydney J. Krause, "Twain and Scott: Experience versus Adventure," *MP*, Vol. LXII (1965), 227–36, is an elaborate exploration of alleged resemblances and differences between the two writers; Ivan A. Schulman, "Jose Marti and MT," *Symposium*, Vol. XV (1961), 104–13, concerns MT's influence upon a Cuban poet. The only Freudian criticism to speak of is in Irving Malin, "MT: The Boy as Artist," *Literature and Psychology*, Vol. XI (1961), 78–84, which is mostly about MT's incomplete or unsatisfactory treatment of the "father-image," and George Feinstein, "Two Pair of Gloves: MT and Henry James," *American Imago*, Vol. XVII (1960), 349–87; the gloves are in *The Innocents Abroad* and *The Turn of the Screw*, and the author's findings are just about as silly as they could be.

The subjects of the following critical articles are sufficiently indicated by their titles: C. Merton Babcock, "MT: A Heretic in Heaven," *Etc.*, Vol. XVIII (1961), 189–96, and "MT and the Freedom to Tell a Lie," *Texas Quarterly*, Vol. V, No. 3, 1961, pp. 155–60; Glauco Cambon, "MT and Charlie Chaplin as Heroes of Popular Culture," *Minnesota Review*, Vol. III (1962), 77–82; William G. Clark, "MT's Visual and Aural Descriptions," *MTJ*, Vol. XII, Summer, 1965, pp. 1 ff.; Hennig Cohen, "MT's Sut Lovingood," in Ben Harris McClary, ed., *The Lovingood Papers*, 1962 (University of Tennessee Press); Max Eastman, "MT, Representative American," *New Leader*, Vol. XLIII (1960), 18–21; Bradford Smith, "MT and the Mystery of Identity," *CE*, Vol. XXIV (1963), 425–30; Tony Tanner, "The Lost America —The Despair of Henry Adams and MT," *Modern Age*, Vol. V (1961), 299–310.

MT's reputation now stands so high that it is natural to expect a reaction. Will somebody try to do to him what Maxwell Geismar attempted for his greatest contemporary in his *Henry James and the Jacobites*? Perhaps, but it has not yet appeared.

The closest we came during the period under consideration was in Lewis Leary's surprisingly disparaging review-article, "On Diminishing MT," *VQR*, Vol. XXXIX (1963), 334–39. Margaret Duckett's valuable book, *MT and Bret Harte* (Okla, 1964) attempts—and, I think, achieves—a successful defence of Harte against MT's devastating charges in *MT in Eruption* and elsewhere. This necessarily involved a certain amount of criticism of MT. Attack is always less graceful and endearing than defence, and Miss Duckett's attitude toward MT is considerably less sympathetic than her attitude toward Harte, in the sense that she always seems more ready to overlook Harte's faults than his. Yet I do not think she is really unfair toward MT; after all, we have always known that he could be fantastically savage toward those who, for some reason, had roused his ire. The unfortunate title of Robert A. Wiggins's *MT, Jackleg Novelist* (University of Washington Press, 1964)—and to some extent the tone of the Preface also—suggested an all-out attack, but the text does not sustain this promise (Wiggins, indeed, seems almost as scared of his own work as MT was of "Captain Stormfield's Visit to Heaven").

The shortcomings which Mr. Wiggins points out will hardly come with a sense of shock or novelty to readers of MT, and whether or not one accepts all his specific judgments, he has produced a perceptive and even graceful study.

VI

We come now, finally, to critical commentary on individual works. By actual count, the largest number of items concern *HF*, but as was to be expected in the wake of Walter Blair's great book, these generally concern odds and ends. The really important critical work has been done on *The Gilded Age, A Connecticut Yankee,* and *The Mysterious Stranger.*

THE GILDED AGE. The most elaborate study is Bryant Morley French, *MT and* The Gilded Age (SMU, 1965), which covers the writing of the book, its background, and its character. French studies the *roman à clef* aspect of the novel in detail, minimizes MT's dependence upon Charles Dudley Warner, and argues that some of the crudeness of the book is to be attributed to its being intended to burlesque contemporary sensation fiction. He also treats the play that was made from it and various related topics. Mr. French has written the most detailed study that has been made of any MT novel except *HF*; has any other work of fiction of such inferior quality ever been considered at such length? Reference should also be made to his article, "The *Gilded Age* Manuscript," *Yale University Library Gazette,* Vol. XXXV (1960), 35–41, and two articles by Hamlin Hill—"Toward a Critical Text of *The Gilded Age,*" PBSA, Vol. LIX (1965), 142–49, and "Escol Sellers from Unchartered Space: A Footnote to *The Gilded Age,*" AL, Vol. XXXIV (1962), 107–13, which concerns Warner more than MT, suggesting that he had more to do with Colonel Sellers than has generally been supposed. Hill also shows that the stories that have previously been told about Escol Sellers are misleading. This man's background is further developed by his grand-nephew, Harold Sellers Colton, "MT's Literary Dilemma and its Sequel," *ArizQ,* Vol. XLVII (1961), 229–32.

A CONNECTICUT YANKEE IN KING ARTHUR'S COURT. Basing his work on Howard Baetzhold's new and revisionary dates for the composition of A *Connecticut Yankee* (see below), Henry Nash Smith, *MT's Fable of Progress: Political and Economic Ideas in* A Connecticut Yankee (Rutgers University Press, 1964), explores and explains the contradictions in the book by reference to MT's changing ideas and fresh experiences during its long incubation. He regards the book as a failure, but the failure of a very great writer. This seems to me the most perceptive study that has been made of A *Connecticut Yankee*, but two articles by other hands are closely related to it in their point of view: James M. Cox, "A *Connecticut Yankee in King Arthur's Court:* The Machinery of Self-Preservation," *Yale Review*, N.S. Vol. L (1960), 89–102, and Charles S. Holmes, "A *Connecticut Yankee in King Arthur's Court:* Fable of Uncertainty," SAQ, Vol. LXI (1962), 462–72. Howard G. Baetzhold's article, already referred to, is "The Course of Composition of A *Connecticut Yankee:* A Reinterpretation," AL, Vol. XXXIII (1961), 195–214, with which should be read his other AL article, " 'The Adventure of Sir Robert Smith of Camelot': MT's Original Plan for A *Connecticut Yankee*," Vol. XXXII (1961), 456–61. In addition to the matter already referred to, Baetzhold has a good deal on sources, and there is more of this in James D. Williams, "The Use of History in MT's A *Connecticut Yankee*," PMLA, Vol. LXXX (1965), 102–10, and John De Witt McKee, "Three Uses of the Arming Scene," *MTJ*, Vol. XII, Summer, 1965, pp. 18ff., who thinks MT used *Sir Gawain and the Green Knight*. Hamlin Hill, "Barnum, Bridgeport, and The [*sic*] *Connecticut Yankee*," AQ, Vol. XVI (1964), 615–16, shows that MT had Barnum in his mind. See also Roger B. Salomon, "Realism as Disinheritance: Twain, Howells and James," AQ, Vol. XVI (1964), 531–44.

THE MYSTERIOUS STRANGER. In "MT's Testament," MLQ, Vol. XXIII (1962), 254–62, E. H. Eby called attention to the fact that the solipsism of the last chapter of *The Mysterious Stranger* belongs to a different manuscript than the rest of the published version; therefore, he argued, it does not necessarily express the meaning of the story as a whole or MT's final intention. As Eby reads *The Mysterious Stranger*, it is essentially "a testament to the greatness of man's imagination." Both John S.

Tuckey (see below) and Pascal Covici, Jr. *(MT's Humor)* agree that Satan does, "in some fashion," as Tuckey puts it, "represent the creative power of the artist's mind," but neither supports Eby's view that the dream conception is not basic to the story as a whole; neither does Walter Blair *(Selected Writings of MT)*. Covici, who sees Satan as subjective to Theodor, believes that the conclusions about the nature of reality expressed in the last chapter of *The Mysterious Stranger* have already been implied not only in the earlier chapters of this story but also in MT's other works. Covici denies the alleged pessimism of the work however: "But the note around which . . . [Satan's] revelation organizes itself is that of optimistic hope that Theodor will indeed 'dream other dreams, and better.' This is not the nihilism of despair."

But the really important interpretation is John S. Tuckey, *MT and Little Satan: The Writing of* The Mysterious Stranger (West Lafayette, Indiana, Purdue University Studies, 1963). The most startling single fact emerging from Tuckey's study is that there is no astrologer in MT's manuscript. Albert Bigelow Paine and the Harper editor, F. A. Duneka, created him! But the most important revisionary conclusion to be drawn is that Tuckey has vitiated Bernard DeVoto's brilliant essay, "The Symbols of Despair" *(MT at Work)* by carrying the composition of the "Eseldorf Version" of *The Mysterious Stranger* back to 1897 or 1898. The last chapter, an anticipated conclusion to the "Print Shop Version," most of which was written in Florence in 1904, was clearly indebted to *Science and Health*, a quotation from which appears in MT's notes for it, and Mr. Tuckey thinks this version might have been completed and published if Duneka, a devout Catholic, had not been shocked by it. Tuckey finds the dream solution in harmony with MT's finished view of the story but insists that it is "explicitly a *story-solution*," not a statement of personal philosophy. He shows that the events MT described in "Stirring Times in Austria" are reflected in *The Mysterious Stranger* as well as other later news events. In "Goethe and MT," *Notes and Queries*, N.S. Vol. VII (1960), 150–51, Martin Klotz added *Werther* to the possible sources of *The Mysterious Stranger*; in *"The Mysterious Stranger:* MT's Last Laugh," *MTJ*, Vol. XI,

Summer, 1959, pp. 11–12, George Knox unconvincingly interprets the work in comic terms. Tuckey's is obviously one of the most important critical jobs that has been done on MT, and it emphasizes the long-felt need for a critical edition of *The Mysterious Stranger* in which all the manuscripts shall at last be printed. Happily, we are at last assured that such a work is on the way.

THE ADVENTURES OF TOM SAWYER. *Tom Sawyer* has attracted little critical attention of late, but the following may be listed: James T. Bratcher, "T's *Tom Sawyer*," *Ex*, Vol. XXII (1964), Item 4; William B. Dillingham, "Setting and Theme in *Tom Sawyer*," *MTJ*, Vol. XII, Spring, 1964, pp. 6–8; Hamlin Hill, "The Composition and Structure of *Tom Sawyer*," *AL*, Vol. XXXII (1961), 379–92; Pastoria San Juan, "A Source for *Tom Sawyer*," *AL*, Vol. XXXVIII (1966), 101–102; Donald A. Winkleman, "Goodman Brown, Tom Sawyer and Oral Tradition," *Keystone Folklore Quarterly*, Vol. X (1965), 43–48.

ADVENTURES OF HUCKLEBERRY FINN. The only study of HF between independent covers during our period is a rather foolish little essay by Tak Sioui, HF: *More Molecules*, which was privately printed in 1962. This piece indicts (or, rather, lauds) E. W. Kemble as having been personally responsible for the indecent illustration on p. 283 which held up the publication of the first edition. The author also discerns a hitherto unobserved indecency in another picture of Uncle Silas on p. 290 and cites a number of passages in the text by which Kemble might have been stimulated. The case, though not impossible, is not clearly established. Both pictures are reproduced, and the one on p. 283 may also be seen in Franklin J. Meine, "Some Notes on the First Edition of HF," ABC, Vol. X, No. 10, 1960, pp. 31–34.

The somewhat unrewarding subject of the rescue of Nigger Jim in HF (previously defended by T. S. Eliot and others) has inspired more articles than any other single theme. Most of these defend this tiresome episode very ingeniously but, to my mind, quite unconvincingly. See Ray B. Browne, "Huck's Final Triumph," BSTCF, Vol. VI, Winter, 1965, pp. 3–12; Bruce Carstensen, "The [*sic*] Adventures of HF: Die Problematik des Schlusses," *Die Neueren Sprachen*, Vol. XII (1961), 541–51, which reviews opinion and denies that the book is first-rate; A. E. Dyson, "HF and the Whole Truth," *Critical Quarterly*, Vol. III (1961), 29–40, which touches also on many other matters and is a valuable piece of criticism whether one accepts Dyson's ideas about Jim's "rescue" or not; Chadwick Hansen, "The Character of Jim and the Ending of HF," *Massachusetts Review*, Vol. V (1963), 45–66; Carson Gibb, "The Best Authorities," *CE*, Vol. XXII (1960), 178–83; C. C. Loomis, Jr., "Twain's Huck Finn," *Ex*, Vol. XVIII (1960), Item 27. Robert L. Vales, "*Thief* and *Theft* in HF," *AL*, Vol. XXXVII (1965–66), 420–29, sees the concluding chapters as tying together "the thief and theft theme" of the novel, it being Mr. Vales's view that MT "sees civilization as composed of thief and victim, both operating legalistically when possible, and frequently thief and victim are one and the same person." Different aspects of the ending are considered by Roy Harvey Pearce, " 'The End. Yours Truly, Huck Finn': Postscript," *MLQ*, Vol. XXIV (1963), 153–56, and William Manierre, " 'No Money For To Buy the Outfit': HF Again," *Modern Fiction Studies*, Vol. X (1964–65), 341–48.

Huck's conscience has engaged at least three critics. Leo B. Levy, "Society and Conscience in HF," *NCF*, Vol. XVIII (1964), 383–91, is a critical examination of the problem posed by Huck's decision not to turn Jim in, in the light of previous discussions of it, some of which are pronounced more schematic than the book itself. Mr. Levy finds it "difficult to accept" the idea "that Huck behaves morally because he has set aside the dictates of conscience." J. R. Boggan "That Slap, Huck, Did It Hurt?" *English Language Notes*, Vol. I (1964), 212–15, argues that the passage in which Huck decides to go to hell is less moving than many have found it because his apparent fear of hell at this juncture has not been prepared for, and that MT, consequently, is deliberately fishing for "a stock response." Sydney J. Krause, "Huck's First Moral Crisis," *MQ*, Vol. XVIII (1965), 69–73, takes stock on Huck's achievement and on what he still has to achieve at the point where the steamboat smashes the raft and MT temporarily set his manuscript aside.

Charles Crowe, "MT's *HF* and the American Journey,"

Archiv, Vol. CXCIX (1962), 145–58, sees Huck as the American folk hero and the voyage down the river as "the fundamental national experience, the adventure of the pioneer and immigrant." Lyle H. Kendall, Jr., "The *Walter Scott* Episode in *HF*," *NCF*, Vol. XVI (1961), 279–81, describes the incident indicated as the "focus of the narrative." John J. McAleer, "Noble Innocence in *HF*," *BSTCF*, Vol. III, Winter, 1962–63, pp. 9–12, contrasts the innocent nakedness of Huck and Jim on the raft with the King's obscenity in *The Royal Nonesuch*, employing cross-references to a number of other writers. William Power, "Huck Finn's Father," *UKCR*, Vol. XXVIII (1961), 83–94, probably has the distinction of being the only writer who has ever taken a sympathetic view of that character. Jessie A. Coffee, "MT's Use of 'Hain't' in *HF*," *AS*, Vol. XXXVII (1962), 234–36, is straight linguistic study, but Robert J. Lowenherz, "The Beginning of *HF*," *AS*, Vol. XXXVIII (1963), 196–201, studies the use of dialect for characterization. Claude R. Flory, "Huck, Sam, and the Small-Pox," *MTJ*, Vol. XII, Winter, 1964–65, pp. 1–2ff., suggests a possible source for the smallpox incident in *Sam Lawson's Oldtown Fireside Stories*, while Abigail Ann Hamblen invokes a more famous work of Mrs. Stowe's in "Uncle Tom and 'Nigger Jim,' A Study in Contrasts and Similarities," *MTJ*, Vol. XI, Fall, 1961, pp. 13–17. John Ashmead, "A Possible Hannibal Source for MT's Dauphin," *AL*, Vol. XXXIV (1962), 105–107, finds a likely original in a "bum" who visited Hannibal in 1853. Two articles compare MT with Faulkner: William Rossky, "*The Reivers* and *HF*," *HLQ*, Vol. XXVIII (1965), 373–87, and an unsigned article in *MTJ*, Vol. XII, Spring, 1963, pp. 12ff.: " 'The Bear' and *HF*: Heroic Quests for Moral Liberation," and three others continue the discussion begun in the fifties concerning comparisons and contrasts between Huck and the hero of J. R. Salinger's *The Catcher in the Rye*: Arvin R. Wells, "Huck Finn and Holden Caulfield: The Situation of the Hero," *Ohio University Review*, Vol. II (1960), 31–42; Devi A. Olan, "The Voice of the Lonesome: Alienation from Huck Finn to Holden Caulfield," *Southwest Review*, Vol. XVIII (1963), 143–50; Deane M. Warner, "Huck and Holden," *CEA Critic*, Vol. XXVIII

(1965), vi, 4a–4b. Huck is compared to Billy Budd in Richard J. Callan, "The Burden of Innocence in Melville and Twain," *Renascence*, Vol. XVII (1964–65), 191–94. In "Twain's The Adventures of *HF*, Chapter I," *Explicator*, Vol. XXIII (1964–65), Item 62, overstresses Biblical parallels in *HF*, underlining what he thinks the ironic effects.

The following articles on *HF* require no description: Clarence A. Brown, "*HF*: A Study in Structure and Point of View," *MTJ*, Vol. XII, Spring, 1964, pp. 10 ff.; Glauco Cambon, "What Maisie and Huck Knew," *Studi Americani*, Vol. VI (1960), 203–20; Sherwood Cummings, "What's in *HF*?" *English Journal*, Vol. L (1961), 1–8; Daniel G. Hoffman, in his *Form and Fable in American Fiction* (Oxford University Press, 1961); James W. Gargano, "Disguises in *HF*," *UKCR*, Vol. XXVI (1960), 175–78; Donna Gerstenberger, "HF and the World's Illusion," *WHR*, Vol. XIV (1960), 401–406; Charles R. Metzger, "*The* [*sic*] *Adventures of HF* as Picaresque," *Midwest Quarterly*, Vol. V (1964), 249–56; Martin Staples Shockley, "The Structure of *HF*," *South Central Bulletin* (*Studies by Members of the South Central Y.M.C.A., Tulsa, Okla.*), Vol. XX, Winter, 1960, pp. 3–10; Eric Solomon, "HF Once More," *CE*, Vol. XXII (1960), 172–78; J. R. Vitelli, "The Innocence of MT," *Bucknell Review*, Vol. IX (1960), 187–98.

PUDD'NHEAD WILSON. There has been one important study— Daniel Morley McKeithan, *The Morgan Manuscript of MT's Pudd'nhead Wilson*, which is No. 12 of "Essays and Studies on American Language and Literature" (Uppsala, A.–B. Lundequistska Bok-handeln, 1961). See also: William B. Jeffries, "The Montesquiou Murder-Case: A Possible Source for Some Incidents in *Pudd'nhead Wilson*," *AL*, Vol. XXXI (1960), 488–90, which deals with a St. Louis event of 1849, involving a French count and his brother; Henry B. Claflin, "Twain's *Pudd'nhead Wilson*, Chapter VI," *Ex*, Vol. XXI (1963), Item 61, which tries to show a closer relationship between the twins and the theme of the story than has previously been established; Edgar T. Schell, " 'Pears' and 'Is' in *Pudd'nhead Wilson*," *MTJ*, Vol. XII, Winter, 1964–65, pp. 12–15; Philip Butcher, "MT Sells Roxy Down the

River," *Classical Language Association Journal,* Vol. VIII (1965), 225–33.

Travel Books. Of the travel books, *Life on the Mississippi* has had the most attention. Two essays by David H. Malone in Hans Galinsky, ed., *The Frontier in American History and Literature,* "Die Neueren Sprachen, Beiheft 7" (Frankfurt, Verlag Moritz Diesterweg, 1962?) analyze the book and consider MT's relationship to the literature of the frontier in general, and two articles by Dewey Ganzel—"Samuel Clemens and Captain Marryat," *Anglia,* Vol. LXXX (1962), 405–16, and "Twain, Travel Books, and *Life on the Mississippi,*" AL, Vol. XXXIV (1962), 40–55—demonstrates the use of a number of literary sources. See also Paul Schmidt, "River vs. Town: MT's 'Old Times on the Mississippi,' " NCF, Vol. XV (1960), 95–111.

Calder M. Pickett, "MT as Journalist and Literary Man: A Contrast," *Journalism Quarterly,* Vol. XXXVIII (1961), 59–66, is a comparative study of the *Alta California* letters and *The Innocents Abroad,* while Henry F. Pommer, "MT's 'Commissioner of the United States,' " AL, Vol. XXXIV (1962), 385–92, gives background material on Dr. William Gibson, who is so denominated in the *Innocents* and who became the butt of Mark's humor there. Another, very important article by Dewey Ganzel, "Samuel Clemens, Guidebooks, and *Innocents Abroad,*" *Anglia,* Vol. LXXXIII (1965), 78–88, demonstrates the use of hitherto unconsidered literary sources.

Franklin R. Rogers, "The Road to Reality: Burlesque Travel Literature and MT's *Roughing It,*" BNYPL, Vol. LXVII (1963), 155–68, is an important supplement to his more extensive studies noted elsewhere. In another article in the same publication, Vol. LXIX (1965), 31–48, "MT's Last Travel Book," Dennis Welland concerns himself mainly with the differences between the American edition of *Following the Equator* and its English equivalent, which was called *More Tramps Abroad.*

Miscellaneous. Of the short pieces, "The Jumping Frog" and "The Man That Corrupted Hadleyburg" have attracted most attention. Hennig Cohen, "Twain's Jumping Frog: Folktale to Literature to Folktale," *Western Folklore,* Vol. XXII (1963),

17–18, explores backgrounds, but Parl Baender, "The 'Jumping Frog' as a Comedian's First Virtue," *MP*, Vol. LX (1963), 192–200, minimizes the regional element, and Paul Smith, "The Infernal Reminiscence: Mythic Patterns in MT's 'The Celebrated Jumping Frog of Calaveras County,' " *Satire Newsletter*, Vol. I (1964), 41–44, audaciously finds the piece a "dark and nearly tragic story," which indicates the "true turning point in MT's conception of man," a point of view which one would think it might be difficult to reconcile with Smith's own slighting estimate of it. See, too, Sydney J. Krause, "The Art and Satire of T's 'Jumping Frog' Story," *AQ*, Vol. XVI (1964), 562–76.

D. M. McKeithan, "The Morgan Manuscript of 'The Man That Corrupted Hadleyburg,' " *Texas Studies in Language and Literature*, Vol. II (1961), 476–80, sheds light on the development of the story during composition. Clinton S. Burhans, Jr., "The Sober Affirmation of MT's Hadleyburg," *AL*, Vol. XXXIV (1962), 375–84, defends the tale against the criticisms of Gladys Carmen Bellamy, and finds that MT's "divergent moral and ethical ideas merge in a view of man which places Twain within a great and positive tradition." Leslie F. Chard II, "MT's 'Hadleyburg' and Fredonia, New York," *AQ*, Vol. XVI (1964), 595–601, nominates, not too convincingly, a new original (Oberlin, Ohio, had previously been, even less reasonably, suggested). See, finally, Nita Laing, "The Later Satire of MT," *Midwest Quarterly*, Vol. II (1960), 35–47.

Finally we have a few articles dealing with scattered minor works, and at least one of these is important: Sherwood Cummings, "*What Is Man?* The Scientific Sources," in *Essays on Determinism in American Literature*, edited by Sydney J. Krause, "Kent Studies in English," No. One (1964). Arthur L. Scott, "*The Innocents Adrift* Edited by MT's Official Biographer," *PMLA*, Vol. LXXXVIII (1963), 230–37, deals with Paine's editing of what emerged in *Europe and Elsewhere* as "Down the Rhone" and adds up to a devastating indictment of Paine's editorial methods. But the article also cites omitted material which illuminates MT in many aspects and by implication calls for a complete printing of "The Innocents Adrift."

Roger L. Brooks, "A Second Possible Source for MT's 'The Aged Pilot Man,' " *Revue de Littérature Comparée*, Vol. XXXVI (1962), 451–53, nominates "The Rime of the Ancient Mariner," and James C. Austin, "Artemus Ward, MT, and the Limburger Cheese," *MASJ*, Vol. IV, Fall, 1963, pp. 70–73, suggests Ward's famous "Babes in the Wood" lecture as the source of "The Invalid's Tale." MT's crotchety attack on James Fenimore Cooper was hardly worth the elaborate and indignant refutation which Sydney J. Krause gives it in "Cooper's Literary Offences: MT's Wonderland," *NEQ*, Vol. XXVIII (1965), 291–311. C. Merton Babcock, "MT's Map of Paris," *Texas Quarterly*, Vol. VII, No. 3, 1964, pp. 92–97, is an amusing commentary on the map as a chart of MT's mind.

Index

This edition of *Mark Twain: The Man and His Work* is set in 11-point Electra on the Linotype. Electra is an original type design by the renowned W. A. Dwiggins. The publishers feel that Mark Twain, whose later life was so much involved with a type-setting machine, is particularly well represented in a face of original American design.

University of Oklahoma Press

Norman